GW01445270

Brighton Stanza Poets Anthology 2013

BRAMLEY

PRESS

Published in Great Britain by Bramley Press
www.bramleypress.co.uk

Copyright © 2013

The moral rights of the individual authors have been asserted.

A CIP catalogue record for this book is available from the British
Library.

ISBN 978-0-9571325-4-2

in memory of
Jo Grigg

Contents

Introduction

One of the many joys of poetry is that it owes no allegiance to place. The Poetry Library and the Poetry Café may be in London, but poets are found throughout the United Kingdom. Similarly, while the Poetry Society has its headquarters in Covent Garden, its Stanza groups exist throughout the UK. They are run voluntarily by Poetry Society members and bring people together in local areas for discussions, workshops and readings.

The Brighton Stanza has been in existence since 2007. Its members come together in a monthly workshop but also take part from time to time in readings in the town. Standards are high. A number of members have their poems published regularly in magazines. Some have published pamphlets or collections. Others have been recognised by winning or being shortlisted for prizes.

But poetry is not just the activity of an informed elite. Its attraction extends to a wide range of people writing on a casual basis or without interest in publication. For these, writing satisfies the need to put down in words the infinite variety of daily life, or to indulge in a love of the English language.

Diversity is a key element in both the membership of the Stanza and the poems produced. What follows in this anthology reflects this in a number of ways. The poems themselves include pieces written more for performance than the page, such as Tommy Sissons' *Rhapsody* or Sue Evans' *Moon on a Stick*. The difference in approach may be self-evident on reading. But even poems intended in the first instance to be read rather than performed vary widely in genre and tone—from Chris Allinson's Japanese-influenced senryu to the nostalgic lyricism of Lynne Hjelmgaard's free verse in *Return to the Tropics*, or from the careful spacing of Andie Davidson's *Departure Lounge* to the sestina form used by Liz Eastwood.

As a result, there is, I hope, something for everyone in this small collection of poems celebrating the creativity of poets in Brighton and the surrounding area. If any reader is interested in finding out more about the Stanza and its activities, details can be found on The Poetry Society's website (www.poetrysociety.org.uk) or the Brighton Stanza's Facebook page (www.facebook.com/brightonpoetrystanza).

My thanks go to my colleagues on the editorial committee, Andie Davidson and Miriam Patrick. Thanks also to Andie for undertaking the task of publication through Bramley Press.

This anthology was originally the idea of Jo Grigg, one of the founder members of the Stanza and its mainstay over the years. It has been a great sadness to us all that she did not live to see the result, which is dedicated to her memory.

Antony Mair

David Agnew

Three poems

1

They say Mount Tateyama
should be climbed in summer.
Mount Fuji should be climbed just once—
Twice is not so good.
Why should I care?
You are my mountain.
I'd climb you every day if I could—
Because you're there

2

Your lack of punctuality grants me
A kind of immortality, it's true—
Even after I'm dead
I'll still be waiting for you.

3

I fall on you
And you fall on me
Like sky divers, together
Falling
              Falling

Forgetting for a moment that we are always apart

The best we can do is
 Fall
        and
              fall.

       And never

                    come to land

                            at all.

Mary Allen

Angels

My walls are scarlet;
gold drips down my columns,
and wooden angels dance
against the lapis vault of my roof.

On my north wall, devils scurry
to the orders of a stern God,
weighing in the balance
naked men and women.

In my darkest corner
an elderly stonemason,
glancing over his shoulder,
carves eyes bulging over a green man's grin.

Envy, lust, avarice and the rest
gouged into choir stalls,
a beaver biting his genitals while men's voices
shiver the angels' wings.

Cheetah

Black tears weep my face, dribbling
the corners of my mouth, while I lie
sideways in the heat.

Two days I slumber in the shade
of a thorn bush beside the road.
Tourists lean from windows,
squeezing shutters, not quite daring
to step from their cars to stroke
my flickered fur, or rub a fingernail
in the soft down behind my ear.

I killed one once, a single swipe
of claws, but I disdain the sweet
ambivalence of human fat and flesh.
By night I sleek into whispering grass,
narrow black pupils towards
a gazelle, pump up my blood
and fly.

Bouquet

Old roses, centres flushed,
bitter-sweet with the smell of almonds.
Purple catmint,
bursts of small blooms snapping along stalks,
heady with peppermint.
And one white lily, breathing syrup-and-honey, hammer-headed
                                                          stamens
knocking yellow dust across my gathering hands.

Wrapping the stems in my palms, I take them to your garden, to meet
your jasmine, sweet williams and heart's ease,
winding ribbon,
binding together our flowers.

In the churchyard I throw my bouquet to you,
down into the dirt,
still hoping you might grab it,
or toss it back.

Chris Allinson

Five Senryu[1]

His teeth stained off-white
by Bordeaux red—he wonders
what colour his liver

&

Lonely and twitching
see the ornithologist
looking for a shag

&

In the looking glass
next the catchlights of her eyes
the disappointment

&

Sunseeker panting
the scorch of the August sands
the sea of bare breasts

&

Cold breath of air as
the moon blacks the searing sun
eyes lowered earthwards

---

1   A senryu is a three line unrhymed poem similar to haiku, though
concerning human, rather than Mother, nature. Senryu are often satirical,
ironic or humorous.

Dave Brooks

Taxidermy for beginners

Begin with what is closest to home,
what died most recently; the dog, the cat,
your love for that girl that meant everything,

hollow it out. The unpacking is often
the hardest part, not the waiting,
whatever Tom Petty suggests.

Rummage around inside the carcass
removing anything vital; organs, sinews.
the passion by which you used to set your clock,
odd concepts that meant so much,
such as loyalty, honesty, commitment.
Rebuilding will come next,
once the carapace is empty.

What you use to stuff it with is personal choice;
hemp, wool, paper lovingly recycled
from weekly local rags; or else fall back on obsession.

Don't worry too much about the final shape,
overloading is a common complaint for beginners,
Filling the void helps to forget what you have lost.

Last Supper

I can see the coffin seams,
the joins show; my dreams
of you are filled with images
where you are working, building. Pages
in the book of your life turn slowly,
all moments we shared; surely
you are not gone, you will return
late in the evening from work; tired and undone
from the day's toil. Grease seeping
from every pore, your laughter sweeping
the room like machine gun fire. No
angry words for those who show
no respect. You dine on something
indescribable, warmed up on a saucepan. I cling
to every word used to describe your day,
I feel you are still here, that you never went away.

Inner space

I mention liquorice.
He predicts the heart,
the steam valve whistles,
a cartoon image as pressure starts to build
to unimaginable levels,
she's gonna blow captain.

I mention my father.
Was it a coronary?
I get a medical diagnosis
complete with labelled diagrams;
does he think this will help?
It's worse than that, he's dead Jim.

He asks was it hero worship?
Living with his two faced history,
I speak in classic cliché and simile,
hoping genetic memory is forgetful.
He was always a tough act to follow,
it's life Jim, but not as we know it.

I once knew a man he proffers,
I add gloss to the surface,
tears dwell at the foot of the well
while my subtlety struts take the strain,
the image of normality is maintained,
as into the night I boldly go.

Lucy Cotterill

Lanes Farm

When I pull up at the shed
by the edge of the chalk track
that ends in this high field,
I like to stand very still and listen
to the sheep crying
from their crease in the Downs.

Inside, the vegetables are sleeping
in their plastic trays
like socks in the launderette
that nobody's come to claim:
sprouting broccoli bundled with twine;
leeks tucked tight in papery shrouds;
the bruised stems of chard
wilting in the dark while
last autumn's apples
shrivel into scent.

Nobody knows I'm here,
but I wait
as if about to be found out,
taking in the stale air
of iron and mice,
a back note of wood,
this taste of being
under ground.

Milk

From this side of the stile he can see them,
veins mapping the breadth of their swaying load.
His girls. He loves that they can't help themselves,
that they tip headlong towards him, stumbling,
rubbing up against each other in the crush.
He knows they're aching for it and now,
behind him, the farmhouse is just a place
from somebody else's life; his wife inside is
somebody else's wife. Out here, it's just him
and the girls, that smell of shit he
could wrap himself up in, the steam
from their nostrils he could breathe all day.

When he gets them in the lane, three abreast,
rumps knocking, he wants to press himself hard
against them, feel himself lashed
by the switch of their tails, but
he waits till the line-up, runs
his calloused fingers along each mole-soft teat,
slips each one into the waiting cup and flicks
the switch, senses the hot teat tingle
as the milk begins to spurt.

Matryoshka

The nesting doll

He calls them blanks
these skins of birch
that barely skim
my bloated hips,
that starve my eyes
of light, my lips of air.
So many layers he's laid
on me. So many layers.
Little wonder
I'm this shape,
bottom wide, bosom sturdy,
strapped inside an apron
that's anchored
to my ever-spreading waist.
What can a woman do?
He's promised me a goose
to clutch, a softener
for all this added bulk.
Says I'll have a basket
of roses, shawl of lace,
blushing cheeks
to capture any man,
a baby locked
inside me
like a nut,
colours shining
in her silent,
perfect cell.

Andie Davidson

Recall

Photographs

are like children   that are memories
with birth times   and wide eyes
exposed to light   and shadows

memories joined to memories
        in
                one
                        timeless
                                        chain

Children

are like memories   that are photographs
that were once   of our family
exposed to happiness   and sadness

times joined to times
        in
                one
                        embracing
                                        moment

Memories

are like photographs   that are children
wide-eyed, free   and happy
exposed forever   as we were

light shining onto light
    in
        one
           sunlit
               fade

photographs	children	memories
being recalled	are as one	exposure of our
longing	and open	eyes

Departure lounge

Silence is a presence in the pressing noise
my ears as unhearing as my eyes can see glass

> *walls*
> *of impending departure sealing sound*
> *without*
> *passport, boarding card or ticket, bag*

and you, in conversation, never looking back
waiting behind your reflection in the glass.

Goodbyes, those precursors to greetings, yours
elsewhere, captured in silence, heart in flight

> *more*
> *in decision than in joy, but its absence*
> *like*
> *the missing kiss and reassurance, bag in hand*

and you, in your other world, spreading wings
waiting, beating, preparing for your flight.

Half-reflections, sun-caught fragments of my dress
glass-printed, unmoving as your body wheels

> *laughter*
> *and anticipation silenced by the glass*
> *recognisable*
> *in your remembered scent and touch*

as you walk and wait, embark and disappear
in the thunder, roar of flight, of lifting wheels.

Bright dots, navigation lights blinking in the sun
silence in the glass as they merge, are gone

> *my feet*
> *are for walking, ticket to a car park*
> *my journey*
> *a returning, wheels to a home alone*

I am fragments of light in silent glass
no longer waiting—reflecting how you've gone.

Visiting

of course there are thoughts

wordless in your unspeaking mouth,
throat lost to utterance, useless
in swallowing—

       though sounds sink in

I cannot tell from your eyes

if you welcome this day—but I sit,
small in talk, infinitesimal
in listening—

       measuring minutes

there is no next anything

maybe tomorrow—maybe I shall come
and talk in spaced words, tested
thoughts and all

       that can't be said

not even spelled by a finger, lifted

drawn against each stroke
resisting the ruin a consultant explains—
describes

       in these white sheets

Liz Eastwood

Book Rape

It was at the Literary Group that I lost my lover,
my *Flesh and Blood: Poems* by C K Williams book.
Today she came back. Two pages missing and the stains
of cigaretty fingers that de-flyed ... no typo ... penetration ... inside
her secret pre-formed, profound, predestined passages It has
bruises on the bottom of page two; no emotions on the cover.

If this happens to you, you won't know how to recover
from the police reports that tell you your lover's
abuser remains unfound. She cannot tell me where she has
been or what or who has been through her. My book
has two pages missing; she's not the same book. Inside
the back cover see twisted, toying digits' disgusting stains.

On page twenty—*The Mistress, The Lover* give us strains
of *a bloody beast* and a *lying bastard*, the next page I discover
is now twenty-three—*Failure* and *Crime*—eyes seek tears turned out
                                                            inside.
I paid five pounds ninety-five to become her lover.
She thought she'd be left on the shelf, just another book
for the spine show; but I covet what's under her cover—so she never
                                                            has.

Perking it up's impossible, now he's prised and poked at private pages.
                                                            Has
any other ... other ... man ... had his fingers inside? Are those stains
sticky coffee, cigarettes, crack line and wine? Look book,
tell the truth. Did you let him? All over your cover?
Is his bookmark bigger than mine? Is he your secret lover?
Scream, book, mime from that vile verb of violation inside.

I should have held on to her, kept her hidden inside
with Plath and Ted, by *The Door* where daring Atwood has
visions; I stuff bloody, honeyed squirrels at wake of sullied lover.
The worst is not the squirrel's guts or gory entrails. Fucking honey
                                                                    stains.
Sixteen years we've been together. I think of me, how I'll recover.
I'm so bloody selfish, I don't think of The Book.

I was so bloody selfish, I didn't think of The Book.
I didn't know where to turn since he'd been inside.
She opened herself at page thirty-eight and hid back cover.
We took our fill of *Will* and *Pregnant*, raw sound of wound has
seen innocence off but, wisely, she opens wide pages to stains
of *Peace* on page thirty-nine, begging me to still be her lover.

If you look carefully you'll see that The Book has
let me back in spite of me. Her elegy, her energy are the breath of
                                                        survivors' stains.
See *First Desires* on page six. Excuse me—I'm off to cover my lover.

Ma Fille de la Rue, My Lady

After Edouard Manet's Olympia (1863)

1865

He sees I'm Sappho, my night brown skin
On his palette, blends of my lady ... pink
Hairs on the brush, touching up her thigh
And breast. I fancy his face is primary red.
I kneel, without obeisance, by her bed
To pose as he said, with flowers, not power.

Black cat paws at flowers. Pussy power!
Green eyes say 'no sin' to her naked skin
Pose for him. Black choker bow, silk laid bed.
On his art whim, he blends my lady ... pink.
Blackie scratches at bushy depths unread.
I sigh, I cry, I die, as he brushes her thigh.

Once, my love, when I caressed her thigh ...
Before this man came with his power
I lit a flame in her, she knows brown blood's red.
My brown slave sin burns pink skin?
Ladies love lush love. Mix me love in pink
And think back how she laid me on this bed.

She blew breath to my brown breasts. By this bed
I begged her moist move high up my thigh.
Now his money brush blends my lady's pink
Shade. She fades. His palette has the power
To get to me, to get under my skin
He sees brown, He sees pink. I see red.

My *fille de la rue* spreads legs; cash for breads?
Now art pays. He blends her nude on a bed
Trying hard ... to force ... on his second skin.
Black cat fur flies, scratches his flabby thigh
I poison his pen with my black power.
No more will his ink blind my lady pink.

1883

On this fine bed, she's laid. Not in the pink.
Grey skin, grey hair and grey dimpled thigh.
Art man has no power to paint free lady in red.

Susan Evans

Silly Shoes

I rushed home from work for him
I went totally berserk for him
I wore silly shoes for him
I sat and had the blues for him
I laughed at all his jokes for him
I ignored all other blokes for him
I went with the flow for him
I stopped saying no to him
I opened my heart for him
I wrote a special part for him
I stopped being late for him
I laid awake for him
I went the extra mile for him
I wore special smiles for him
I stopped seeing my mates for him
I started baking cakes for him
I cleaned out my flat for him
I totally lost track for him
I danced drunk in the street for him
And I threw up and I reached for him
I gave thanks and praise for him
I thought I'd end my days with him
But it wasn't really happening ...
It was just a fling to him.

Moon on a stick

How come you're single? I mean you're gorgeous, he said
Another mister mingle, filling me with dread; sees me in his bed
I'm selective, la la la
You mean what's wrong with me? Blah blah blah
Chit chat chit chat cut to the chase;
let's be honest It's all fucking base
I'm a symphony, bitter sweet symphony; fifty-fifty fire and ice
I've done sympathy too much sympathy
I've gotten to be too bloody nice
Come on mister under cover, what's in the bag?
You think I'm a potential lover to recover from the Ex. Shag?
I'm a person; a whole person, not just a goal;
done love on a roll, love on the dole;
full on full off, it's taken its toll,
I feel like a fucking rag doll
Enough's enough. I'm married to me not you
but you can huff and puff and make mountains move
Yeah, move me a mountain, make me a fountain
I want nothing but devotion, I want poetry in motion
I want potion after potion of feel good lotion
I want slow motion
I want to be emotionally arrested, don't want to be molested
I want to be amused not confused
No compromises only nice surprises
I won't be bent over a stove, I don't want to be made mauve
and I don't wish to live in Hove Actually!
I want the moon on a stick, dick
Does that answer your question?

I think I've lost my edge

I used to go in for poetry slams
where voices were vexed
no language was banned
With an open mind
at the open mic
I spat my words so they would bite;
the crowds lapped up these anarchic nights
My mates would cheer
and the drunks would jeer
as I felt the fear and did it anyway
Then suddenly, I lost the urge for performing my emotions
I had a sudden surge to put some healing into motion
No more entertainment from spilling woos and woes
'Tis time for something useful besides dwelling on the lows
I do have a confession
I think I've lost my edge
since I buried all my anger
and found new love down at the allotment ...

John Feakins

Waterhouse—The Lady of Shalott

Only the candle (one of three) caught
in the breeze and the lantern's flame
hints at the twilight through the trees
on this white-dressed pale lady's
last journey; note the black band
around her waist, despite the fresh
embroidered colours of a counterpane
and touches of light bird plumage, her red lips.

The trees behind are dense and matted,
the waters almost stagnant, reeds tangled,
as she releases the chain, lifts
her head for a last song, watched
by the dead Christ on her prow, and drifts,
heart blazing into the night.

Skirmish

He's like an imperial intruder, wary, threatening,
she like a cautious, watchful native,
he snake-boots, solar topee, sunglasses, rifle at the ready,
she body exposed, but concealing pipe and poisoned darts.

They circle each other never losing sight of the rifle
or the hands held behind the naked back,
manoeuvring the opponent into shade or light,
watching, if only out of the corners of their eyes.

Listening for change of breath, gesture or move,
keeping an eye on the eyes, the hint of a nod or frown,
ignoring the deceit of a deflected flicker over a shoulder
waiting, pausing; any hesitation, false move could be your last.

Out to Sea

A city drowned in a storm
where no-one hears church bells,
or sees the thriving market;
no smells of dung, no curling smoke;

there's no hint of breath or quarrel,
no banter, haggling or anguish,
no candle-light in taverns, no raucous drunks,
no coupling, births or deaths;

now slipped from sight or touch,
all this is beyond the unwelcoming shingle;
only our imagination's reach
lightens the rough edges of history.

Little remains but still-crumbling cliffs,
a sea-voice reduced to a stammer,
a dead-end high street, a ruined abbey,
empty fields and brambled paths.

Behind the last uncertain bank, the car-park
cowers in a dream; above the waves people lie
between the idle boats, stare out to sea,
where only weed and fish float round sunken walls.

Clive Findlay

playing happily

muddy shoes
grubby fingers
dusty face

watching me gran
pegging clothes
grey wisps in the wind
brushed away with trembling fingers

coal piled high
on the street below
waiting for the men to come home

down near the river
rusty rails filled with rubbish

bare brown mountains
empty houses

the men swaying home
faces black
pockets full of lambs tails
knowing the pit would close soon

and me, not knowing

playing happily

you didn't deserve it

I don't know why I keep coming
you don't deserve it

I've brought fresh flowers
my favourite roses
not that you knew
you never bought flowers for me

Diane's at college now
doing well
not that you'd care
you never liked her

Alan's here too
took a day off work
a proper job
not like you had

we're in a new house now
one with no shouting in it

we used to love you, you know ...

but you didn't deserve it

that's despair

sitting cross-legged
grubby, wet
and cold

mangy dog snuggling
better fed, better shape

biscuit tin lid
scattered with coins

feet passing by
splashing the rain

never see faces
never see smiles

only see pavement
never see sky

that's not begging

that's despair

Joanna Grigg

Anzacs Memorial, Sydney, 1970

Scarf shadowing her face, she visits for the final time,
avoids the attendant wanting to explain.
The walls carry photographs—please, not one of him –
she almost leaves but no, this is as vital as the day
they first met in the County offices, the wonder
of stillness when he stopped, and turned, as though
the sheep he sheared, the mines he worked, were under
his control and he could, with a nod, still them, too.

She has his silk embroidered postcards, warm below
the crease of breast. Her skin, reddened from the heat,
pales underneath the dome of stars, his face drawn
in the patterns of the Milky Way. She takes an envelope,
places into it the postcards, letters, telegram, drops it
behind a cabinet, walks in the direction of the wharves.

The First Equation

*Megalithic monuments, dating from the 3rd millenrium BC,
incorporate geometric figures such as circles, ellipses and
Pythagorean triples.*

An angle of grass-head, bud to stem.
Bypassers stop, query how this statement
should be described: a painting on a wall,
sketch in sand, both inadequate
to draw more than the *there* while, as they watch,
it grows. Uprights brush and chivvy,
form familiar arcs.

Fingers in the air, they try the careful
placing of a cross to symbolise *another*,
tilted to construe *more*. A recognition
by those who enjoy symmetry.
A surprising constancy.
The perturbation of subtraction.
The joyful discovery of brackets.

From The Edge

The wind was braying that night, stamping its hooves,
as we who stood launching Chinese lanterns
in memory of our dead found ourselves sucked
into the moon-like globes, carried for miles
before dying flames set us to stutter, tumble, crash

then up went the empty lanterns to be caught on guttering,
shucked across roofs in a waltz, singletons at tea dances
feeling the movement of air, the warmth of a glancing touch.
They paused over the power station chimney,
inhaled lungfuls of warm gas, headed for France.

My kitten tells me it's dawn. I push her back. Even then
she anticipates the excitement of today—*Look*—she purrs—*Games.*
A bowl of cream. That other world outside.

She's so close to boundaries, I can't let her out
any more than I let myself onto the storm beach
where pebbles fly like bullets, undertakers wade
the violent wash, embalming everything they find.

Birth and death are huge within her. *One day*, I purr back,
you will meet fox, squirrel, toad. Gull, snail,
grass, tree. Some you will eat. Others will eat you.

I don't even know the name for it, this sport
in and above the sea, tiny black people,
arms outstretched, legs bent, bobbling across the surf
like speeding vans on a pot-holed planet

until a kite buckles against the wind, angle of woman,
elements, the energy of froth, the crescent curve
of a kite aerodynamic as bird's wing. She rises until I know
that when she crashes all of her will break

but she flies

further towards the fractured clouds,
a brush of sunlight catching her

as it would have been for Armstrong had he not
tied the laces on his weighted boots, his giant leap
taking him to orbit. See him—*there*—observing
the airborne, the leaden-footed on the beach.

Jeanne Hewton

Looking On

Your world
from a chair.
Square.

No smell, no feel,
no taste, nothing real.

Images mesmerize.
Words juggle for meaning.

No wind, no sun,
no kisses, no fun.

Friends on screen
Facebook phenomena.
Friends unseen
Twittering.

Amazon Street tempts.
Cheap. Quick delivery.
House bulges.
Bigger screens.

You
smaller.

Machico (Madeira)

I choked back tears
as many families emerged from the Gothic doorway—
Machico celebrating a Holy Day with Mass.
In the town every cafe filled
teenagers joined in happily with grandparents and toddlers.
We sat with our coffee
watching.

Later I wept for something we have lost,
for a time when families lived close, supporting each other.
I wept for children everywhere who struggle alone to find
love
security
food
and a rite of passage.

Our nuclear age has blown us apart.
Like spade-dug ants
we scatter across the Earth
seeking new environs
wealth
somewhere different.

Lynne Hjelmgaard

Return to the Tropics

I sit child-like at the edge of the cliff,
and hear my name chanted by geckos
when I close my eyes.

The mountain on the tropical coast, in silhouette
(moon rises just behind it), no longer knows
its way to me.

Still, the island has a pointed rock-shape
like the head of a black lizard;
there is a ruin now
where there used to be lights.

A cactus has died,
its thick-skinned shadow more obtuse
and creature-like in the star-shine.
The tamarind have all but disappeared.

Trade winds occupy
our house on the hill:
they blow me in
they blow me out.

But I longed to get back!

Midnight howling gales
clear the way for morning,
summon the new.

Waves no longer operate in threes:
break on the rocks,
die down,
start up.

I remember local men
fishing in a small boat
seemingly buried in a swell.

They'd disappear,
then rise up again,
yell excitedly
to *Annalise* higher
on the top of
a foamy green crest.

Their boat appeared
out of nowhere
the way geckos do.

On land the men's gait
is laboured and slow.
Though I know them
they pass me blankly.

But still I want back.

Threads of black clouds
seem to tease the moon
off its axis.

I close my eyes, dream—
it drifts and spins aimlessly,
shows its never-before-seen side.

Connections

Yachts are tied to wooden pilings,
(patient in their tortured movement)
they lean, bow and rise, lean, bow and rise.

Dock lines twist and stretch,
(forgiving and strong, tightened
to the maximum).

A captain rubs the hull
of his enormous yacht- smooth to shine.
(Methodically, in no hurry).

As you and I had once rubbed
our smaller *Annalise's* hull- smooth to shine.
(Methodically, in no hurry).

Clumsy, I step aboard a friend's yacht,
afraid to tumble. Instantly I sense
the distance travelled, know this space.

The thrill of sails and hull that work
with water and wind. My upturned
face in the happiness, its salty smell.

Or a night sail under the milky way,
taken in by rawness, the immediacy
of the unknown, an embrace.

But then, uneasy again, disconnected.
I lie in this strange bunk, surrender to the motion,
the clatter, the groans, rattles and thumps.

This rock-and-roll.
This bull with a harness on,
tamed by cowboy wind.

Robin Houghton

Poem beginning with a line by Emily Dickinson

Make me a picture of the sun:
a collage. Use what comes to hand:
yellow dusters edged in red
and orange zest to represent
the summer high noon overhead
blaze that burns the backs of ears,
mix with salt sweat and chalk
from the cliffs, narcissus petals,
the pale yolk of an egg when stale,
add all the unwanted Yellow Pages,
history's turncoats, jaundiced faces,
Doris Day songs, a little blond hair.
It will be big and bright and hot.
It will be bigger than its parts.
They will see it in the Arctic Circle,
in all the dark places, from space.

Sports photography in the 1970s

The captions are little more than clues:
Kevin Keegan heads past Zender
three grainy figures on a grainier background
—could be a crowd, a forest or a curtain -
the ball and Keegan's hair (he has no face)
are *tête à tête*, or it could be a plate he's
rolling up his arm or balancing mid-air
in a magic act. Zender, oddly, lacks limbs,
his lunge a diagonal curio while another,
unidentified moustached player is gazing
into space as if in a spot-the-ball tableau.

In this other one, two sportsmen seem to do
a pole dance, the first resting his head
awkwardly on Keegan's elbow, the latter
higher in the air. On closer inspection
I see the pole is none other than a pillar
to the main stand, rising up from the grey
pea soup of blank faces. At least I think
they are faces. But the well-fitting shirt
and shorts I recognise. Definitely Keegan.

Tess Jolly

Tiger

My lover prowls the room watching me write.
Poised beneath thick sleek hide

he senses my fingertips tapping keys
as forms rise behind glass, settle into chains.

Moonlight seeps through a gap in the curtains
onto his fur, the bands of orange and black.

In the space between lines I imagine
going to him, resting my head against his heart

to hear my voice echo in the cage of his bones.
I imagine curling into the pads of his paws,

his warmth, our muscles flexing as we sleep,
then I tilt my face to the cold bright screen.

My lover presses his tongue to the scruff of my neck.
Hot mute breath rises with my own.

Peter Kenny

Minotaur

Forehead gored by migraine;
pain has sharpened my senses.
I hear mosquitoes in the garden
there are clouds of them conspiring,
one for every promise.

You promised me this garden
somewhere private; somewhere lovely,
now it's empty bar some black dog
whose hairs I find everywhere.
And still I sense it panting
among the sculptures, *fin de siècle,*
made by someone very clever.

Rose-choked, the garden walls break
over the cracked slabs. I tread petals,
I make the divine slime of rose heads
the ecru of ex-white petal falls.

Or I listen to the radio,
snorting with uncontrollable laughter,
or I read my leisurely books
near the ornamental fishpond,
the copper-coloured fishpond.

The one I can never look in.

Train in Snow

Face at a window
I hatch these crazy theories:
the track is a snake totem,
a Peruvian spaceship runway
and all the grey stars
of these English towns
were built to summon you.

I print your name
to be read from space,
letter by letter,
on each passing
paperwhite field.

For you are the woman
who would fall to earth;
supergirl, correspondent,
my Aphrodite.

With all your graces,
I believe
you'll bring me something:
like spring
but everlasting.

Erbaut 1942

I peer through the grim slit
of the Nazi bunker
into the green of Guernsey
in its April ecstasy
and think of the forgotten.
Perhaps you were a Pole,
your father's farmstead
overrun by clanking tanks.
I imagine your belly flop
into the concrete slop
of these foundations,
your body splayed forever
in the attitude
of an inept swimmer.

Antony Mair

Damage

Seawind gusts across the yukkas' spikes
but here he's screened, his noontime shadow short
against the astroturf's hard green—like the plastic
fields through which, at home, his little trainset

obediently runs. He's holding the club
just as his father said; still feels the echo
of his father's body moulding him to the shape
of older men in larger spaces. The hole,

a distant disc across a narrow bridge,
joins in the mockery of the insolent ball:
Go on, sucker, try and see. Fear's a knife-edge.
His father's checking texts on his new mobile.

He gulps and swings the putter back: a light
tap on the ball's smug whiteness, like a rebuke,
that starts his own home movie, as the ball hits
the tiny parapet, then moves oblique-

ly to a ridgelet, hesitates
and—unbelievably—slips downhill
with a soft clunk into the hole. Rockets
explode inside him and the sunlight's full

of stars and exclamation marks. His father
looks up and says, pocketing his phone,
*Well done, lad. Let's be going. Your mother
wants you back.* Where's this from, this pain

that hotly swells in the eye, blurring the green?
The distant whoops of children on the beach
sound like jeers. A silent chasm opens
as he shrinks from the approaching touch.

Cloudless

Water juggles with silver
under a blue emptied
by the invading wind, save for

gulls cawing in the gusts—
Manhattan weather,
with fire-escapes and radio masts

etched by sunshine, flat
against retiring shadows;
or Australia, where the light

glares at eucalypts
—and in each place I've walked
in tunnels thick with dark, then stopped

and sensed a diamond horde
hurtle down passages,
glittering in the sluggish blood.

Today too there's
an atavistic tug
responding to the light's fierce call,

senior to the mind:
a primeval echo
behind the curtain of surrounding sound

but captured by the waiting
heart, instinctively.
Do you see how these simple gulls are floating

high in the turbulent air?
playing with the wind
with that freedom that we long for?

Agnès

Friday morning, and I'm polishing the brass:
the knocker, doorknob, letterbox, arranged
like medals on our front door's uniform.
Spring sunshine paints the street with light and shade.

The wind's turned to the south southwest, and if
I travelled up its path, unravelling
the seam of its trajectory, across
the sunlit Channel, up the gentle Seine

past Paris, down the idling Loire and on
to Angoulême, I'd come to Ribérac
and market day; and if wings carried me
as high as the migrating cranes that coast

in ragged arrowheads above the town
I'd see the shimmering Dronne, the glint of cars,
and hear, perhaps, a distant buzz of talk
rise through the chestnut trees, the *paysans*

sun-wrinkled, square, exchanging pleasantries
beside spruce carrots and plump aubergines.
This was the day you cleaned our double doors
fronting the square; and if I travel back

against time's current, I can hear you chat
to passing friends, while bringing out the shine
on two brass handles, carefully restored
to pristine gold. In England now, above

the rippling sea, I rub our foreign brass.
Its liquid gleam dissolves all boundaries.
I see you pause, look up, shading your eyes,
and watch the cranes regroup, then travel north.

m.g.neal

Midwich Mother

After John Wyndham

A hammer rests on the kitchen table,
claw sticking two fingers up.
It should be hanging around
with its own kind,
tools on hooks in a garage.

In a kitchen it arouses suspicion,
I try not to imagine it splintering bone,
but know the comfortable balance
and weight of its swing; easy to wield,
easy to smash the aquarium, or make smithereens.

I resist touching lest it sway me
to do something irrevocable,
with its dull scuffed-iron face,
gracefully curved head, blind eye,
chiselled cheeks, bluntness.

I keep my hands pocketed
and don't think the word 'weapon'
in front of the children.

Heliopause

On reaching this unmarked boundary,
ignorant of its existence before,
she discovers an intangible void.

Along a trajectory, perhaps pre-determined,
certainly uncharted, a course far out

beyond the tonguing of flames,
beyond the magnetic field, to where your sphere
is light years from this astronaut's universe;

she feels her way through a wallow of night
succumbing to the vacuum, its limbo, free-floating.

Turn around, the golden rays are tarnished,
she refuses to rise or fall with the solstice;
re-entering your orbit her skin no longer feels the scorch.

Synaesthesia in a Department Store

Cacophonous perfume counter smothers her
like a bazaar stall of saris in a breeze,
vocalists jostle in a jazz choir for ascendance,
until she passes the aftershaves
announcing themselves like bassoons in a concerto,
or piccolos trilling around her upturned nostrils.

Through the grapefruit and mango flavoured clothes
hanging from rails of tangled vines,
she flounders towards the toy section.
Candied Barbies waft like frosted cup-cakes
a bakery of dolls with custard tart hair;
from legions of plastic military models
a stench of trenches and open sewers.

She runs to the double doors
where sunshine washes through,
lemon juice in cream, curdling fluorescent light.
A flashing blue alarm of a security guard's grip
on her arm, he gaoler-bawls 'Madam'
she seems to have slipped a rainbow in her pocket.

Miriam Patrick

Still Life with Vegetables

Dusk was his time
and even then reluctant,
he would return from a day
at the allotment, announced
by the rumble of his barrow
over cobbles, the sneck lifted
and the gate flung open,
bringing him in at the yard
to stand a moment, breathless,
before his sing- song tenor
called, 'I'm home'
at the kitchen window.
He was a one man harvest festival,
the barrow piled with marrows,
lettuces and beetroot, thick pink
sticks of rhubarb bound in bundles.
After unloading in the scullery,
he'd stand a while, admiring
summer's glut, then cup his hands
beneath the tap and scrub until
no more than traces of the black
half-moons beneath his nails remained.
Exchanging boots for slippers
he'd go in at last to find his mother;
bringing, gracious as a suitor,
freshly cut sweet peas, and talk
of growing plans and weather.

At Kamierz

Their smiles catch you first.
Six boys, all wearing the yarmulke,
arms round one another's shoulders,
posing for the camera
on a dirt road,
in a village that was home,
somewhere in central Poland.
The photograph is dated 1936.
The boys are ragged, all but one
barefoot, his boots gone
beyond repair.
Unbearable to see them, smiling
and walking unprotected
on the road to history.

Tim Rancelant

Meniscus

Glistening there on top
only words could break its surface
so we wrote letters past it
expressed beside it
gurned into its mirrored lid
Only words could break the tension
so we pinned notes to its stem
mimed in front of it
slapped on a smile
& went about our day
Only words could break it
Don't say a word &
I won't say a word.

Busy

Busy—yeah busy—
selling counterfeit placebos on the internet
Busy—yeah busy—
arranging bodyguards for celebrity bodyguards
Busy—yeah busy—
getting keys cut for that burnt-out house
Busy—yeah busy—
forging my own signature

Present

Aware of the Register being called
are we still sat at the back of the Class laughing
after having been moved so many times
Beal, Bowyer, Burstow, Coffin, Howells
When you were looking out there
I tried to hold a candle to you
Our formation became the opposite of rehabilitation
Inspiration made us wilder
enough to make us eat our own young
selves.

Robin Renwick

The Ram

Later in life I discovered how it worked,
a simple pump, driven by the flow
of a small stream, needing no power
and little maintenance.

All that we knew
was that it was yellow, and it had
a black swastika emblazoned on its side.
And it ticked, a slow relentless sound
that never faltered.

The danger was clear.
We kept our distance, dared each other
to get closer, included it in our games,
hurling grenades of clay from the long grass
and the dead ground.

We learned to live with it.
And something has remained over the years,
part of our world, drifting into dreams,
touching us, like a light breeze from childhood days
that carries the sound of bells, a distant siren.

Prism

Take this piece of glass.   Place it between
your words and mine, and those you hear me say.
See how reflection and refraction change
their meaning.
                        I did not begin the day
with the intention it should end this way.

If

If, my darling,
I could take all the sadnesses
that you have ever known, that are
turning to stone within you still,
and hold them in my cupped palm,
I'd make of them a white dove
all feathered with soft caresses
and let it loose on the green hill
for the world's winds to carry.

And, my love,
if I could take your every smile
and keep it in a precious jar
then, once in a while, I would try
to ease away the sorrow from your soul
and use your own sweet balm
to show you who you are.

Helen L Scott

Full Circle

You hoped I'd had a happy childhood.
What can I say to that,
looking at you with tubes in your nose?
How clever of you to ask me now.

I held your hand, even now
so much bigger than mine.
My other clutching a damp paper tissue.

There wasn't going to be an epiphany.
A washing away of years of disconnection, pain.
But, still, in the bright lights of this sterile room,
your shallow breath filling the silence,
we went full circle, my father and I.

Spreading Wings

The conditioning of thirty years,
the work ethic etched in stone—
no negotiation, no retraction. But what
if that were to change? And how would it
change?

The mind is a fragile tool,

but it can be bent, without being broken.
And even when broken, it can
be repaired.
To bend or repair is to grow;

spreading wings.

Tommy Sissons

Early wakers

Rise here with the early wakers,
the break of sun pacers, the fry-up creators
and the desperate for caffeine hot coffee makers,
rise with the homeless.

Leave home for your purpose,
for what will put promise in wallets and purses,
walk with the hermits
and then walk on.

Outweave the job seekers
and climb the sky scrapers,
race the work suck-ups to the top and then beat them,
if they could they'd leave you hanging like the window cleaners,
distance your metres from them.

But watch the street sweepers
that blend with the sun,
in fluorescent jackets
and let them become,
lend them one
moment of time.

Stop
and notice the line,
of standing guards at Buckingham Palace,
for hours they cannot emote,
some pay to be ravished,
some pay off the savages hoping they'll be left alone,
some are paid but will always stay broke.

The same scissors cut both the umbilical cords
of the marble floor stroller and the mud walker
who inherit the dirt from their ancestors' work,
but it never comes off in bath water.

And when the day's done with the corporate jobs,
Pall Malls in the mouths that inhale them,
leave the office and hear the door slam on the novice
floor to floor, door to door salesman.

Flag a taxi,
to the insomniac in the driver's seat
imply your needs
and watch him back track streets
till you arrive and then leave him.

Then sit,
and in the mirror, you may see that you're faceless,
convince yourself that you're not like them,
as you sit in the dark with your papers,
but should you drink too much
or stay awake till late, face it,
when that first glimpse of sunlight
slips through your window,
you'll still rise with the early wakers
and relive it all over again.

John Taylor

Under High Spy

Face stinging wind whips up the valley
walkers form a file, sheltering
like Wenceslas' page following
in the snow, a path more clearly
seen afar than at foot

one side of the valley bright
with fresh yellow spring bloom
of rampant gorse strewn
the shadow-side still not quite
from winter born

ancient lead-mine now at rest
fading snow on sun-warmed soil
like echoes of past sweat and toil
crooked hard hewn stones re-dressed
with lichen, moss and fern

Swiss October

Face alive in grey mountain air announcing
a long winter whose snow-bearing breath
brings life to the shuttered ranks of apartments
masquerading as ancient chalets bloated on wealth.

Lifting clouds show flanks of topless mountains,
newly sprinkled with early snow like sugar-strewn
fresh baked rock cakes. Glaciers, yesterday grey,
now sparkle in the momentary sunshine.

Old friends, fresh snow, knee deep. Once more
a walk whose mad joys, memorable
insanity and lack of safety adds it to a
relationship both precious and fruitful.

A field only two days ago green and sunny
now blizzard-bathed. The lake which had
offered prospect of lazy circumnavigation
only visible as snowflecked slate glimpsed

through the swirling flakes. Chairlifts, though
static no longer incongruous, wait the opening
of the runs, not yet due. The closed
café offers no shelter and the train waiting

room locked but sliding doors amenable
to being pried open. The cold concrete space
protects from wind and snow. A family also waits.
Even the children can no longer face

being out in this sudden winter landscape.
The final train of the day appears
to rescue us from the shaken snow-dome
and bring us to warmth and calm our fears.

Now head back to the airport as cloud
wisps stick like cotton wool to the lower slopes
of mountains whose new snow-capped peaks
sharply defined in the sun whose heat soon melts

Simon Tilbury

walking with elm-seeds

blossoms wander the sky, their idling
engines lending the airborne wilderness
a grainy feel, a low low
in-the-bones sub rosa rhythm.
an envelope—empty—jitters underfoot,
i lift my heel and it goes
skittering away, down the hill,
like me, toward the
      crossings of the steine, where,
millioned, teeming and profligate
the elm seeds are dancing up a storm.

tiny bits of paper, their
folded-up voices overspilling my pockets,
i aim them happily at passers by.

glossy rivulets blink in the gutter, while
inklings of some molten, never-was alphabet
ricochet from windscreens and shopfronts.
the museum announces a new exhibition:
'figments, fragments and everybody's love affairs'.

seen a-glance,
a toyshop is selling all the little lost things,
bright with memory, blankly gazing,
blinking out from worlds-ago,
senselessly
      enchanting.

a fox slips behind a skip and vaporizes.
my tempo does not slow. in the breath
    between each footfall
immaterial, insurmountable
 bacteria wreck and wreak,
etching signs of heartbreak into
    all the eye is eating —

Eliza Wyatt

Bloody Jane Eyre

My family only pretends to listen
in the evening gloom
my adulterated wife, my sons, their girlfriends
my in-laws planning to dispose of left-over chicken
and the governess who is supposed to teach
sits and picks her teeth.
Two weeks holiday in Provence with this bunch
provided for by my city acumen
commuter sweat
me, the only one who knows how to think.

'I came in good faith, sir!'

I never know what she means
my sons' art teacher carefully lured
into sharing our summer vacation.
Sometimes I don't remember her name!
Give yourself licence to change it, she pertly says
as if this is something I could admit.
It is Selena, sir
isn't that the name of a witch?
Isn't she a shade anaemic?
Her stick figure, all bosom, turns me on.

'What can I say, sir?'

All the bloody girl does is wash up
breaking plates
which sets them off
insanely laughing?
If only she could teach me
now that I've a leisure minute
how to take abstract photographs
or I'll learn by watching her paint

from ten to one and two to four in the afternoon
that is, if she has nothing else to do.
'I'm sorry sir!'

She was invited here to impart art
calls me patron but plays Scrabble
with my sons and beats them.
Their girlfriends think she's amazing
we can do without their admiration.
Even the mosquitoes are boring!
Especially killing them.
I drink more than anyone.
She's allergic to wine.
'Not in France' I shout

'I'm in danger sir.'

She's obviously subversive
My wife gets undressed
and I want to be sick: my headaches increase
I'm the one in danger
of becoming a homicidal maniac.
My wife asked me last night
if I ever wanted to kill myself
knowing the answer was yes, yes.
The governess combs her long hair!
No questions asked, she must leave us.

Bloody Jane Eyre
who asked her here?

Ashes

wide-eyes innocent   blank attention
knotted scarf around   allowing him
to touch his loss   his lost hair

while hers erupts fiery furnace-heated
combed through with wrongs

he hides   on the edge of ardent forest
running with leaves   soaked in deer sweat

unrefreshed by hurt

                    regret reaches towering pines
                    in a place where sky escapes

                    she let go his hand
on the crumbling path
before it crumbled

                    words become a laugh

promises to wed   a wedding skit
thrust through wooden doors

her face a torch   contemplating the 'if'
doubt a sour dry berry

Judas Kisses

She takes her smell with her
    incense from Kerala

going west in search of hardship
    clothed in memory

torn shirts stained orange and red
    left

in India, a continent of infinite
    leisure

she's flying past nightmares
    animal myths

leaving ash and me upstairs
    sitting on my hands

two weeks later
    smoke still lingers.

The Poets

David Agnew
enjoys sharing poems with the other poets at Brighton Stanza meetings. 'The criticism is always constructive and it's interesting to read others' work during the writing process.' He sometimes takes part in other local pub poetry evenings around Brighton. David tends to do shorter poems and writes them quickly: the ideal would be to leave the pen and paper out overnight and let the poem write itself entirely.

Mary Allen
read English at Cambridge and then went on to be an actor for several years. A varied career in arts management culminated in her becoming Secretary-General of the Arts Council of England in the 1990s. She started writing poetry in 2006, and joined the Brighton Stanza when she moved there in 2012.

Chris Allinson
is a writer and copy editor based in Shoreham-by-Sea. With an academic background in education and social policy, he has worked as a development advisor in central and eastern Europe and central Asia. Chris has a longstanding love of all forms of short verse, and is a former committee member of the British Haiku Society.

Dave Brooks
works for an investment bank in the City, commuting from the Three Bridges area. He has been writing poetry for more than 15 years and recently completed a module in creative writing with the Open University. He has been attending the Stanza Group workshops for two years, and participated in the Stanza Bonanza readings that took place at the Poetry Café in 2013.

Lucy Cotterill
was shortlisted for the 2012 Keats Shelley Prize with her poem *The Bracelet*. She is currently completing a Masters in Creative Writing at the University of Chichester. She lives in West Sussex with her husband and three children.

Andie Davidson

is a writer, musician and sometime artist, who earns a living writing about machines and relaxes by writing poetry about life. She is also a publisher (Bramley Press) and regular blogger in her spare time (www.andiesplace.co.uk). *Realisations*, a volume of poetry relating her experiences in coming to terms with her transsexuality and the way people responded, was long-listed for the 2013 *Polari* First Book prize.

Liz Eastwood

was born in the UK and educated in the UK and Cyprus. Having spent some years in the Middle East, she now lives and works on the South Coast. She is a performance poet, plays in a band and runs. *Book Rape* won the Sunny Worthing Arts Group Competition prize in 2009. She is currently working on a collection of metaphysical short stories.

Susan Evans

is an East Londoner, now Brighton-based Performance Poet. Her one woman show 'A bit of oral' premiered at the 2010 Brighton Fringe Festival, *Komedia* Brighton, with encouraging reviews. Susan's thrilled to be contributing to Brighton Stanza Anthology, especially having recently performed alongside a number of fellow contributors, in *Stanza Bonanza* at the Poetry Café, Covent Garden. Susan is pleased also, to be performing on home ground, at Waltham Forest Literature Festival, in November, 2013.

John Feakins

is 72 and spent 40 years teaching English in the UK and abroad. Having grown up in London he now lives in Eastbourne, where he pursues his interests in swimming, walking, history, cooking, real ale and rugby. He is the president of Eastbourne Rugby Club and has just published a history of the club. Future plans include a book of landscape poetry and photographs.

Clive Findlay

was born in the Welsh mining valleys. He first worked in the hotel, restaurant and conference business in the UK, then in consulting in the Middle East, before moving to Brighton and management education.

His first poem was written while at primary school. The next one came 40 years later. He now writes on a regular basis, publishing poems, short stories and haiku on his website (www.memoriesandimaginations.com).

Joanna Grigg

founder member of the Brighton Stanza and current Stanza representative. Until her untimely death shortly before the publication of this anthology, Jo worked as a freelance educational consultant and creative facilitator/lecturer, after a varied career spent largely in the education sector. She authored thirteen books and her poems have been extensively published, notably in *The Rialto*, *The North* and *Interpreter's House*. Two of her poems were long-listed in the 2012 National Poetry Competition.

Jeanne Hewton

studied at The Royal Academy of Music. Her career has been teaching music in Secondary Schools followed by Music Therapy in Special Schools. More recently she has become increasingly interested in literature and started writing poetry. She is retired and married with one son.

Lynne Hjelmgaard's

latest book, *The Ring*, was published with Shearsman Books in 2011. Her latest sequence of poems, titled *A Boat Called Annelise*, was a runner-up in the Poetry Wales Purple Moose Pamphlet Competition in 2012.

Robin Houghton

won the 2013 Hamish Canham Prize and the 2012 *New Writer* Poetry competition, and was commended in the 2012 Poetry Society Stanza competition. She has had work in a range of magazines including *The Rialto*, *Agenda*, *The North*, *Iota*, *Poetry News*, *Mslexia*, *Obsessed with Pipework* and *Ink, Sweat & Tears*. Her 'how-to' manual, 'Blogging for Creatives', was published in 2012. Robin blogs at Poetgal (www.poetgal.co.uk).

Tess Jolly

has had poems published in a wide variety of paper and online magazines including *Magma, Mslexia, Agenda, The North* and *Iota*. She fits working part-time as a library assistant and running Tiger's Eye Writers—creative writing workshops for 6-11 year olds—around looking after her own two children.

Peter Kenny

lives in Brighton and has strong links to the Channel Island of Guernsey. His poetry collection *The Boy Who Fell Upwards* was published as half of 'A Guernsey Double' (2010) which also featured Richard Fleming and was supported by the Guernsey Arts Commission. A creative collaboration with classical composer Matthew Pollard resulted in the album *Clameur* (2012), while his comedies *Wrong* and *Betty the Spacegirl* ran in Brighton's Marlborough Theatre (2011).

Antony Mair

was formerly a commercial lawyer, then a French estate agent. He now lives in Hastings, East Sussex. He has had poems published by *Acumen* and *Ink Sweat and Tears* and is about to undertake a Creative Writing MA with the University of Lancaster.

m.g.neal

studied Philosophy and Literature at the University of Hertfordshire, and has an MA in Women's Studies from the University of Sussex. She has a poem published in a National Anthology which was used in an exhibition of paintings by Rachel Plummer, and in a film to mark the tenth anniversary of the Lewes Flood. She has been a member of Brighton Stanza since 2010. She lives in Lewes with her daughter and son.

Miriam Patrick

is a part time teacher. She has been writing poetry for over twenty years, drawing on memories of growing up in Manchester, biblical texts and ideas triggered by reading other writers. An MA at King's College, London, focussing on Middle English, left her with an abiding devotion to Langland's *Piers Plowman,* and she has recently been reworking extracts from this little-known masterpiece.

Tim Rancelant

is a member of the Safehouse Experimental Music Collective. In 2003 his *Opéra des Figues*, written for the No Hay Banda Puppet Theatre Company, was performed in Toulouse. His poems are spoken word pieces, which have been performed live with a number of musicians, including the 4thirtythree Jazz Trio. A review of their 2010 CD described his poems as 'aphorisms from the mind of a racetrack mystic'.

Robin Renwick

was born on a farm in Sussex and studied Design at the Royal College of Art. He has spent most of his working life as a designer/printer and lecturing in Art and Design. He retired from full time lecturing in 2001 and now works as a rock climbing instructor. He has had poems published in *Agenda* and its online supplement.

Helen Scott

has recently reclaimed her childhood passion for reading and writing poetry; perhaps due to a recent significant birthday. Her work is broadly themed around personal experience, nature and mental health. Helen also plays with micropoetry on Twitter @honestcelt and randomly posts on her blog (honestcelt.wordpress.com).

Tommy Sissons

is a 17 year old Spoken Word Poet and Playwright from Brighton. He is the current Hammer & Tongue South East Poetry Slam Champion and is ranked 5th nationally, following the 2013 finals. He writes about politics, urban lifestyles and working class values and is currently compiling his first collection. His plays have been performed at the Chichester Festival Theatre, the Unicorn Theatre and the Dome Theatre among other venues.

John Taylor

has lived most of his life in Sussex, mainly in the leafy middle, while commuting to London to work in the financial services sector. A few years ago he gave up full-time work and moved to Brighton. A liking for poetry, which had previously found its expression in occasional

comic verse, developed into a more serious activity following his
Brighton move.

Simon Tilbury
is a singer-songwriter living in Brighton. With a passion for poetry,
he has experimented with words for as long as he can remember. 'My
mind is too unruly for any formal technique—for me, every poem is
unique. A poem only comes about through successive 'passes', each a
kind of performance, where the poem finds its own coherence via
internal music, intersecting ideas, real and imagined scenarios.'

Acknowledgements

Liz Eastwood's *Book Rape* won the Sunny Worthing Arts Group Competition prize in 2009.

Tess Jolly's *Tiger* was commended in the 2012 Poetry Society Stanza Poetry Competition and published at www.poetrysociety.org.uk/lib/tmp/cmsfiles/File/12%20Stanza%20co mpetition%20poems.pdf.

Miriam Patrick's *Still Life with Vegetables* was published in *South* in April 2012, and *At Kamierz* in *Weyfarers* in 2011.

Robin Renwick's *The Ram, Prism* and *If* were published in *Agenda*.

Lightning Source UK Ltd.
Milton Keynes UK
UKOW04f1557211013

219474UK00003B/8/P

Author photograph by Jenni Lee Photography, Tavistock

Anna West is the name used by Jackie Waddle to write contemporary romantic fiction. Jackie was born in the village of Lytchett Matravers in Dorset. She now lives in the market town of Tavistock in Devon, and is involved with creative writing in the community. She began writing when her two sons started school. *Breaking New Ground* is her first novel.

BREAKING
NEW GROUND

Anna West

Best wishes

Anna West.

Aspiring Writers

To Mum whose imaginative bedtime tales I pleaded
for as a child inspired me to write my own stories.

Prologue

'I know the competition judges have the final decision, but we could sway them in our direction and I have good vibes about the 'Orchard Court' entry.'

Crispin Grainger waited for a response from the 'Breaking New Ground' team. He opened a fanlight window at the end of the conservatory, moved a tray of geranium cuttings and sat down on his director's chair with his pen poised. Ruby shivered, then picked up the photographs and began flicking through them.

'But there are four separate plots in this garden Cris, they won't go for it, it'll be way over budget for a start.'

'It's one of a kind Ruby, we'll never find a project like this again. The whole garden is like a hidden world, it's so whimsical.'

Cameraman, Barry leaned over Ruby to take a look.

'I thought there was only allowed to be one winner for the competition boss?'

It was just the sort of dim, unimaginative response they all expected from Barry. Crispin paced the floor with tight lips and exasperated snorts, while Ruby smiled and sipped her café latte through a bright pink plastic straw so as not to smudge her perfect crimson lipstick. Crispin removed the photos gently but firmly from Barry's grip and laid them out methodically on the table.

'Look everyone, I'm putting it to you, what are the alternatives? We have the long thin terraced garden in Leatherhead not touched for ten years. Then there's the cottage garden in St Andrews. Remember? The owners had a problem with sea mists damaging their plants. Or we could go for the equally scintillating patio and window box area in the concrete jungle of…'

'All right Crispin we get the point.' Ruby examined her tiger-striped highlighted hair in her handbag mirror and sizzled the last inch of her cigarette to an early death in the dregs of her coffee.

'I don't want you to look stupid, that's all,' she said.

Another cameraman, Colin pointed to the photo showing all four plots.

'Do you know what the residents are like Cris? You'll have to get their agreement first, only Mrs Parker entered the competition, she can't vouch for everyone.'

'Yes, yes I realise that. I telephoned her yesterday to ask her to put it to the neighbours and get agreements sent to the studio as soon as possible.'

Ruby stood up to smooth out the creases in her pale blue linen suit. She turned to Crispin.

'So did Mrs Parker tell you what the neighbours were like Cris? For all we know they could be a right awkward bunch.'

'I spoke to Mrs Parker. She's a quiet, friendly girl, but with an air of determination. She's a shop assistant and her husband's high up in the fashion industry.'

'That's interesting, what sort of line is he in?'

'I don't know Ruby,' Crispin replied brushing her off and continuing. 'Next door to her is Miss Dolce, then there's Mr and Mrs Cunningham and their four sons and finally Mr Harper on the other side of the garden, he's recently been widowed.'

Ruby shifted in her seat and wondered about Mr Parker's connections in the fashion world along with how old Mr Harper was.

'So shall we put Orchard Court forward to the judges as the best proposal?' she said.

'You've changed your tune Ruby,' Barry piped up in surprise.

Colin and Crispin stared at him and he shrunk back into his seat.

'I'll go and email them straight away,' Crispin said decisively, 'while all our tunes are still in harmony.'

Chapter One

Adele Parker set her alarm early today so that she could have breakfast with Ben before he left for the fashion conference. She stood barefoot on the terracotta tiled kitchen floor, feeling the coldness of the tiles and the sharp prickle of toast crumbs beneath her feet. A long white towelling robe covered her thin T-shirt and the front of it gaped open to reveal slender honey coloured legs.

'More toast?' she offered, juggling the last two pieces, hot from the toaster and placing them in the rack in front of her husband.

'Any more butter?' he mumbled back, glancing up momentarily from his laptop and looking expectantly at her.

'Yes, just a sec, I'll soften it for you in the microwave.'

She lingered patiently for the 'ding' from the machine and refilled the butter dish. Ben was e-mailing a supplier and reached blindly for the butter and knife while Adele continued to stand calmly, waiting for the kettle to boil for the second pot of the day, the first served in bed this morning just after her alarm at 5.45 a.m.

Ben had been very successful so far, climbing the managerial ladder in the retail industry and Adele was giving all her support to his training. He'd taken on a new position two years' ago which meant long hours and many of those on the road travelling. Adele had taken on more of the household tasks since they had moved to the West Country from Croydon. It was all part of her effort to rectify what was wrong in their marriage. She'd found a part-time job, leaving behind her full-time position at the department store in Croydon and her job now at the mini-market gave her more time to tackle washing, ironing, housework and shopping before Ben came home. Having some free time allowed her to experiment in the kitchen with new recipes and to sample the selection of wines on offer at her new place of work. There was always time for Ben to relax with a glass of wine when he finally arrived home in the evening. Adele had great plans for redecorating the house and had even considered doing something with that nonsensical fragment of garden that went with the property. If it all went wrong now she could tell herself that she'd tried her best and if her best wasn't good enough, well...

The water bubbled up and Adele covered the tea bags and replaced the lid. Ben was still typing away as she stared out of the window that looked over their plot of garden while she waited for the tea to infuse.

'Do you think we should have some raised borders in the corner that catches the most sun? We could grow a few herbs. It would save buying all those small plants from the supermarket.'

Ben continued to look down at his work.

'I'll be back late tonight, about 10 o'clock. We've got a regional conference on "Changing the Style of the Power Suit." It should be over by 6.30, so I'll be on the road by quarter to seven.'

He snapped his laptop closed and waited for her response. Adele's eyes were fixed on the sun's position now and where it would be at lunchtime today.

'Del, Del, did you hear me? You really are in cloud cuckoo land lately.'

He planted a perfunctory kiss on her cheek.

'So, see you about ten tonight?'

She forced a smile and murmured, 'Okay, at ten.'

Ben loaded his briefcase and laptop into the trunk of his silver BMW. He selected three of his favourite CDs to play at random on the journey, hung his jacket on a hook over the back seat and pulled away. By the time he had reached the turn-off for the motorway he had relaxed and stopped worrying for a while that he'd brought all the right files.

Adele put on her jogging trousers and a brand new pair of green Huntress Wellingtons. The Wellingtons were a recent purchase from the local farming store and up until now she hadn't realised that there was a fashion code in countryside clothing. She wasn't due into work until lunchtime today, leaving her a few hours to take a look at her patch of garden and make plans. She straightened the pile of CDs in the kitchen. 'The Lighthouse Family' was missing and she guessed Ben had taken it with him. The CD was a few years' old now, but it always managed to calm his nerves and yet fire up enthusiasm at the same time. Adele and Ben had been to see them live in concert. They didn't seem to find time to go to concerts, theatre and cinema since he'd started the new job and he was no longer relaxed enough to spend an evening with her any more. The cuddles and chats over a shared bottle of wine that Adele had so enjoyed when they were first married had faded into the past.

10

Adele's mother had said that the new mini-market job was a bit of a come down for her, but she hadn't taken much notice of her mother's comments. She had to make some sacrifices for what she believed in and maybe, just maybe she and Ben would get it back again, back to where it was before, before he changed. Her new lifestyle was quite sedate and verging on boring. It didn't challenge her at all but she did have the high-class night time functions to look forward to, although even they were tinged with an unsettling air of disrespect. Ben always made a point of showing off with her on his arm at company functions. He said she was all class, sleek and fashionable and not at all cheap in any way. He told his boss that he hadn't tired of his wife like so many of his colleagues and so far she was continuing to be an asset to him.

Adele climbed the steep steps by the side of her neighbour's patio and made her way across to her own plot. The access to the garden was enough to put anyone off before they even thought about buying packets of seed. Except for the patio with its boundary neatly marked by a white plastic picket fence, the border-lines were all lined with the occasional metal post with thick wire strung between them. The wire had once been taut but had slackened over the years and one or two of the posts had rusted out of their sockets and lay unattended in the long grass. Adele wriggled through the gap between two pieces of wire. There was supposed to be a wooden gate and she was sure that the estate agent had shown her where it was when they viewed the property, but that had been in winter and now the early spring shoots and leaves obscured the entrance.

Their plot was a regular rectangle, facing south-east. Adele stood in the middle of it trying to visualize a tidier affair. Even if she did tidy it up, bought a barbecue and some garden furniture, imagine dragging Ben's work colleagues up the steep steps and through this jungle. She looked through the hedgerow of dense shrubs to see if there were any recognisable plants. She hadn't had very much experience of gardening yet as she and Ben had only been married for five years and lived in a flat in Croydon before this house. Most of the shrubs were distorted and tangled together, but in a shady corner was a truly beautiful specimen hiding behind taller, stronger plants. Its delicate fern-like arms arched themselves elegantly out of the dark corner, although not in an ostentatious manner. Each succulent frond bore clusters of heart-shaped pendants along its main stem and each individual crimson bloom displayed a tiny droplet of white, squeezed from the base of a flattened heart. Whilst she didn't want to damage the shrub, Adele gently picked one bloom to identify it when she got home.

Back in her kitchen, she sipped her camomile tea while watching the gardening slot on daytime TV. The presenter plugged a competition for a garden makeover. To enter all that was needed was a photograph or a sketch of the garden and an explanation of where it was in the UK. Adele made a note to enter later sending in one of her sketches and a photo. She suspected that as usual in competitions of this kind that she would be one of thousands, but wouldn't it be wonderful?

She picked up the fragile heart-shaped bloom selected from the garden earlier. It lay in her pale elegant palm resting against the ridge of her antique gold wedding band. The presenter went on to talk about 'easy-to-grow' perennials and among the plants he showed to the audience was her plant. He picked it up to talk about it. It was an exquisite flower and its name was dicentra or bleeding heart.

'Well what a coincidence, I'll certainly be keeping you,' she said dropping the flower on the kitchen table and getting up to look out of the window at the garden. The kitchen was on the first floor of the house, with an unoccupied flat on the ground floor. The most recent tenants had moved out when the property was sold and Ben had been reluctant to let it again, uneasy about sharing the house with strangers.

Ben was always suspicious when it came to making new acquaintances, but after only six months of moving into Orchard Court Adele knew all the neighbours and some of the town folk as well. There were three other houses in Orchard Court; Eileen in the cottage to the left, followed by Rory and Viv and their four children in the two cottages knocked into one large house at the end of the terrace. The garden, divided into four plots was situated in front of the houses and on the other side a small cottage housed Miles. Adele sat at her kitchen table where she could see the garden as well as the goings on of the all the houses through the window. She was in need of some help if she wanted to do anything with that garden and she wasn't sure that she'd get any help at all from Ben.

Chapter Two

Viv Cunningham rubbed the base of her back while gazing out of her upstairs window on the landing. She'd had a minor accident a few days ago when she slipped on a moss-covered step injuring her back. Her window overlooked the rambling garden shared with her three other neighbours. A gnarled old apple tree in the middle of all the plots encroached onto everyone's space and Adele and Ben's out of control grass strangled the last few perennials in the corner. Eileen's pocket handkerchief-sized patio was nearest to the lane as was Miles's green sanctuary next to Eileen's with its ancient wooden bench shrouded by amethyst encrusted buddleia.

The different plots used to be clearly marked out and each sectioned lawn neatly clipped. Now all peripheries were a mass of cancerous brambles and weeds entwining into disarray. Viv and Rory had cultivated the garden just before they moved into the house ten years ago. It was whilst they were living in rented accommodation and the builders were knocking the two cottages into one house. Their eldest sons, Justin and Drew were younger then. They had helped her make fat balls for the birds in the winter and used an empty cooking oil drum from a local restaurant to fill with sandy soil and grow carrots the following summer. As soon as the conversion was finished they moved in and house decorating took over. Then life seemed to take on a faster pace. They'd added two more sons to their family since then. Harry and Jake were at primary school now, but there was still a lot for Viv to do looking after four boys and a husband. She'd kept up the herb garden for a while, but all that remained of it now was an over large bay bush and a spindly rosemary with more bark than sprigs of the herb.

Rory Cunningham crept out from his house and into the lane at Orchard Court carrying a mug of tea. He climbed the steps leading up to the garden to find they were covered in a fine slippery moss, the top one having an imprint of a large skid.

'What was she doing up there in the first place?' he murmured under his breath.

He leaned over to the gate half hidden by rotten leaves. Even leaning on those steps he could feel his feet sliding. It was a death trap. He collected a bucket of grit from his shed, spread it over

13

each step and then stood in the lane, away from his house finishing his mug of tea and his cigarette. He stubbed it out on the saucer, wafted the air around a bit then pushed his bike out of the shed, eyes wide open in search of his wife looking out for what he was up to. He started the bike in the lane, dribbled down to the main road, fixed his helmet strap and was off.

Viv wiped the rest of the crumbs from the breakfast table. The forecast was for a clear dry day. They'd had rain for so long now that she'd forgotten how long it was since she'd hung the washing outside. The small courtyard at the back of the house was just large enough to house a rotary line and tiny shed for Rory's bike. She wished that the area was bigger and more of a garden for the family to sit in or have a barbecue in the summer months, but Viv didn't really relish the idea of heavy gardening work any more. She much preferred spending time with her children.

She pegged the last shirt on the line and before returning to the kitchen paused to close the shed door left open by Rory earlier. There on a small wooden shelf was a brown Denby saucer full of stubbed out cigarettes and an empty packet of Benson and Hedges.

'Damn you Rory,' she said to herself. 'You told me you'd given up.'

Back inside the kitchen she abandoned the rest of the cleaning, her back was aching slightly and she needed a walk. She grabbed a fleece and her purse and made off in the direction of the mini-market. She needed milk and vegetables for Justin's favourite beef stew tonight. As she mulled over what to buy she planned what she would say to Rory over the smoking later today. She spotted Adele at the till as she wandered around with her wire basket and wondered whether she would have stood a chance for the job at the mini-market had she not withdrawn the application. She remembered why she'd withdrawn it and in turn it reminded her that perhaps she shouldn't be too harsh on Rory. She paid for the shopping and after a quick 'hello' to Adele left the shop.

Adele had hoped that Viv would stop for a chat. She needed to ask her something today. She'd received a phone call about the garden competition she'd entered the other day. She'd finish her shift in an hour though so perhaps she could call on Viv then.

After much knocking, Adele found the door of Viv's kitchen open and walked through the hallway to hear her clattering pans for the meal tonight.

'Viv,' she called out, 'can I come in?'

Viv came to the hall and invited Adele into the kitchen.

'I saw Rory this morning and he said you'd slipped and hurt your back. Are you okay now?'

Viv looked out of her window in the direction of the garden.

'I'm okay, but we really should do something about that garden. If we'd been looking after it this never would have happened.'

'Don't feel too guilty; our plot is much worse than yours...In fact that's why I've come to see you.'

'Sounds interesting Adele. Go through to the lounge and I'll make us some coffee.'

Viv made coffee. She waited for the boiled water to cool slightly before pouring it onto the fresh coffee grounds. She normally relished the smell of fresh coffee, but today as the aroma drifted upwards to meet her she felt sick. She sat down and before taking the tray back into the lounge to join Adele, she sipped at a glass of cold water.

Viv put the tray of coffee down, poured two coffees and handed one to Adele.

'We're lucky to have the back two plots you know and you're the furtherest away from Eileen's precious patio. She thinks she owns the place, sat there in her deckchair like some kind of queen. My boys go up there to play and she always seems to be there to tell them off and shout at them for no real reason.' Viv sat down and prepared to listen to Adele.

'So what is it about the garden?'

Adele placed her coffee down on the table.

'I entered a competition recently for a garden makeover. The TV company telephoned me after I sent them a photo and a sketch saying they were interested not only in my plot but all the neighbours' plots in Orchard Court.'

'So how can I help?' Viv questioned.

'I need everyone's consent that they would like to think about sharing the garden between all of us and making it into a larger more usable area.'

Viv moved forward on her seat with interest.

'What a good idea, I'd never have thought about doing that. Tell me more.'

Rory pushed his bike wearily into the shed that evening, but came running out again followed by a flying dustpan and brush.

'Bloody hell woman, I'm too tired to clean it up now I've just finished a shift.'

'Wish I could just swan off and leave all my responsibilities behind me for someone else to look after.'

'Your trouble is you've got too many responsibilities and now you've just gone and landed yourself with another one.'

Rory drew breath and before Viv had chance to reply, screamed out, 'You're like the woman that lived in the shoe in Jake's nursery rhyme book.'

'Can't you understand? It really was an accident this time and I can hardly help having the reproductive system of a rabbit. You can blame the hospital waiting lists I say. If your name had come up on the vasectomy list like we planned I wouldn't be in this situation.'

'You told me you'd had a coil fitted.'

'I did. Is it my fault it's become dislodged from where it should be?'

'Bloody kid will probably come out holding the flaming thing, with a big grin on its face.'

Rory bent to retrieve the dustpan and brush. Viv started to follow, still not satisfied with his reaction. Then she marched off upstairs and as Rory entered the house again, his eldest son Justin gently removed the dustpan and brush from his father's grip and said:

'It's all right Dad. I'll do it. Go and see Mum.'

On the way through the lounge Rory stopped to kiss Harry and Jake, their two youngest sons. They were sitting by the TV in their pyjamas looking at a magazine. Harry still enjoyed the television programme it had originated from, even though most of his eight-year-old peers had long forgotten it. Jake was eager to look at any book or magazine since starting school last year. He was determined to go some way towards catching up with his brothers Harry, Drew and Justin at school.

'I'll see you two scoundrels later', Rory winked at them.

Viv lay on the bed when he got to their bedroom. Stripes of tearful mascara streaked her pale complexion. She allowed her shoulder length deep red curls to fall over her face, hiding how emotional she had become in the past few weeks.

'Justin said he clear up all those cornflakes on the kitchen floor.'

16

'He's a good lad,' she sniffed.

'Listen, sorry...' they both said in unison.

'Are you sure you're feeling okay.' Rory sat on the bed moving his hospital uniform to the chair.

'I'm just tired, but it's a different sort of tired to how I felt carrying the boys. That's why I think this time it must be a girl.'

'We could have a whole football team before a girl comes along and besides what about that job you applied for? That's all gone to the wall now hasn't it?'

'I was going to tell you about that. I withdrew my application when I found out I was pregnant and I've since heard that Adele next door has got the job.'

Rory puffed as he pulled his leathers off from over his porter's trousers.

'Thought she'd have gone for a job in the city, like her husband.'

'She told me she spent five years working for a large department store when they lived in Croydon. She'd had enough of it and wanted some time off to decorate the house and revamp the garden.'

Rory lifted the cushion on the chair to look for his gloves.

'Well I hope her husband's earning a good salary. They'll need it, three days work at that pathetic little mini-market isn't going to bring in much.'

'Oh, so it was alright for me to go for the job, but not good enough for Miss Adele next door.'

'Christ woman, you don't half fly off the handle. Never met anyone with a shorter fuse. It's a good job I'm a forgiving bloke.' He flashed her one of his comic grins and as she turned away in a huff he could see the corners of her mouth curling up. He could always manage to bring her round and coax her out of her angry mood. He was confident of that, well... that was until next time.

Chapter Three

Miles Harper moved his unwilling body on autopilot up the garden steps to his own segment of wilderness. Climbing first over the lower branches of the ailing apple tree, entwined with woody honeysuckle, he made his way to the cracked wooden bench beneath the now bare branches of the buddleia tree. The dishevelled picture his eyes took in registered as a clouded image on an old TV screen. A background fuzz to a radio station no longer tuned in. There was no one to share a vista of a more organised and picturesque nature since his wife, Janet had died so tragically last year.

Adele and Viv sat in Adele's kitchen, drinking coffee and watching Miles sympathetically.

'He has a very vacant look about him. What do you think Viv?'

'Yes, I've noticed that about him. The district nurse has been looking in on him whenever she can. She says it's the anti-depressants he's on. It's suppressing any small spark he's got left in him.'

'Well if it protects him from thinking about the accident, that's a good enough reason to carry on taking them. What about his job? Will he be able to go back to the office eventually?'

'I think he will in the long run. I saw his partner, Cameron in the town last week. He said Miles has been signed off for at least the next three months. He's organised a temporary solicitor to take on his cases for the time being. And what makes it worse is that compensation for the relatives is unlikely to be sorted out for at least six months. The insurers of the plant company are trying to establish whether it was the driver's fault for not securing the arm on the digger or the manufacturer's for producing defective machinery.'

'Is he still having counselling?'

'Not as far as I know. He went to see a young woman at the local surgery for the first few months, but then that petered out. At least he didn't have to face what the police did, arriving on the scene. Rory told me that they have in-house counsellors for police attending horrific accidents, particularly if victims have been burnt in car accidents. It's not as gruesome and appalling as parts of the body strewn all over the carriageways though is it?'

'It doesn't bear thinking about. Poor Miles it's a horrendous situation for him, all that grief and loneliness and no family around him to fall back on.'

Miles sat forward on the paint flaked wooden bench with his head in his hands. He covered his face with his hands to block out the light and the world. He sat so still, hardly breathing that even the curious Eileen had not noticed him when she hung out her washing.

Miles had a skip outside at the beginning of the lane restricting the walkway so that Rory could only just squash his bike through the gap. It was already half filled with rubbish cleared from his house. He had been going through each room in the house in a methodical fashion. He put off the task of clearing out after Janet's death and his tidying was long overdue. He couldn't focus on what would happen in his life after the monumental clearout and re-organisation. Viv had helped him just after Janet died by taking clothes to an Oxfam shop. She'd made an excuse about seeing her mother and dropping the clothes at the local Oxfam shop in her mother's town. Miles knew her reasons. He may have been suffering from shock and the onset of depression but he certainly wasn't stupid. Her mother lived a good two hours drive away and with more than seventy miles between them he knew as well as she did that he would be unlikely to see Janet's clothes on display or on anyone else. He was grateful to her for that.

Most of the rubbish accumulated from upstairs had been his: old paperback novels, back issues of Yachting World and a yellowing ream of revision notes for his law degree. The tin box thrown out earlier belonged to an old lady's estate he had dealt with. It was used to keep various bits and pieces to do with his interest in sailing. Inside the box before he threw it out were three items, a book about tying knots, some thin ropes and a framed wall hanging of the finished articles. Miles kept everything and threw the box out. He hadn't done very much sailing since he and Janet had married. He'd taken her for a few romantic trips on his friend's yacht when they'd been engaged but she had always ended up in the galley with her head poised over a bucket, looking far from seductive.

With the upstairs finished, he tackled the lounge next. The room was north facing and full of darkness. Shadows threw themselves randomly on the cream carpet and across two bottle green sofas.

The sofas were centred on a blackened grate and marble mantelpiece. Above was a gilt-edged mirror and on either side of the mirror, oval-shaped arrangements of pressed flowers, collected by Janet on one of their weekend walks. Two church candles on tall stands still held the drips of encrusted wax and in the fireplace a half-burned log rested on a pile of spent ashes. There were two alcoves on the west wall of the room where cupboards and shelving had been built. The shelves held books, videos and photos of their wedding including one special photo of the two of them sat at a table holding hands as the sun sank into a warm horizon on a Greek island. Thankfully Janet had been very methodical with the labelling of the videos and photograph albums and he left them all in their neatly stacked piles. The room was just as Janet had left it.

Miles polished the oval coffee table next to the window and straightened the green velvet curtains. He dusted the shelves and the photos and although he tried hard not to look, he couldn't help gazing at her eyes in the holiday photograph. She'd had the most unusual eyes, exposed by the fact that she always wore her shoulder length hair tied back in a pony tail. Her hair was light brown, thick and wavy. She had said it got in the way when she wore it loose. Her eyes were pale green and solid in colour, not streaked with marbled shades. Sometimes their colour had made the pupils look small giving her the appearance of a frightened gazelle. In the photograph, even though she was smiling her eyes would pierce the soul of an onlooker. He put the frame down but her eyes followed him around the room like laser beams of light, searching for a reason. The reason for her death was as nonsensical as his life now. He stood up and stared at himself in the mirror over the fireplace. He certainly looked all right from the outside but the thread by which he was holding on was not visible to the human eye. If anyone could have seen it they would have seen a silken gossamer strand close to breaking point.

Chapter Four

Eileen Dolce carefully carried her steaming bucket of water and bleach down the steps from her patio to the front door of her cottage. It was quiet in the lane today so she talked to the cat, slopping milk into its bowl in the kitchen. He purred contentedly as he lapped up the milk and Eileen starred longingly out of her window, willing someone to come outside. She left the cat to it and returned outside with bucket and long handled hard broom.

Scrubbing her steps and patio was part of her daily routine, except when the weather curtailed the pursuit. Eileen knuckled down to her cleaning with vigorous rhythm and energetic pace. She stopped only momentarily to flick an annoying wisp of grey hair behind her ears. The bleach etched out a river of white on her path by the numerous cleaning sessions it had suffered. Many years ago Eileen remembered watching her mother scrubbing the steps and path in their family home in Scotland. A similar river of bleached pavement marked their entrance making it stand out from all the other houses in the small village just outside Edinburgh. Her mother was just as committed to her daily task as Eileen was now and she would tell Eileen about the women back in Italy and how every morning they would all be out at the same time scrubbing their steps and engaging in conversation.

Eileen leant on her hard broom and sighed. It must have been so difficult for poor mother to leave Italy and come to Scotland. It was a different culture and the weather in Scotland was a complete change to the daily sunshine she would have grown up with. Perhaps it was the similar mountainous scenery that attracted her or the numerous Italians who also made the decision to emigrate to Scotland after the Second World War. Meeting Eileen's father must have been a deciding factor to make her stay. Now, when Eileen heard from her cousins they mentioned the large clusters of Italian descendents all over Scotland, many opening exclusive restaurants, bringing a Mediterranean flavour to a cold country. Eileen however, had no desire to return to Scotland, besides her brother, Robert lived in the West Country and she wanted to be near him. She picked up her broom and swept the last trickle of water away, then scooped up her bucket, went inside and closed the door.

Adele folded the daily newspaper neatly and picked up the information file on the garden project. She had reservations about approaching Eileen. She meant well, but her fussy manner would soon start to annoy the gardening team as well as the rest of the neighbours. Adele told herself as she walked towards Eileen's cottage to keep calm and ask her nicely and firmly.

She knocked on Eileen's door. It was surprising anyone could hear the weak tapping from the obscure little wooden woodpecker she used as a doorknocker. She knocked again. Eileen was the only one who paid any attention to her patch of garden and Adele was unsure of how she would react.

The hollow tapping of the woodpecker's beak against hardwood interrupted Eileen from her dusting. She carefully placed her mother's precious statue of the Virgin Mary back into its alcove and peeked around the side of her net curtains to see Adele tugging at the decorative chain activating the carved woodpecker door-knocker. He was a replica of a green woodpecker. Her father had made him many years ago and Eileen loved the idea of a woodpecker tapping at her door. Anybody visiting always remarked on how quaint he was. She opened the door to a smiling Adele.

'I…I err…I've come to ask your advice and to tell you about an offer regarding our gardens,' Adele chose her words very carefully while Eileen stood resolute in the doorway.

'I suppose you'd like tea?'

She ushered Adele to the kitchen and pointed to the stool next to Bertie, the cat. Adele proceeded to perch on it, her legs hanging and toes balanced on the rung half way up.

'I'd love a cup of tea Eileen, thank you.'

Eileen moved the letter she was finishing writing to her niece, Claire and placed a magazine over the top to hide it. She didn't want Adele asking any awkward questions about her brother Robert and his wife Carmel. She passed a blue cup and saucer filled with weak tea to Adele and sat frowning while the details of the garden plans unfolded. She took in the information, but couldn't stop her mind from returning to thoughts about Claire, her niece. Maybe Robert would be able to bring Claire when she came to stay. At eighteen surely she wasn't too old yet to have her father bring her. Besides the train times were inconvenient and the station half an hour away and Claire hadn't passed her driving test yet. It would be lovely to see Robert without that tiresome Carmel tagging along. She was always so jealous of the closeness between brother and sister. She told them it was an unnatural relationship and she even made Eileen feel uneasy about a mere telephone call to her baby brother. The fifteen years between them didn't make a difference to their devotion and over the years they'd kept in contact every week, especially since their sister, Margaret had emigrated to Australia ten years ago. Robert generally rang Eileen from the office in the week and she occasionally returned the call when the icy Carmel went to the supermarket on a Saturday morning.

Eileen could still hear Adele's voice rambling on about the garden project and she snapped back to listening. She had to admit that it did sound a good suggestion, but she wasn't going to be forced into accepting any new-fangled ideas.

'Just so long as I can keep my nice clean patio. I'm not being bullied into having it replaced by one of those awful wooden decking thingy contraptions.'

'That's precisely why we want you involved Eileen. We can discuss and agree together as residents all that goes into the new garden and I can assure you that you'll get what you want.'

Eileen nodded, but she couldn't quite take in the details today. Writing to Claire had stirred up her feelings and stifled her normal forcefulness. Adele began to reverse out of the kitchen and Eileen was happy to see her leave.

'I'm going to make a move now Eileen, I'll let myself out,' she said hurriedly.

Adele turned quickly and made for the front door. She pulled the door shut with a bang and the woodpecker rattled on its perch. That was easier than she'd thought it would be. She was lucky to have encountered Eileen in such an unusually subdued mood today, but she doubted that it would always be this easy. She didn't even appear to be listening properly today, but after much explaining and repetition Adele had finally got her to agree as long as she invited her for an opinion when the T.V. crew came. She only had Miles to visit now. She'd knocked on his door twice already and he hadn't answered. She suspected that he wouldn't really be bothered what they did to the garden, but she still needed his agreement nonetheless. There were only four groups of people to come to an agreement about the garden and although they could all agree on the revamping being carried out Adele could already foresee a diverse range of needs emerging. She glanced again at the details sent from the TV gardening show. It was such a good idea and she had to have faith that in the end they would all be able to compromise enough to make it work.

Chapter Five

Viv walked slowly around the garden, holding the base of her back. The doctor had told her that it was only bruising to her coccyx bone, but she should be careful now that she was pregnant. Adele watched from her kitchen and wondered whether she should go and help her down the garden steps, but she must have got up there in the first place and besides she was an independent woman and Adele didn't want to interfere. She watched her movements carefully just in case help was needed. Viv tried to make light of struggling through Adele's plot back to her own. When she got to the steps leading to her property Adele almost knocked over her mug of tea. She slid down the metal handrail in the middle of the steps as if she were a ten year old. Then she edged herself along the wall and made her way back to the front door of her house, stepped inside and closed the door.

'And she slid down the pole just like a fireman.' Adele stood up and imitated Viv, as she related the morning's incidents to Sheryl in the shop later.

'You'll have to try it yourself next time, could be fun.' Sheryl stacked the women's magazines on the shelf.

'Let me know when you're going to do it and I'll be around to make sure you don't fall,' Bradley smirked. Bradley Blake, the manager of the mini-market didn't miss a trick when chatting up women was on offer.

'We'll do without your sort of help thanks,' Sheryl frowned, displaying the harsh pencilled lines where her eyebrows once were.

'Oh come on Sherrie baby, you know you love me really,' and he flashed a grin at her as he squeezed her shoulder. 'Coffee girls?' He asked as he whisked the tray from under the counter and made his exit before she got her own back with the magazine she was rolling in her hands.

'He was only joking wasn't he? He's quite harmless really isn't he?' questioned Adele. She'd heard about sleazy men like Bradley, but hadn't encountered any after attending an all girls' school and a career in textiles and fashion.

'I wouldn't give him the chance to be anything other.' Sheryl thumbed through some of the glossier magazines and paused on a page for spring and summer fashions for this year. 'Hey, that skirt you've got on is exactly the same as this one.' She pointed to a model wearing a rust coloured skirt with the hemline cleverly cut, sides sloping downward towards the middle of her legs.

'Yes, it is. I copied it from that magazine.'

'What you mean you made it yourself. How?' Sheryl's painted blue eyes widened in amazement. She fastened her peroxide blonde hair back with a clip as if to take in everything Adele had to say.

'I started making my own clothes with a group of friends when we were still at school. We used to order clothes from catalogues or try them on at high street shops to see if the style suited us, then we'd pick the best of the bunch and design the patterns and make it ourselves.'

'Wow, you could save a fortune and have a huge wardrobe.'

'Well I don't do so much of it now. Ben's in the fashion industry; he often gets discount on designer clothes and besides he prefers me to wear the real thing. He says it creates the right image when I'm with him.'

'He's mad. You're brill Adele.'

'Would you like me to make you one?'

'Oh, I couldn't, you're probably too busy.'

'No really, I'd love to, I don't get the chance to make so many clothes these days and I do miss it. I could make it in any colour you like.'

'If you're sure, purple would be nice or maybe cyclamen pink. My legs wouldn't look as nice as yours though.'

'Oh come on Sheryl you've got lovely slim legs.'

'I'll second that.' Bradley waltzed in carrying the tray of coffee, plus samples of new chocolate flakes on sale in the next few days.

'Like to try one Adele?'

Adele took one from the tray and Sheryl helped herself but had to put it under the counter while she served a customer. Adele sat in the alcove behind the till, unseen by the customer. She sipped at her coffee and bit gently into the chocolate. Bradley was at his usual leaning post filling in a questionnaire for the new chocolate. He glanced at her soft mouth enveloping the flake and the delicate flick of her tongue catching the escaping pieces from the corner of her mouth. He very quickly scribbled comments onto the sheet of paper. Adele looked over and their eyes froze together for a second, then hastily he broke the glance and crossed through everything he had written on the paper.

Sheryl slammed the till shut knocking the dregs of her coffee over Adele.

'Sorry, it's this bloody till, you'll have to get it fixed Bradley. Are you okay Adele?'

'Yes, I'm fine. Don't worry, I'll go and sponge my sleeve with some water.'

Bradley flashed a smile at Sheryl and helped her mop up the mess with some tissues.

'Trust you Sherrie, clumsy clogs.' He gently put his arm around her waist and added, 'I'll send her home in a minute then we can go for a drink after work if you like.'

'I'm not having you getting me pie-eyed like last time.'

'As if I would Sherrie, what do you take me for?'

Sheryl smiled as she watched him serve Mrs Clooney with some cigarettes. He was good looking, medium height and hair a rich shiny conker brown. He had eyes to match, like dark pools that drew you towards him. He had the cheek of the devil and made her laugh with it, but she knew what he was like and she told herself to steer well clear. The only trouble was, all that internal advice flew out of the window after several gin and tonics on a Friday night.

Adele picked up the letter on the hall floor and went upstairs to the kitchen. She sat at the table overlooking the garden and ripped open the brown envelope. The TV company wanted to visit and inspect the plots. They found the structure of all the gardens such an interesting challenge and they wanted to try and do something for the Orchard Court residents in their next series of programmes. All Adele had to do was to finish getting the agreements and they could make preliminary plans. They also asked her if she would mind co-ordinating procedures amongst the neighbours. She couldn't believe it, after all her thoughts on the garden, what a piece of luck for all of them. She put the letter on the kitchen table so that Ben could see it later on. She wanted to involve him and for him to be proud of the way she planned to organise the project. Adele kicked her shoes off in the hall and went upstairs to change. She put on a comfortable pair of pyjamas for now, meaning to have a bath before Ben came home. Then brushing her hair in front of the mirror she stared at her reflection and had a sudden change of tack.

She ran back down the stairs into the kitchen and grabbed the letter, flying back to the computer to compose a reply. She typed up a response agreeing to organise plans at her end. She could tell Ben about it later, when she found the right moment. The programme was scheduled for the autumn and would go out at 8.00 p.m. on a Friday night. Adele's mind was bursting with ideas for plants, shrubs and furniture for the garden. She hoped that they'd allow the residents enough input and what a perfect name for the programme - 'Breaking New Ground'.

Chapter Six

Viv eased herself up from the comfortable sofa and made her way slowly to the kitchen. Her back was beginning to feel better, but it was replaced by the sickness and washed-out feeling that had accompanied pregnancy. She'd been trying to stick to Dr Lethbridge's instructions and rest while she could, but it was difficult to curtail her active spirit. She daren't tell the doctor what she'd got up to sliding down the rail in the garden the other day. Still, nobody had seen her and she hadn't hurt herself. She made herself a mug of tea and armed with Turkish Delights from Adele and a video from Rory she returned to her rest.

As the trailers flashed by on the screen, snapshots of Miles and his tragic circumstances displayed themselves inside her head. The first scene of the film was half way through and just as she made a move to rewind to the beginning again, the phone rang. It was Rory.

'Hi, how are you, like the video?'

'Thanks, very thoughtful, I'm just about to watch it now.'

'How's...ing...on'

'You're breaking up, where are you?'

'In the car park, I'll walk up towards A and E. Is that any better?'

'Yes.'

'I'm on a break, so I thought I'd check up on you.'

'It's alright. I'm doing exactly what I've been told to do. I'm lying on a sofa, getting fat with a box of chocolates and watching TV.'

'Perhaps it's just as well you didn't go for that job at the mini-market.'

'The way I feel at the moment Adele can keep the job! Anyhow, I'm refusing to get depressed about hanging around doing nothing. Chocolates and a good film are the only answer!'

'Chocolate is your answer to any problem,' Rory laughed. 'See you this evening sweetheart. Bye.' Rory replaced his mobile in his jacket pocket. Maybe he'd have to keep feeding her with a regular supply of chocolates if it was going to keep her from getting agitated about resting. Any amount of money was worth it to stop Viv becoming agitated.

Viv watched the trailers for a second time before Miles throwing a large metal object into a skip outside disturbed her again. She looked across the deserted garden with the oasis patio and observed the scene of her neighbours. Almost as soon as the old tin box hit the side of the skip, Eileen was outside and down the path to Miles's house bearing a cup of tea and a freshly baked rock bun. Viv saw the levels in the skip rise as Miles kept finding new junk to fill it and almost every time he came out from his garage, Eileen found an excuse to chip in with a bit of conversation.

Viv was glad that she'd helped Miles with the initial clearout of Janet's clothes and personal possessions. It was the hardest part of dealing with a close relative passing away. If the clothes were left in the wardrobe and the coat on the peg in the hall it was as if the person had only gone away on a long holiday and they weren't really dead at all. Her auntie had left uncle's cap hooked onto the umbrella stand in her hall for two years after he'd died. Viv had found it rather eerie, especially as it had retained for the first few months, the smell of her uncle's hair cream he used to spread on his almost bald head.

The video showed the beginning of Viv's film for the third time and unable to fight the feeling of tiredness any more, she clicked the control to the standby position and drifted off to sleep.

Adele sat at her kitchen table observing the whole of Orchard Court and all the gardens. She smiled to herself as she watched Eileen scrubbing her path, muttering away quite openly before sending the remains of the bucket cascading into a bleach river down the lane. She got up and pulled a small bag of potatoes from the vegetable rack. Then running a bowl of water she fixed her eyes on the gossipy morning programme on T.V. while she sat peeling potatoes, plopping them into a saucepan of fresh water. The squeaky clean presenter announced that after the break Joey Brooks would be showing us how to make Spicy Caribbean Chicken and 'Knock Your Socks Off' Rum Choc Pots.

'Stay with us after Joey's culinary delights for a live chat with Sammie Wilkes, the woman who had to live with the aftermath of a disastrous mistake following an operation for a breast implant.'

'And finally,' her co-host added. 'We will be revealing the winner of our competition to give a garden a face lift this year on the T.V. programme, Breaking New Ground.'

They were about to announce the winner for the garden competition after the break. Adele pulled up a stool and sat poised for the announcement. She stared out of the window at the garden below. Eileen's bleached patio looked pristine, yet stark and clinical against the natural backdrop of the unkempt partitions. Access to all the plots was fairly complex except Eileen's and she almost defied anyone else's entrance to the wilderness The whole area was fairly large, but made completely unusable by the muddled sections. The television was blaring out a really annoying jingle which ended abruptly as the hosts froze their perfect smiles in a split second silence and the cameras clicked in on the example of a perfect garden.

'You may remember our 'facelift for a garden' competition. The winner's garden was to be featured on the new Friday night programme, 'Breaking New Ground'.'

The cheery female presenter smiled as if she had a surprise in store.

'Well, we have not just one winner, but four! The original winner is a Mrs Adele Parker from Orchard Court in Hexbury, but the very generous team from Breaking New Ground has offered to refurbish everyone's garden in Orchard Court. The finished garden will be shared by all the residents, but will be far more practical and usable for all concerned. Breaking New Ground says it was a unique opportunity that they couldn't turn down, so well done Mrs Parker, good for you and all your neighbours.'

Adele turned the volume down and smiled to herself. So Mr Grainger's recommendations and the returned agreements must have worked. It was lucky that she'd managed to get Miles's agreement at the last minute. She felt like jumping up and down with excitement. This venture presented itself as such a new challenge to her and she could do with some mental stimulation. The job at the mini-market was fine, but it wasn't exactly scintillating. Adele put the lid on the freshly peeled potatoes just as the phone rang.

'Hello, is that Mrs Parker?'

'Yes.'

'It's Crispin Grainger here, from the Breaking New Ground TV programme. I thought this would be an opportune moment to phone you. You didn't by any chance see the slot on morning TV did you?'

'I certainly did,' Adele replied, soaking up the sexy smooth baritone voice on the end of the line.

'It looks like we're on course now Mrs Parker.'

'One thing Mr Grainger, did you receive the consents from myself and the other neighbours in plenty of time?'

'Yes, they arrived in the post at the beginning of the week.'

'That's good and I'm sorry it took longer than I thought. I had to wait to see Mr Harper. He's been a bit of a recluse since his wife died, but I think that the garden refurbishment could be a project to help cheer him.'

'Yes, hopefully it will give him something to become involved with. I wanted to let you know Mrs Parker, I think there might be a lull in the proceedings for a while, but it'll give us time to think of ideas when Breaking New Ground finally arrive on the scene won't it?'

'How much of a lull?'

'Not too long, but I'll give you a ring when we know more details. Are you still okay for making arrangements at your end?'

'Yes absolutely fine. I can't wait.'

Adele couldn't wait to see if the person matched the delectable voice. Crispin hadn't been seen on TV yet, but from viewing past shows they weren't in the habit of choosing anyone dull or unattractive. They had their viewing counts to think about after all.

'There's one more thing Mrs Parker. If we are going to be communicating over this assignment can we use first name terms?'

'Of course we can. It's Adele.'

'And as you already know, Crispin. So I'll speak to you fairly soon Adele.'

'Yes, and we're all looking forward to hearing what you have to suggest. Goodbye.'

Adele tried not to let on too much about the neighbours' personal problems and hoped that the new garden would focus their attentions. She would have to be ready herself to keep them all in check. Miles, the poor soul was too depressed to think of anything, Eileen would have the whole garden rigged out in pink and white slabs and a few tubs and Rory and Viv would never stop bickering for long enough to decide anything. Rory had told Adele yesterday at the shop that Viv was pregnant.

'Is she? She didn't tell me when she came round the other day.'

'She's only recently found out.'

Rory didn't seem particularly pleased and although Adele didn't say anything she couldn't imagine coping with five children.

Adele changed for work that afternoon fired with a sense of enthusiasm. The move to Orchard Court had been the right thing to do, but the last six months of settling in had something missing, just that extra spark that makes life worthwhile. Ben would be home tonight and she could tell him all about it. That would be after she'd heard his spiel about the recent conference and sales targets. After his long soak in the bath while she cooked and put washing on. After he'd eaten his meal, drunk his bottle of red wine and obsessed with late night politics programmes. Perhaps she'd leave it until tomorrow.

Crispin was glad that Adele had agreed to help with the garden plans and even from the short telephone call he could sense that she had just the right balance of a caring nature, with a sprinkling of calm determination. It was quite a contrast to his present impulsive, uncaring assistant on the team. Ruby was a 'do it now and think about it later' person and he was thankful that Adele would now be around on this project to force her to hold back, just a little. He read her response to his letter asking if there were any specific requests from the residents of Orchard Court for the design of the new garden. She'd told him that she would talk to the other neighbours and get back to him. She sounded very thorough and organised. He was very much looking forward to meeting Adele and the sooner the better.

Adele was at ease with visiting Miles and Eileen, but when it came to Viv she could sometimes sense a chill between them. She'd asked Rory about it in the shop.

'It's probably because you're a lovely looking girl Adele. She gets very jealous when I as much as look at another woman. I'd only need to mention your name once or twice and she'd be on the defensive.'

'But I've hardly spoken to you. I've served you at the shop for your cigarettes a few times and that's it.'

'That's another thing she's always trying to get me to give up smoking.'

'Well that's not my fault Rory, I can hardly refuse to sell them to you.'

'I know and don't take it to heart. Don't worry about it, leave her to me.'

'Have you thought what you would like in the garden Rory?'

'Yes, a barbecue. A nice brick built one, nice an' easy to clean. How about you Adele?'

'I'd like a nice stretch of soft lawn to lie on and read a book, oh and a bench for when it's too damp for grass.'

'How about a hammock or even a trampoline?'

'Now come on Rory, let's think relaxation not breaking our necks. You'll be asking for bungee jumping ropes from your roof next!'

Rory laughed. 'Listen Adele, I'll work on sweetening my wife for you and I'll let you know when to go and call on her.'

'Thanks Rory, but make it soon.'

Rory waved at her with his usual cheeky grin and his thumb up as he left.

Chapter Seven

Adele arranged the tins of spaghetti and baked beans into neat rows. It was buy two, get third free this week and her next job was to make a small poster to draw attention to the offer. It wasn't quite as chic as displaying cerise silk evening gowns with matching feather boas, but the job was turning out to be convenient and gave her time to settle into the new area. She'd been asked to come into work an hour earlier today, but as Ben was away in Manchester on a conference her time was her own.

With the boxes empty and all the tins neatly stacked Adele went to find the marker pens and some yellow card. Bradley sat in his office, glancing up from his work to see her go past to the stock room. Adele pulled the wooden stepladder out from behind the door and climbed to the top shelf where the stationery was kept. It was in a cardboard box towards the back of the shelf and she ran her hand along the dusty metal and felt for the box in the darkness.

'Why don't you put the light on?' a voice said from the shadowy corner before the room was suddenly lit up.

'Thank you Mr Blake. I didn't know where the switch was.'

'Anyway, what are you looking for?'

'The stationery box, Sheryl said it was up here.' Adele put her cold hand to her flushed cheeks and held on tight to the shelving to steady her legs. She hadn't bargained on Mr Blake to go snooping around checking up on what she was doing.

'Come into my office. The stationery's in there now and besides we have to fill in some forms for you.'

Adele got down and followed him. As he ushered her inside she felt the heat from the cramped workplace. An opaque sheet of condensation obliterated the view from the sash-cord window in the corner of his office. The swollen wood prevented it from being opened and air from circulating in the stuffy atmosphere. Slate-grey metal shelves stacked high with Lever Arch files lined the sky blue painted walls. Adele looked up to see where the intense heat was coming from. Her eyes met a two-barred electric wall fire operated by a pull cord. Her mother had had one just the same in her bathroom. She had never seen one like it anywhere else.

'Mrs Parker? Adele?'

'Yes, Oh Yes, Sorry...'

He indicated to her to sit down on a comfortable grey striped fold up chair and he sat on a blue swivel office chair next to the computer screen.

'Nothing to worry about. Just a few forms to sign for Head Office's records.'

He placed the forms on the edge of his desk and indicated to her where to sign. Adele leaned over his desk to read the form quickly before putting her name to paper. As she handed the pen back to him, he looked up quickly and smiled at her. She smiled back at him.

'Anything else, Mr Blake?'

'Err...no, but if you'd like ten minutes off to nip back home and change your tights it's fine with me.'

She looked down to see a fifty pence sized hole in her black tights, just below the hemline of her short camel coloured skirt. She pulled her skirt down in embarrassment and disbelief of his nerve.

'Oh, and take this out with you, I believe it's what you were looking for just now.' He handed her the box of marker pens and card.

'Thank you, Mr Blake,' she said picking up the box neatly and efficiently.

'No need for formalities if we're to be working together. I insist you call me Bradley. It's all right for me to call you Adele isn't it?' he questioned.

'Yes, of course,' she croaked. Her throat had gone dry in the heat of the room.

She put her hand up again to cool her already red face, now increasing to crimson. She closed the door and made a quick exit back to the shop. What a cheek to notice her ripped tights, but perhaps he was just being polite. He couldn't be one of those shifty men she'd only read about could he?

It was fairly quiet and under the counter Sheryl was trying out the new glitter nail varnishes.

'What do you think?' she asked as Adele walked back in carrying the stationery box.

'I like the vibrant colours in that range. That one's very tasteful, looks good on you. Mind you, quite expensive.'

'Oh, I didn't buy it. I'll just put it back on the shelf afterwards.'

'But what if Mr Blake finds out?'

'He won't and anyway if he does I know he won't mind.'

'Well as long as we don't get any complaining customers.' Adele paused and placed the box of stationery by the till She didn't know what to think of her boss now. What sort of a manager would ignore using the goods and replacing them on the shelf?

'Is he a pleasant man?' she questioned Sheryl.

'Who?'

'Mr Blake.'

'I guess he's okay. Same as all the rest of them.'

'All the rest of who?'

'Men, of course. Anyway, where have you been to get a bright red face like that? You're almost the colour of this nail varnish.'

'I had to sign a few forms in his office. It's like a Japanese sweatbox in there isn't it? Now I know why he wears short-sleeved shirts under his suits.'

'He said I could go home and change my tights,' Adele added. She felt the need to go and change them since he'd mentioned it and she certainly didn't want to give him any cause for making more unnecessary comments. She fingered the tear, pulling it up from view under her hemline. 'I must have snagged them on that rotten old ladder in the stock room. I won't be more than ten minutes; you don't mind do you Sheryl?'

'You go ahead. Insisted that you call him Bradley yet, has he?' But Adele had already walked out of the door and didn't reply.

Rory leaned against the wall at the back of the Accident and Emergency Department of the hospital. He was on a break and had to get away from the wards to think. He'd had a letter in his pigeon hole this morning to say that his name was near the top of the list for a vasectomy. He only had to confirm the appointment, but since finding out about Viv's pregnancy he didn't really know what to do. It threw a different light on things altogether.

Only the ambulance drivers could see him from here, to all other staff he was obscured from view, except if they looked more closely at the spiral of smoke. Before he stubbed out the first cigarette he lit another from it. He drew on it, feeling the tightness in his lungs and the subsequent rush as it entered his blood stream. He gave a determined kick at the first dog end, sending it flying into the mud. Dr Lethbridge had suggested that he should go on the waiting list and while he was waiting think about the operation for a few months just to be sure he'd made the right decision. If Viv wasn't pregnant the decision to accept the appointment would be easy; he would go ahead as planned, but now…well now he was confused about what he really wanted. The last stub was also kicked into the mud and Rory made his way back to work. He was working with Ted for the next hour.

'What's on then Ted?'

'I've already done the first one mate, where were you? Chatting up those student nurses in the cafeteria?'

'Something like that, sorry. Right where next.'

'Mrs M French in Bluebell ward, floor 9.'

Mrs French turned out to be a pretty young girl with dark curly hair, accompanied by her mother. Rory and Ted wheeled her into the anaesthetic room where the anaesthetist administered the final shots into her left hand. Seconds later she disappeared into the operating theatre. Ted took the bed and Rory consoled the mother, who'd forgotten how distressing it was to see your own child pass into an unconscious sleep before your very eyes.

'Don't worry. She'll be fine, it always looks worse when you're a relative looking on.'

'I just hope it works for her. My poor Melinda, she's been trying for so long now. She's been on the IVF programme for two years and then they discovered a new surgical procedure to unblock the fallopian tubes. The only trouble is that it's a very tricky and delicate operation and there's always the risk she'll end up completely infertile.'

'Poor girl, but I've got every confidence in Mr Pashnaev, haven't you Ted.'

'Absolutely. Best surgeon in the gynaecology department.'

'Just go home and grab yourself a cup of tea and she'll be out in no time.'

Mrs French's mother smiled through her tears and murmured a croaked thank you.

'Thanks, that's all I need right now.' Rory muttered to the empty blue sky as they wheeled the bed back up to the ward.

'What's that mate?'

'Nothing Ted. Nothing at all.'

Chapter Eight

Bradley Blake arrived earlier than usual today. He had the stock room to tidy and reports and records to prepare for the area manager's visit tomorrow. Sitting in his blue swivel chair, he swept his hand through his gelled hair. The screen in front of him flicked to an imaginary screensaver, a tessellation of Adele's breasts.

He had to stop this, he'd spent more time thinking about her lately than he had stock-taking and office work. It had meant staying late every night last week in order to catch up with the work missed because of day dreaming of her. Opening up the computer diary he was reminded that Mick, the Cadbury's rep was due to call today at 11.30 a.m. Maybe this could work to his advantage. Mick was a good sort, Bradley had been for a drink with him many a time. He was quite a smooth talker and Bradley knew he wouldn't let him down. Perhaps he could arrange a lunch at the local riverside pub. Maybe Adele would like to come as well. Sheryl could manage by herself. Tuesday was never a particularly busy day.

'Hi Mick, how's it all going on the road?'

Mick cut in and out on the mobile and eventually asked Bradley to ring back on the car phone, which had a much better reception. Bradley had written the number down on an advertisement flyer for the new chocolate Mick had been promoting. It reminded Bradley how Mick's skin resembled the molten chocolate, silky smooth and brown like pure cocoa.

'That's better, any problems Brad?'

'I was thinking of a business lunch for you, me and a new young lady who I'm considering recommending for assistant manager.'

'A young lady you've got the hots for?'

'Well not exactly, she's really nice, but...'

'But what? But nice tits, legs, skirts up to her arse?'

'But married that's what. So no go this time Mick. Just worried about stopping myself. She comes into my office to see me, seems to want to make a friend of me.'

'When all you want to do is screw her, like all the others.'

'All the others weren't married Mick.'

'Does it make a difference to someone with a sexual appetite like yours?'

'I have got some morals and besides I've been warned countless times by my sister. It's like juggling emotional dynamite so she says.'

'I'll believe it when I see it. What time then, for lunch I mean?'

'I'll book a table at Gillie's Rest, the one by the river just before the bridge, 12.15 alright for you?'

'I'll come to the shop first, do the business then I can enjoy watching this new girl of yours.'

The Gillie's Rest was five minutes' drive from the shop and there couldn't have been a better day to lunch there. The moorland river passing by the inn's garden was at a perfect level, running gently past over large granite boulders. Hanging baskets and wooden barrels full of multi-coloured annuals adorned the walls. It was truly a setting to impress and Adele was delighted that Bradley had asked her. She'd told him, 'It's so sweet of you to try and make me feel welcome in a new job and area, but won't Sheryl be put out that you haven't asked her?'

He put her mind at rest, telling her that he'd taken Sheryl out on previous occasions so now it must be her turn. At the bar, Mick joined Bradley briefly to carry the drinks.

'A pretty little naïve Miss you've got yourself this time Brad.'

'Pretty yes, naïve yes, MISS NO and it's no this time. She's just gonna have to be a poster on my wall to enjoy looking at.'

Mick flashed him one of his ear to ear brilliant white grins, against his smooth dark skin, but said nothing in return.

Mick said his goodbyes outside the shop and indicated the huge queue inside. Sheryl was slamming around and not at all happy that she'd been left to deal with the heaving mass of people descending on the shop.

The queue was eventually diffused. Viv was the final customer and she stepped up to Sheryl to be served, allowing her to witness the close conversation between Adele and Bradley.

'Thanks for coming with us today Adele. Mick was so impressed with the way you talked about improving sales.'

'It was a pleasure Bradley. It felt good to be treated as an equal and what a wonderful spot. Mick said he'd been there before, I didn't know it existed.'

Bradley's warm smile was fixed as his eyes did the roaming work for him. He reached into his pocket and pulled out a small crumpled blue bag. He handed it to her.

'Oh Bradley, there was no need but thank you.'

Saving her blush he added 'thought you'd like that colour and it's not from stock. I picked it up at the new little shop in the town. They've called it "A Penny for your Thoughts…" weird name for a shop if you ask me.' He stopped talking and before disappearing back to his office, glanced into her eyes and smiled.

In the crumpled bag she found two pink candles with a delicious smell. Bradley had tried to rip the price tags off and succeeded in obliterating the name of the candles as well. 'Nice touch.' She murmured while wrapping them up again. The receipt fell out as she wound the tissue paper around the base and twisted it around the wicks. Adele glanced at the price, £3.49 each, 2 x "Haze of Seduction".

She screwed it up and threw it in the bin, trying to tell herself that it was the price she was embarrassed about. Then straightening her skirt she made her way to the till to serve the next customer.

Cascades of pastel pink and mauve petunia swaths spilled from the white plastic pots on Eileen's matching pink terrace of scrubbed slabs. There were one or two dead heads hiding in the greenery waiting to be found and ripped out by her tidying hands. She wiped the splash marks from the pots rendering the containers spotless and pristine once again.

'Slug pellets,' she said, smoothing Bertie's head. 'I must remember to get some from the shop next door to the market.'

Above the green woodpecker doorknocker hung a basket of bizzie lizzies swinging in the breeze. Their gaudy mixture of colours clashed with the supermarket carrier bag lining and the bright orange plastic washing basket at Eileen's cottage door. With the cyclamen pink duvet cover billowing dry in between showers Eileen stood back to admire the kaleidoscope of colours created by her work. She picked up Bertie and he snuggled into her chest.

'Look Bertie, a perfect rainbow, and I've written to Claire and told her she's welcome to come and stay any time she likes.'

The cat purred contentedly.

'She'll love to see you again. Have to keep an eye on the washing. Don't want it to get wet again do we. And we have to get the spare bed made up quickly just in case she calls and wants to stay for a night or two.'

Carrying the cat back inside she placed him on his stool while she ran warm water and vinegar for the windows in Claire's bedroom. It was the front room that had the best view over the gardens. If only the T.V. folk Adele mentioned could get a move on, then Claire would have a good view when she came.

Adele knocked at Miles's door clutching a glossy gardening magazine. She waited patiently for what seemed like several minutes before Miles came to the door. He managed a forced smile for her and eventually invited her in for a cup of tea when she calmly explained what the visit was about. Adele moved some of the papers from the chair into a pile on the kitchen table and sat down. The kitchen looked a mess. There were papers everywhere and several boxes laced with dust piled on the floor. Miles opened a number of cupboards before he found some loose tea.

'I hope you don't mind tea leaves. I think I must have thrown the strainer out in the last skip.'

He poured the leafy brew into her cup and added some clotted milk from the jug. The lumpy bits made an oily film on the top of the tea and Adele winced when it tasted as sour as she had expected. She laid the gardening magazine on the table and wondered if when she'd gone it would be thrown out with the rest of the rubbish in the kitchen.

'Miles, is there anything you would like to see included in the new garden for Orchard Court?'

'The only thing I'd like to ask is can we keep the buddleia bush.' He stopped short as if the words had crashed into a brick wall. Then his eyes started to water and he got up and poured himself another tea. Adele wanted to ask about the buddleia bush, but didn't really know where to start.

'That sounds like a good choice of shrub to keep Miles.'

He sat down and began talking again in a choked voice.

'Yes, as you can see I'm trying to get myself sorted out, make a fresh start if you know what I mean.'

'Good idea,' Adele started off tentatively, not too sure of Miles's reaction to her acknowledgement of his grief. 'It's best to get rid of things you don't need or that cause any painful memories.' She picked up an old rusty music stand on the table. It had a sticker with Janet Harper written on it.

'What instrument did she play?'

'Oboe, she was good, she was in a big band at university. She didn't play very much after we married, although she had her favourite pieces.'

Adele smiled and decided not to pry too deeply.

'Thanks for your time. I'll leave you the magazine to browse, it might give you another idea.' She went to open the magazine and put her hand onto a plate sticky with jam under a newspaper. Miles didn't seem to notice.

'Miles, do you mind if I wash my hands in your bathroom, I seem to have picked up something sticky?'

'Of course not, it's upstairs on the left.'

Adele climbed the stairs. The hallway and galleried landing were tidy in comparison to the kitchen. Perhaps he was using the kitchen as a sorting room. At the top of the stairs on the left were two doors, both closed. Which one was the bathroom? Adele opened the first one nearest the stairs. It wasn't, but the room she had opened was something else.

The room was like a show case at an historical museum. There was a bed with a hand-made quilted eiderdown and on it, a white cotton chemise with intricate lace and a black velvet skirt. On the floor ready to wear were matching black patent court shoes, on the arm of the chair black stockings and underwear and a clutch bag on the seat. On the dressing table perfume, makeup and hair brushes were displayed and by the window was a wooden music stand holding sheet music. By its side stood a beautiful black oboe on a stand, the silver keys had been recently polished and gleamed in the light. There were framed photographs of Janet all over the room. It was a shrine to her.

Adele came out of the room and closed the door quietly. She wiped her sticky hand in her skirt and went downstairs.

Chapter Nine

Ben slammed his glass down on the kitchen table and Adele mopped up the red wine.

'I don't want you slopping around muddy gardens in a pair of old wellies 'Del.'

'Crispin says there won't be an awful lot to do yet and when there is it's unlikely to be manual work.'

'So why are you still in your scruffy old jeans now; that's not my little wife and her usual style. And by the way who the hell is Crispin?'

Adele stood by the kitchen sink and pulled off her rubber gloves to reveal well-manicured immaculately painted nails. She wore faded blue jeans and a soft mauve polo necked jumper with the sleeves casually rolled up. The pastel colours made the auburn of her hair even more striking and although tonight she had dressed in a relaxed way it didn't undermine her natural prettiness.

'And why didn't you ask me before you signed up to have our garden ripped apart by some amateur bunch of would-be horticulturists?'

'I didn't think there was any need to ask; I thought you'd welcome the idea, especially if it was free.'

'Well you thought wrong, but you've done it now. If you go back on your word now it'll make us seem complete idiots, especially to that bossy bitch Viv.'

Ben picked up the tea towel and started to dry the dishes.

'Why don't you go and have a bath? Take off those old jeans and get into something sexier. Go on, I'll finish these dishes.'

Adele poured ylang ylang essence into the steaming water. Ben didn't even know Viv, so what gave him the right to call her bossy. And more to the point why did she not tell him how judgmental he appeared. Maybe it was because his hypercritical anxious state went hand-in-hand with his short temper. The manner in which he delivered the comments was spiteful and mean and she didn't want to add any more fuel to the vicious fire. If only she could have the Ben five years before who would have made a friend of Viv. She laid her black silk Elle camisole on the bed and undressed from her casual attire. Ben nearly always wanted sex when he returned from a stressful business trip. He told her he couldn't wait to hold her, kiss her and make love to her. She used to look forward to his powerful manly way of pleasing her and the way he took the lead and up until now she'd always wanted him.

Tonight she didn't. She remembered when he'd taken an interest in what she'd been doing during the day, before he'd started to apply his bossy commanding attitude fresh from the workplace to their home life. She lay on the bed caressed in soft silk and her green eyes reflected the beginning of sadness.

All the lanes were open on the Tamar Bridge and Adele's car moved steadily with the rest of the traffic over the Cornish border. Beyond the grey shadow of the parallel Brunel's railway bridge were the bobbing corks of brightly coloured fishing boats on the murky river Tamar. Viv sat in the passenger seat and chided herself for previous thoughts regarding Adele and Rory. After talking with Rory she was now thankful for the company of her younger friend. Adele had understood when Viv talked to her about her pregnancy and she now saw her as a good confidante.

There was something about leaving one county for another that allowed all life's irritations to be left behind. Between the two of them life's aggravations were enough to line up in boxes along the whole length of the bridge. As they left the bridge and the small town on the other side the jumbled information in Viv's mind filed itself away into neat pockets of order; all except those peculiar round marks she'd seen on Adele's arm earlier before they were obscured from view by her cardigan.

The two friends were on their way to visit a heritage garden in Cornwall where Crispin had done some work. It was before he joined the TV gardening team when he was part of a team of garden design experts working for West Country Heritage Gardens. Adele wanted to show Viv the spectacular displays; she said it might give them a few ideas for when the T.V. crew arrived in a few weeks' time. They approached the garden via the lane, with a stream running beside the beech hedging. Crispin had managed the heavy work in the garden for six months and the proprietors, Veronica and Hector sang his praises to the full. Veronica had been delighted when Adele rang saying that she'd been recommended by Crispin. She answered the door in a floaty green skirt topped with a deep purple sleeveless top and mauve cardigan. Adele looked up to her and smiled. Veronica smiled back over the top of her reading glasses from her lofty height. She looked like a cultivated iris on the front of a designer bulb catalogue.

'Veronica? Hello, I'm Adele and this is Viv. We'd like to look at your garden if you don't mind.'

'Adele, of course I don't mind. Any friend of Crispin's is a friend of mine. Do come through to the conservatory.' She chivvied Adele and Viv through the kitchen to the patio door where the smoke signals from Hector's pipe rose up in spirals. Hector rose from his seat and signalled to Adele and Viv to sit down. His wife reached for the teapot and he leant over to offer the two ladies some shortbread.

'It's wonderful to see visitors my dears.' Hector moved his panama hat to another chair and neatly pulled his trousers up a few inches to sit down. Adele pointed with her teacup to a vase of chrysanthemums, the colour of white cotton sheets with virgin green centres.

'I love the flowers,' she said.

'They're very nice,' Veronica replied unenthusiastically. 'He bought them,' she said nodding to Hector. 'I would have liked another colour, but…'

'Never satisfied, thinks I'm a mind reader.' Hector smiled at his wife understanding their differences. He picked up 'The Times' and quietly puffed away like an old incinerator. Veronica beckoned Adele and Viv outside.

'Bring your tea dears and come and see what Crispin has been up to.'

Veronica pointed to the separate borders.

'That's my border on the left and his on the right.'

Adele looked to the left onto a crowd of flamboyant blooms, haphazardly placed at random heights. The right was not as eye-catching in a colour chart of varying whites, creams and greens although it did have shape and form.

'Yes, you can certainly see the difference.' Adele smiled, holding her tongue.

'Well it's all thanks to Crispin. Did he tell you he used to call me Lady Chatterley? That's just about right with him stuck in there in his chair.' Veronica nodded towards Hector in the conservatory. Adele gulped her tea and stifled the laughter.

'Not that I was ever thinking about getting up to anything with Crispin dear. I suppose he'd be what you call a toy boy for me, wouldn't he?'

'I'm sure that he'd be very flattered Veronica,' Adele replied, wondering even more now what Crispin would look like. He'd certainly hit it off with Veronica and he must be quite a bit younger than her. How much younger...well she'd just have to wait and see. Hector appeared holding on to his stick for support.

'Are you ready my love?'

'Ready for what?' Veronica turned frowning.

'The neighbourhood watch meeting at Cyn's house.'

'Don't let him push you out early Adele.' Veronica held on to Adele's arm.

'Can't you see they haven't even finished their tea yet?' She snapped in Hector's direction.

'Actually Veronica, would you mind if we stay for a while in the garden while you're out.'

'Of course not my dears. Stay as long as you like. I'll make you a fresh pot of tea before we go and if you leave before we get back put the tray in the potting shed.'

'No, there's no need.'

'Yes there is dear. I insist.' And she walked off briskly to the kitchen.

Adele strolled to the front of the house with Hector, while Viv waited for Veronica and even though Hector hobbled along the paths he gestured for her to go first and held the gate open for her. He looked very regal despite his condition, in his smart blazer and cream flannel trousers. He took his panama off as he said goodbye to Viv and Adele and very sedately levered himself into the passenger side of the bright yellow VW Golf. He'd hardly got in and pulled the door shut when Veronica rushed out.

'You stay as long as you like my dears. Tea's on the patio table.'

And she was off down the lane, a scuttling of chippings from the drive settling behind her.

For a moment they sat at the patio table with eyes closed, listening to the surrounding sounds of birdsong and leaves and branches rustling. The ticking of the garden clock just inside the kitchen porch could be heard just gently in the background. Adele wandered further into the garden watching a blackbird pull a worm and a cloud of honey bees disperse from a huge clump of lavender.

'Doesn't it give you inspiration?' Viv murmured in a library voice.

'You're so right. It's beautiful and so tranquil.'

A squirrel ran onto the lawn and dug up an acorn. So that's how the tiny pits in the lawn appeared. The squirrel buried the nut again, climbed the fence and scuttled along the ledge before leaping with bat-like limbs into a hazel tree.

'How are you feeling now,' Adele asked Viv. 'What about your back and is the pregnancy making you feel sick?'

'Fortunately the back is getting better, but the sickness has replaced it along with a dreadful feeling of tiredness. I have to rest from time to time but if anything it's given me time to rethink certain aspects of my life. How much time have I wasted not doing what I'd really like to do? How many minutes and seconds would it amount to in a squirrel's life?'

The squirrel was still in the hazel tree dangling from one of the branches.

Adele tipped out the contents of her bag while she mulled over her thoughts. She pulled out a sketch she'd done earlier. She had a talent to draw without a doubt. It was a skill too good to be wasted. She gently rubbed her bruised arm where Ben had grabbed her earlier. He'd brought the garden project up again in the morning and when she insisted that she was going to help with the arrangements he'd lost his temper and told her that they should employ their own workers and not expect her to organise it for nothing. Perhaps she should have kept quiet about being involved, but...maybe she had been wasting time as well, too much time with a snappy neurotic husband to even notice what talents she had to offer.

Chapter Ten

Viv defrosted chicken from the freezer for a curry she planned to make later. There didn't seem so much to do in the daytime now that all the boys were at school. Still, that wouldn't last long. She had become used to the idea of having another child in the last few weeks. At first it had been a shock, but at least she felt needed again and she did love being with small children. Rory hadn't said very much about the pregnancy after the initial outburst, in fact he hadn't been himself at all lately. When she met him sixteen years ago he was a fun-loving person and it was that and his sense of humour that first attracted him to her. The last few weeks had shown him quiet and withdrawn and unable to settle to a conversation however hard Viv tried to pin him down. It was starting to become unbearable.

As the noisy washing machine cycle finished she could hear a telephone message being recorded. She heard Adele's voice and stopped the answer machine to talk to her.

'Viv, how are you?'

'I'm so glad you phoned. Can you come over? I'd come to you, but, well to be honest I think I've overdone it this morning. My legs are aching and my back feels so stiff.'

'I'll be right over. I could do with a break. I've just finished some sketches of our gardens to send to Crispin.'

Adele let herself in through the back door. Viv had returned to the sofa in the lounge.

'I thought I was doing so well this morning, but I suppose sliding down the rail from the garden the other day didn't help.'

'You did what!' Adele reacted with surprise, trying to hide the fact that she'd actually seen Viv do it.

'I thought that it might be easier than encountering the steep steps.'

'But Viv, sliding down poles is not a usual thing to do even when you're in the best of health.'

Adele was about to offer to make Viv a hot drink, but before she had the chance to leave the room Viv started to cry. Adele sat next to her on the sofa.

'I thought that you were getting better and in good spirits when we visited the garden the other day Viv.'

Adele gave her a tissue and Viv tried to sniff out her explanation.

'It's me and Rory. We're not getting on since I discovered the pregnancy. I couldn't believe it when I found out. I did a pregnancy test at home and when it turned out to be positive I had to make myself go to the doctor's to have it confirmed. Rory and I had agreed that he would have a vasectomy, so as you can imagine this wasn't planned.'

Adele held her hand.

'Go on Viv, what did the doctor have to say and what about Rory?'

Viv blew her nose and poured a glass of water from the carafe on the coffee table. She sipped the water.

'I couldn't believe Dr Lethbridge's suggestion. He said I could consider having a termination, especially bearing in mind my age and the fact that I already have four children to cope with.'

'Many people do Viv. It's just that we don't hear about them and besides it's nothing to be ashamed of under the circumstances.'

'I couldn't do it Adele. I know it will be difficult but I'll find a way of managing. It's just Rory…'

She burst into floods of tears.

'We argued about it at first and I could handle that. But I can't survive this never-ending silence he's gone into. He goes to work in silence and returns the same way. I feel as if he blames me for everything.'

'Don't worry Viv, I'm sure he'll come round. After all it's not him who'll be staying at home looking after the new baby is it? He's probably taking time to adjust to it.'

'It was just like the turning off of a switch. One minute he was at loggerheads with me, waltzing around being his usual rowdy self and the next minute silence. I've never known him so quiet.'

'Be patient Viv. Give him some time to mull it over, he'll come round.'

The two friends sat in silence for a few moments, before Viv looked up, dabbing her eyes.

Adele closed the front door and crawled up the stairs to the kitchen, while the kettle was boiling she warmed soup in the microwave. She knew she should try and eat properly when Ben was away, but lately she'd lost her appetite. Today had been a long day and she'd worked overtime with Bradley to help stock take before the area manager's visit next week. He'd thrust a long red package of chocolate into her bag as she left and thanked her for staying. She poured hot water onto a tea bag and pulled the chocolate out to look at it. Baci – the Italian word for kisses. What was he getting at?

The steamy water plunged onto the bath salts causing a fresh aroma to rise in waves. Adele dropped the blind and returned to the bedroom to slip out of her clothes. Although she missed having the company, she rather liked the freedom of Ben not being there. She could eat, drink and shower whenever she liked and if she felt like watching a late night film while finishing the ironing until 2.00 a.m. she could please herself. She put on her short black satin and lace night robe and transformed the bathroom to her liking. She lit a honeysuckle incense stick on the window sill and a large white candle on a Gothic stand by the door. Then she pulled out the carefully wrapped 'haze of seduction' candles given to her by Bradley from her lingerie drawer. She stood them in some pebbles at the end of the bath so that she could watch them burn from the far end. Lastly, a glass of warmed red wine and a flight sized fashion magazine, also from Bradley. Dropping her robe onto a chair she sunk into the warm water and sighed. Her aching muscles melted into the balmy atmosphere and the flames flickered dissolving her thoughts. She sipped the wine, closed her eyes and attempted to drain her mind and relax. She tried to think of what she would be doing with Ben at the weekend and how she could make him warm towards the garden project. Then about going to see Eileen tomorrow and Miles's dilemma, but how ever hard she tried thoughts of Bradley kept returning like laughing demons. She knew that he fitted the 'Jack-the-Lad' character that she'd only read about before, but he was fun and easy to be with. Surely he couldn't be that bad and what harm was she doing just thinking about him. So Adele welcomed the demons into her mind and they didn't laugh in a mocking way, they were seductive and fanciful. She gulped down the red wine and more of them entered her mind. She soaped her body all over with a soft natural sponge and massaged oil into her shoulders, neck and breasts. The magazine curled its corners with the heat and steamy droplets of oil spoiled its glossy cover.

Rivulets of oily water clung to the sides of the bath, emitting the smell of her cleansed skin throughout the room. She wrapped a soft pink bath wrap around her and extinguished the candles. Then, dropping the towel, she lay on top of her bed with a thin cotton sheet covering her naked body. She reached for the Baci chocolates and as she unwrapped one the heat still in her hands melted it. She licked the chocolate from her fingers and wiped them in a tissue. A flimsy piece of paper fell out of the chocolate. It was a feature, a thought or love note inside the wrapper in Italian and four other languages. Typical Italian crossed her mind and perhaps typical Bradley. She liked the sound of the French best – *Il n'y a que l'amour qui nous fasse voir les choses banales sous un jour extraordinaire.* She repeated it to herself several times, then she fell asleep clutching the note – *Only love lets us see normal things in an extraordinary way.*

Adele could smell Eileen's baking coming from her open kitchen window as the woodpecker knocked twice on the cottage door. Eileen answered the door with oven cloth still in her hand.

'Ah, you're just in time for a nice piece of warm bannock cake. It's my own grandmother's recipe.'

Adele didn't usually eat cake or biscuits, but couldn't refuse Eileen's enthusiastic offerings. It was a welcome change from the rather icy reception she'd received from her a few days ago. The tea was ready to pour as Eileen handed Adele a plate with a huge triangle of the fruity bread spread profusely with melted butter. She followed the cake with a cup of tea for both of them and sat down opposite Adele at her minuscule kitchen table. Adele got out her notepad, sketchpad and a pencil.

'About the garden Eileen, is there anything specific you would like to see included?'

'I would like to keep my pink and white slabs. They're so clean and scrub up well don't you think?'

'I suppose you could call them practical,' Adele replied, not wanting to stifle Eileen's cheerful mood today, 'but there must be so many alternative products available now. Perhaps we should order some catalogues over the internet to see what's available in the way of natural stone patio coverings.'

'Could you do that for me, I haven't got a computer and wouldn't know how to work one if I had. We might be able to find some up-to-date pink and white stones, you never know.'

'You never know Eileen,' Adele replied holding in her smirk.

'Come to think of it I had a garden magazine in the post the other day.'

Eileen started to sift through the pile of mail by the toaster. The leaflets and post slid over the work surface and an envelope in pink recycled paper landed on Adele's lap.

'You dropped this letter Eileen.' Adele handed it back to her. Eileen passed the gardening magazine over and she took the letter.

'This looks ideal Eileen, it'll give you some ideas anyway. Look at this patio made from natural Bath stone.'

Eileen was reading the letter, ignoring Adele. Adele saw her wipe away the tear at the end of her nose. She sniffed, folded the letter up and put it back in the envelope.

'Do you want to talk about the garden some other time Eileen?'

The jovial atmosphere had been wiped clean away by whatever was in that letter and Eileen's face dropped into glumness.

'No, no it's alright, now is alright. Yes, the Bath stone looks very modern…she doesn't understand about me and Robert.'

'You and Robert Eileen?'

'Yes, Carmel she doesn't understand. Robert's my brother and Carmel's his wife. They have one daughter, Claire and I'm sure that Carmel has poisoned her against me. I want her to come and stay with me, but she doesn't even reply to my letters. I bet her mother's intercepting them.'

Adele sat back on her stool, surprised that Eileen would even begin to open up to her.

'Why would she do that Eileen?'

'She's always hated the closeness between me and Robert. She's jealous. We've always been really close, but when he met her it was like having one of my limbs amputated. She took control as soon as they were married and now we have to correspond in secret because she makes so much fuss. Obviously there are times when I will ring the house when she is there and I send birthday and Christmas cards and presents, but she doesn't miss a chance to put me down or criticise the way I live.'

'How long have they been married Eileen?'

'Nineteen years.'

'And you've put up with that kind of treatment all this time?'

Adele hadn't realised that organising the garden project would include the role of an agony aunt, but she sympathised and continued to listen.

'It wasn't too bad when we lived in the same town. We could meet each other for lunch and Carmel would never know. It was only when I moved here that it became a problem.'

'So how old did you say Claire was Eileen? Eighteen was it? She should be able to make her own mind up now shouldn't she?'

'If only I could persuade her to come and stay Adele, just for a few days.'

Adele put her key into the front door and made a mental list for her phone call. All she had to report to Crispin was that Miles wanted to keep the buddleia and Eileen her precious pink and white slabs, but then there were the other things - Miles's shrine to Janet, Eileen's desperation for her niece to visit and Viv and Rory's upset over her pregnancy. She hesitated. The neighbours' anxieties had nothing to do with the garden project, but on the other hand...Adele didn't want Crispin to be put in a difficult position just because he wasn't kept informed and Crispin would be discreet, she was sure of that. They'd had several conversations over the telephone recently and she sensed that even though she hadn't met him, he was someone she could trust.

'I don't want to put you or the BNG team off the project, but there are a few personal obstacles. I'm hoping that they can be overcome, but I wanted to let you know, just so as you're aware. I trust that I can also rely on your discretion.'

'Absolutely Adele and it doesn't sound too bad with Eileen and Viv and Rory, but what about Miles, that's more worrying. The bedroom you discovered is like Janet's own personalised museum. I'm no expert but has he come to terms with Janet's death?'

'Perhaps that's just the way he deals with the situation, but I agree it's not really moving on. The thing is he doesn't know that I found the room. I'm not sure whether to mention it to his G.P. or the lady counsellor that he went to see? Should I tell them, I don't want him to think I'm meddling?'

'Why don't you leave it for a while? You can keep more of a vigilant eye on him and decide what to do according to how he is in the next few weeks. What do you think?'

'Yes that's probably best and perhaps I could look out for Eileen at the same time.'

'And for Viv and Rory. I'm sure they'll all sort out their problems in time and I won't mention any of this to a soul. It sounds like we're becoming a pair of garden doctors Adele.'

'What shall we call ourselves? Is it to be Gardens in a Swirl or Neighbourhood Botch?' They both laughed together before their sincerity returned.

'We shouldn't joke about it. It's a serious concern for each of them.'

'You're quite right, it is serious.'

Eileen sorted the brown envelopes from today's post. She put the bills to one side and held the pink envelope. Her fingers shook as she pulled out the single sheet of matching writing paper...

Dear Eileen
We received your letter requesting Claire to come and stay with you. It's very kind of you to offer, but Claire is awfully busy trying to sort out a flat in readiness for the autumn term when she starts her new course in food technology and design. She is also extremely busy with social engagements meeting friends of her own age. She has asked me to write and tell you that she is finding it very difficult to find a suitable time to come and see you. So rather than disappoint you we thought it best to decline your offer now.
Fond regards
Carmel

Chapter Eleven

Rory and Justin stood outside their front door in Orchard Court and watched Veronica and Hector walk back to their car. Veronica was wearing a bright orange chiffon suit with a bright green wide-brimmed hat and Hector wore the usual panama, cream suit finished with matching bright green bow tie.

'Who the hell were *they* Dad?'

'Shh Justin, they own a heritage garden in Cornwall. They were returning a carrier bag of sketches to Adele. The old boy looked a bit shaken up didn't he?'

'Not as shaken up as I was this morning when Tony told me I'm not in the trials.'

'No! They haven't picked that wally Ben Rose have they?'

Rory sat astride his Suzuki 250 and he and Justin watched Hector being manoeuvred into the car by Veronica. Justin gave the petrol tank a final polish, screwed up the cloth and stuffed it in his pocket.

'I can't believe it. Rose hasn't played more than two matches this season.' Rory continued.

'I know Dad, the rest of the team think it's a shit decision. Bill called earlier, asked if I wanted to go down the field and play penalty shoot outs, but I can't be arsed after they picked Rose over me.'

Rory wheeled his precious motorcycle into the shed.

'Thanks for helping me clean the machine.' He said patting the seat. 'Don't let the trials worry you too much, there'll be other times.'

Justin ruffled his hair back into shape and shrugged his shoulders.

'You don't need me any more do you Dad? Think I'll take my board and go down the ramp.'

'No waxing the pavements on the way down. I don't want to be liable for any little old ladies breaking their necks in the gutter.'

Justin rode the board all the way down to the half pipe in the corner of the playing field. To start with he sat on the steps and watched. Chris Gates was pretty good at his 180 turns since he'd last been down. He ought to be, he was down here for hours every day. He was always with Lynch, sitting on the bar smoking fags. Justin took his board and climbed up by the bar. He just about had the courage to drop in and sufficient bend in his knees to power him up to the other side. He nodded at Chris by the bar. Not much was said between anyone using the ramp; they needed all their concentration to stay upright. Two or three other bladers were there as well and one guy he'd never seen before on a BMX. Justin took a few turns and then sat out next to Lynch by the bar.

'Got any cash on you Just?'

'No, why?'

'Want some more fags to go with our stuff for later.'

'What stuff?'

'No, I'll ask Chris's brother. It's okay.'

Justin stayed watching the BMX bloke do his tricks. The ramp was less busy now. Maybe he could get to have a go without being so embarrassed. Lynch had come back with Chris's brother, but they'd be okay. They went behind the ramp anyway so they wouldn't see him make an arse of himself.

Justin plucked up more courage and twisted his board round at the top of the ramp. He didn't quite make it and skidded down on the hard shiny metal burning his elbow.

'You okay?'

They were the first two words that Chris had uttered.

'Yeah, I'm fine.'

He picked up his board and watched Chris. Someone on blades was standing on top of the railings. Chris had got off the ramp as well now. It was Lynch!

'Shit, he's not gonna drop in from up there is he?'

Lynch screamed out, 'Just watch me, fucking have it,' and jumped off the railings onto the cold hard steel. Miraculously he made it to the other side to join Chris's brother. They both looked drowsy and were pushing each other around and when Lynch passed Justin again he could smell something strange. It was a bit like the paint his Dad had used to do up the shed with. Lynch and Joe (Chris's brother) had freaked out and were jumping off the railings, trying out moves that they would never normally dream of. Some of the time they made it and a few other times they slid to the middle of the half pipe. Justin and Chris were so amazed at what they were doing they didn't notice the two Coppers coming up behind them. The next thing they knew, all four of them were down at the police station. Their parents had been called and Lynch had been sick in a bucket.

Joe and Chris started an argument about whose fault it was.

'You know Lynch used to get asthma don't you?'

'No…'

'No, well no's too late when my mate's lying dead on the floor.'

'Well they can't have us anyway.'

'They can't get you for sniffing, but they'll make damn sure they get you for nicking the stuff and me and Justin too.'

'But we didn't do anything.' Justin looked over to Chris for reassurance. Chris looked away. Justin sat with his head in his hands. He'd never been so pleased to see the friendly face and robust figure of his father come through the door.

Later at home he lay with his head on his father's lap while Viv slept upstairs. The doctor had told her to rest and she'd gone to bed early complaining of tiredness, not that she'd said much to him about the incident when she was downstairs anyway. Either she wasn't bothered or she didn't believe that he hadn't been involved in some way.

'How come Mum thinks I've been sniffing stuff before.'

'She doesn't, she's just tired, must admit though she did look a bit vacant about the whole thing.'

'You believe me don't you Dad?'

'Course I do, but…'

'Yeah I know, next time choose the penalty shoot out.'

'Exactly. Go on, up to bed, I'll come up and have a chat with you in a minute.'

The encroaching dawn brought no fresh light to Miles Harper's world. He threw off his sheets, damp with his sweat and padded slowly and barefoot to the kitchen. With shaking hands he filled the kettle and grappled in the drawer for his pills.

'You know you should have listened to the district nurse old boy.' He pricked himself on the prongs of a fork and remembered her words: *'Now Mr Harper, it's no shame to be on anti-depressants, especially after what's happened. I should go on taking them for a while if I were you. It's what Dr Lethbridge recommended and when you do want to stop taking them you must go and see him first to get his advice.'*

Miles felt like death, it hadn't occurred to him that the pills were the sort of drugs he'd have to wean himself off. He decided to go back to the usual dose and gulped one of the plastic coated capsules down with water. Four days ago he'd decided to give up the pills. The dosage was three a day and he'd gone from that to nothing overnight. The hours wore on and he felt worse and worse from headaches to hot flushes, cold sweats and panic attacks. He knew what the term 'cold turkey' meant now. He didn't know what was worse the despair he'd felt before the pills, the fuzziness of his life while on them or the terror and fear that surrounded giving them up. He'd have to devise a plan of cutting down gradually.

Miles climbed back upstairs and turned into the room at the top of the stairs. He lay on the bed and felt around for Janet's chemise. He held it to his chest and tried to inhale any last remnants of her body scent. He climbed inside the covers holding the shirt and closed his eyes. He was with her now, he put his arm around her imaginary body and fell asleep with the soothing memory of his wife in his mind. Later he got up and replaced everything just as it was. He smoothed out the bed sheets and plumped the pillow. He arranged the quilt and placed the clothes precisely in the exact spot where he had found them. Then he sprayed her favourite perfume around the room and left closing the door firmly behind him.

It was a beautiful sunny afternoon and Adele noticed another sprinkling of freckles across her nose when she came in from the garden. Her mother had always said her freckles were cute, but Ben didn't like them at all. Perhaps she could put some concealer on them later on, after her bath. Ben was on his way home now and Adele stood in the kitchen preparing bruscetta for starters and tagliatelle served with Chianti for the main course. She crushed garlic and chopped cherry tomatoes and green olives. The red peppers and single cream stood waiting for the next course. She laid the table with a red cloth and matching candles, napkins and place mats. Finally she filled the top shelf of the fridge with bottled beers. By 8.00 p.m. Adele was ready, scrubbed up, seductively dressed, freckles hidden, but still no Ben. He hadn't rung her and she was expecting him home by 7.30 p.m. at the latest. She sat down on the sofa to read her magazine. 8.05 p.m. and he still wasn't home. She poured herself a glass of wine and put her feet up on the sofa. As her feet hit the cushion Ben walked in.

'It's alright for some isn't it? I've had one hell of a day and the hold-ups on the M5 were horrendous.'

Adele slopped wine over her silk blouse. Ben dumped his case in the hallway and shouted, 'I'm just going to have a quick shower and then can we eat? I'm bloody starving, they didn't even provide us with lunch.'

Adele got up and went to the kitchen. Typical of him to come in through the door the moment she sat down and he didn't even greet her with a kiss. It was off to get changed as soon as he came in.

By the time Ben had showered and changed into jeans and designer t-shirt the food was ready to serve. He couldn't fail to pay compliments to his wife's cooking ability, but there was still a sting. He put his hand on her arm.

'Great food 'Del, but then that was one of the main reasons I married you,' he patronized. 'You were a much better cook than that blonde I was seeing at the same time.'

Adele smiled pretending to see the joke, but by now it was beginning to wear a bit thin. She took the dishes out to the kitchen, returning to find Ben lighting the two candles she'd left on the mantle piece – *haze of seduction.*

'These old things smell nice 'Del, where did you get them?'

'A new shop in town I think it's called *Penny for your Thoughts* weird name for a shop if you ask me.'

'Yes,' he said and flumped onto the sofa. Adele brought coffee on a tray and some Baci chocolates she'd had left over from the ones Bradley had given her. Ben sipped his coffee and picked up one of the chocolates.

'These look chunky, have they got nuts in?'

'Yes, and inside they have…'

But Ben wasn't listening to the rest of her sentence. He unwrapped the chocolate and crunched the walnut sized lump up all in one go. Then he screwed up the paper and aimed it at the fireplace. Adele ate hers and folded up the motto to read later.

'Is that a new camisole you're wearing there 'Del?'

He undid her blouse and slid his hand inside. He stroked her breast under the silkiness of the cream laced satin. She closed her eyes as he picked her up and carried her to the bedroom. As he placed her gently on the bed he removed her blouse and kissed the edge of the lace where her flesh met the garment. It was dark in the room and the curtains were closed. She took off the rest of her clothes and he removed his leaving them in a heap by the side of the bed. They lay naked under the thin cotton sheet and she kept her eyes gently closed all the time. The pleasure was all hers. She shared it with the laughing demons, she welcomed them into her bed to share her seductive, fanciful thoughts. They stayed with her until she opened her eyes, then they disappeared like a wisp of smoke blown away by a gentle breeze.

Chapter Twelve

Sheryl chatted to Adele as they stacked boxes of chocolate bars in the storeroom. She revealed the tale of how she had had too many gins last Friday and slept in on Saturday until 11.30 a.m. She omitted to tell Adele that Bradley had been with her and a few other friends and he'd ended up sleeping on her lounge floor in a sleeping bag. She wouldn't want nice quiet Adele thinking that she was a tart. Adele told Sheryl about the meal she'd cooked and her freckles.

'I agree with your mum Adele, your freckles are cute.'

'Yes, but Ben hates them and I don't want him to find me unattractive.'

'I can understand women who go on diets, have their hair cut a certain way or wear certain clothes to please a man, but freckles? It's all a bit picky Adele.'

'I don't mind though Sheryl.'

'Do you like them yourself?'

'Well yes, but...'

'Well what then, if you like them tell him to go and take a hike with his concealer, the bossy sod.'

Bradley walked into the storeroom with the invoice sheets.

'What do you think of Adele's freckles Bradley?'

'They're cute; they make her look sweet and innocent.'

'See told you Adele, and Bradley's an expert on a woman's appearance.'

'Hey, watch it Sheryl you'll give me a bad name.'

Sheryl laughed and started taking some of the boxes out to the shop to restock the shelves. Bradley stayed in the storeroom to chat to Adele. He knew he'd have to do something about his living arrangements soon. It wasn't the first time that he'd slept on Sheryl's floor when he'd stayed in town drinking until late.

Until two months ago Bradley had lived with his wife and two year old son in a village nearby. She'd been looking for an excuse to kick him out for nearly a year now and when word got back that he'd stayed with Sheryl overnight for the third time that was the perfect reason. He'd arrived home on Sunday lunchtime to find his clothes in black bin liners on the front lawn. That, coupled with the sight of his macho brother-in-law looking out the window, arms folded, frowning deeply was enough to make him retreat. He'd thrown all his bags in the car and left. He managed to find lodgings with a friend in the village, but they had only given him ten weeks before their son returned home from Belgium. So in a few weeks' time he was officially homeless.

'Adele, I need to talk to you about something important. I'm hoping you'll be able to help me, you and Ben that is. You'd have to ask Ben as well, of course.'

'Yes, what is it Bradley?' It wasn't like Bradley not get to the point.

'You know you and Ben have that flat of yours on the ground floor?'

'Yes.'

'Well, I'm looking for somewhere to live. My time's come to an end at my present lodgings. They've been good to me, but we did agree that I'd go two weeks from now.'

'It is free at the moment, but Ben's been a bit touchy over renting it. He says it needs redecorating and renting is a lot of responsibility. It makes sense though, for you to rent it. I'll see if I can bring the subject up in the next few days.'

'Thanks Adele.' Bradley leant over and kissed her neatly and quickly on the cheek before returning to the shop.

Adele finished stacking the boxes neatly before resting on the stepladder. Oh damn, what had she done now? She should have put him off. Perhaps she could paint a bad picture to Ben and then it wouldn't take much for him to refuse Bradley. And there must be plenty of other rented accommodation available in the town for a single man such as him.

Miles counted the rings on the other end of the line as he held onto the receiver. Viv picked up after six, but promptly dropped her phone on answering behind a shoe cupboard in the hallway. By the time she retrieved it the person had hung up. Miles listened to the distant voice saying 'Hello'. The voice wasn't so distant in reality, but Miles croaked a few more hellos into the mouthpiece at his end before assuming that he'd got the wrong number and hanging up. He poured a large tot of whiskey into his tea and went to lie down upstairs.

Eileen saw him go past the large picture window on his landing. She yearned to go and knock on his door and ask if he'd join her for a cup of tea, but he'd spurned her too many times now. Instead she finished her sweeping and washed the dirt from the front door with warm soapy water. It was nearly lunchtime and she was late with her path cleaning today. Maybe Adele would be coming home soon. She could chat to her. Eileen went inside to collect more water to rinse the door. When she returned Ben was there waiting for her with his arms folded.

'Eileen, I just wanted to ask if you've seen Adele.'

'No,' Eileen replied and before she could speak Ben continued.

'I've been to the shop. She's not there and not at home either. The blonde girl seemed to be the only one around at the shop and she didn't have a clue.'

'Sorry Ben, I haven't seen her.'

'I only wanted her to come and have lunch with me. If you see her you will tell her won't you?'

Ben gave a business-like smile and walked away from Eileen. His request sounded more like a command that she should tell her. He walked back to his own house and within minutes he had returned.

'Are you sure that you haven't seen her Eileen?'

'No, I haven't seen her for a few hours dear. Last time I saw her was this morning when she was talking and laughing with Rory, you know the hospital chappie.'

'I see, thank you very much Eileen, you've been most helpful.'

Eileen smiled and returned to her pavement cleaning while Ben flew back to his own house.

Adele fiddled with her key in the front door. She'd come home for lunch and a change of scenery. She pulled her carrier bag in around the door and bumped right into Ben sat on the stairs.

'Where have you been hiding?'

'What do you mean? I've been working all morning, have you got some time off?'

'Yes and I was hoping to spend it with you if I could find you.'

'Did you come into the shop?'

'Yes and that dim blonde girl said you weren't there.'

'I did go out to the stock room to tidy up after the last delivery.'

'Oh well, you're here now. Come and sit on my lap.'

Adele couldn't get past Ben as he sat stretched across the stairs so she reluctantly sat on his lap, gave him a quick hug and got up again.

'Shall we have lunch?'

Their conversation was interrupted by the door bell ringing. It was Rory.

'Did you leave this outside Adele?'

Rory handed Adele her handbag, which she realised had fallen off her shoulder on to the pavement when opening the door.

'Thanks Rory.'

Adele took the bag and turning her back on Ben she carried on the conversation with Rory. It was general chit-chat about the weather, the garden and the lack of parking spaces in the area. She closed the door. Ben had disappeared upstairs. When she got upstairs to the kitchen he was throwing saucepans around and trying to heat up some soup. He rooted around in the freezer turning everything upside down.

'Where are those crusty rolls you bought the other day?'

He looked up at her with a face like thunder. He continued turning out every item.

'Okay Ben, you don't need to snap.'

'Don't need to snap? Why shouldn't I snap, when I come home to see my wife and first she's nowhere to be found and then off talking to that bloody lowly hospital porter?'

'There's nothing wrong with Rory. He's a nice guy and funny.'

'Oh I can see he's got you hooked. His wife was looking out of her window earlier; she's obviously worried about him.'

'You must have got the wrong end of the stick Ben. Viv and Rory are okay. It was a bit of a shock about the new baby, but they're getting used to it now, so Viv tells me.'

'So that's what she's called, Viv. Yes she's another one. You make sure you get them all on your side won't you.'

Ben slammed two bowls of soup down on the kitchen table with a plate of sliced bread. They ate in silence and Adele stirred her soup around. She couldn't eat for the lump inside her stomach.

Adele made her way to the study. She opened up her emails to find a new one from the Breaking New Ground gardening team.

Dear Adele,

Tried ringing you this morning, but no answer…

The Breaking New Ground team are planning to visit Orchard Court to make preliminary plans regarding the TV show. We're looking for accommodation in the area for a few days (in about

two weeks' time) and wondered whether you could make any recommendations. The budget for the show is not exactly huge so we might need to economise in a few areas. Looking forward to hearing from you and to meeting with you and your neighbours soon
Yours BNG team

This was great news, at last it was all beginning to fall into place. Adele phoned Viv for a few ideas and emailed them back straight away.

Dear BNG team
Great to hear that your team will be here soon. Here are a few recommendations for accommodation, from B&B to hotel:
Bluebell Cottage B&B, Tel: 895745 (£28 per night, ensuite rooms, walking distance of town)
Lavender House B&B, Tel: 897612 (£30 per night, ensuite rooms overlooking river)
The Rose and Crown Public House B&B, Tel: 898045 (£25 per night, double and single rooms above the pub)
The Hexbury Green, Hotel, Tel: 875412 (£50 per night, ensuite rooms with lounge area, TV and mini-bar)
Hope this is okay, Eileen and I also have room for 2-3 people if you get stuck booking rooms.
Best Wishes
Adele Parker

'I think you've been a tad ambitious mentioning 'The Hexbury Green,' Viv said when Adele showed her the email. 'I didn't mention that one and I thought they said the show was on a budget.'

'I didn't want them to think we're bereft of any posh hotels in the town.'

'I suppose you're right, it's definitely worth showing off. It's very stylish and fashionable, very pricey as well though.'

'It'll be interesting to see who stays there, if anyone does.'

'Yes, it certainly will.'

A skinny boy in school uniform hung around the car park at the General Hospital in the city, kicking a plastic bottle. The attendant caught up with him.

'Shouldn't you be at school young man?' He said more out of annoyance than concern.

'Lunch hour.' The boy mumbled back and hoped the man didn't understand as much as he did about school regulations. A woman reversed very close to the ticket machine and thank God the attendant was distracted.

Drew walked at his fastest pace past the main entrance and towards A and E. He knew that if he hung around the back staff door, well away from the ambulance bay his dad would come out for a fag at some stage. Sure enough after five minutes Rory crept out tapping a cigarette on the packet. He looked straight over at Drew.

'What the hell are you doing here?'

'Bunking off school and wanted to see you.'

'What do you mean "bunking off school" and how did you get here? I hope you don't make a habit of bunking off.'

'Caught the bus in and said I was going for a blood test and that you knew about it.'

'Oh great, get yer poor old dad into trouble as well.'

Rory could see however, that his son was upset about something and he put his arm around him.

'Want a cup of tea in the refectory upstairs?'

'Okay dad, and a doughnut?'

'Okay, I'll get you a doughnut as well.'

Rory put his cigarettes away and the two caught the lift up to the fifth floor. Drew watched his dad balancing the tray with two mugs of tea and a jam doughnut. He pulled his socks up on his scrawny legs and winced at the bruise forming on his left shin. Then he spat on his finger and rubbed it onto his sore ear. Eric Bullen had sat on him and twisted it round. It was still throbbing now. Eric had made Drew's life at school a misery, it had started not long after he joined the school and Eric, although he looked two years older from his thick frame was in the same year as Drew.

'No bastard's gonna diss me and get away with it.' He'd yelled at Drew as he held him by the throat after the offending French lesson.

'If all the others can keep their mouths shut why can't you?' Eric shook him as he shouted. 'Always got an answer for teacher haven't you. Gay little boff.'

Madame Paon, along with many other adults found Drew to be very polite and pleasant to talk to. 'A boy to be trusted,' she'd told other members of staff. He was trustworthy enough to have the guts to tell her who had tipped Coke straight from the bottle out of the top floor window. Unfortunately, the definition of a trustworthy person in Eric's sleazy slang book was 'dobber'.

Rory stirred the milky tea and placed it in front of Drew. He tucked into the doughnut first and Rory was pleased to see him eat. He could do with a bit more meat on him; he was far too thin and small for his age.

'So what is it all about Drew? Why the running away from school?'

'Wanted to ask you if you and mum were okay now. You are okay with her having another baby now aren't you?'

'Yes, of course I am, but is that all you're worried about?'

'Yes.'

'Sure about that Drew?'

'Yes, sure dad.'

Drew ate his doughnut in sticky mouth-filled silence. Rory walked him to the bus stop and made him promise not to bunk off again. As Drew sat on the bus for the half hour journey home he thought of his mother when he'd gone home for lunch yesterday. She had sat down and flicked through the Mother and Baby magazine on the table, carefully brushing the drops of vegetable water from the front cover. Placing a glossy shot of a cute baby girl in front of him, she touched him on the shoulder.

'I wonder if it'll be a baby sister like this one.'

Drew had forced a smile in his mother's direction and sipped his warm tea.

'I know it's supposed to be unlucky,' she said. 'But I've started a collection of baby clothes already. Look!'

She produced a screwed up carrier bag from the bread bin in the larder and fished from it a selection of miniature vests, socks and two lemon babygros embroidered with ducks.'

She handed him one of the babygros.

'Feel how soft it is.'

Viv put her hand on his.

'Listen Drew, you won't tell your father about this collection of mine will you. I know you understand my feelings, you always have. You've always been willing to listen when the others walk away. I don't mean I'm keeping it a secret from your father. It's just that he needs time to adjust to the idea.'

She picked up the two cups and wiped the table.

'Don't worry Mum. I'll keep it quiet. But Mum…'

'I reckon he'll change his tune in just a few weeks. He'll be as proud as he was when all of you boys were on the way.'

Drew pulled the leg of his trousers down and gave a sigh.

'I'd better go back to school now Mum.'

'Okay love, see you in a few hours.'

Drew closed the front door and took a detour up the garden steps. He walked over to the apple tree in the middle of all the plots. He and Justin had carved their names on the tree about five years' ago. The bark had darkened around the area of the carving and a white fungus attached itself to the trunk in raised patterns like miniature clouds. Drew picked up a stone and scraped away the fungus in a meticulous fashion until the tree was clean again. Then he hacked away at his own name until it was obliterated from the bark. If only it were that easy to scrub the likes of Eric Bullen from the face of the earth. Checking his watch he realised he'd be at least five minutes late for his first lesson this afternoon, but late and detention from Mr Valcheva, his science teacher was far easier than meeting up with Bullen and his cronies. Drew had been collecting detentions recently; forgetting to bring homework in on time, answering back to teachers he knew would rise to the bait and defacing school property such as desks and books with vulgar graffiti. Detentions were a safe haven, a quiet place to work guarded from the torture waiting outside the school building. Nobody would make the connection, discover the plan. They'd just assume that he was about to undergo metamorphosis into yet another twelve year old with no reason to non-conform other than to be 'cool'.

Chapter Thirteen

Rory was working on the Urology ward this morning. It was a full schedule for Doctor Shaw and a busy time for the nurses having to reassure men who changed their minds about their operations at the last minute. Rory chatted to the ward clerk, Sheila in her office. She organised the general administration of the ward and thank God she hadn't noticed or chosen to comment on Rory's appointment to go ahead with the vasectomy later that afternoon. He'd made up his mind for sure only the night before and he'd also decided, perhaps foolishly to not tell Viv that it was today. Well, it wasn't as if they hadn't discussed it and agreed upon it. She was generally a fit and healthy woman so she should be alright with this pregnancy. For Christ's sake she'd rested enough and she hadn't had any more silly accidents on garden steps. He could make some excuse to stay at Ted's tonight until he got over the soreness following the op and then he'd tell her in a month or so. He knew for sure that it would make him feel better towards Viv at home. Things had been really icy lately between them. He hadn't wanted to bring the subject of the vasectomy up in case she'd changed her mind, what with being pregnant, but he still believed it to be the right thing for him to do. He'd nearly had a fit when Drew had turned up unexpectedly this morning. If he'd decided to turn up this afternoon he probably would have discovered his secret. Thank God he'd been able to get rid of him before he stumbled on the truth. Maybe he should have grilled Drew a bit more for bunking off school and done a bit more digging for the truth as to why he'd done it, but he had a lot on his mind today and he was relieved to get his son back on the bus to Hexbury and to school.

Sheila shuffled the papers on her desk and Rory continued to chat to her.

'Hey Sheila, how's it going between you and Andy.'

'I'm still plucking up the courage to ask him.'

'You'd better get a move on. There are only a few tickets left for that 80s disco. Actually Andy's on his break now.'

'I can't go now. I'm on duty here for another ten minutes.'

'You'll be the loser, if you don't get it sorted.'

Sheila looked at Rory and smiled.

'I don't suppose you…'

'Yes, course. I'll man the phone for the next ten minutes and make out you had to go to the toilet urgently.'

'Thanks so much Rory, you're a gem.'

The phone was silent and Rory's eyes wandered around Sheila's office. It was nearly lunchtime and his stomach was rumbling. He'd only had a cup of tea with Drew earlier this morning and nothing to eat. He was off his food lately and besides he was fasting before the op this afternoon. Sheila had left her workspace in the logged-on mode and in front of him was a list of today's operations. Rory scanned down the list of vasectomies and checked his name on the list. They'd all been ticked off for admission to the ward for this morning. Whoever was next on duty would do the afternoon admissions. Rory moved the cursor up to where Sheila had left it and as Carole arrived to go on duty to relieve Sheila he left the office.

Rory went straight upstairs to tell Sheila that she could go home as Carole had arrived for her shift. He took himself off to the admissions clerk and after half an hour's reprimand for being late he found himself in a hospital bed. Mobile phones were banned, but Rory knew he'd have to let Viv know that he wouldn't be home at the usual time. He set his mobile to silent and sent her a text, *'Viv, forgot 2 tel u Arney has stag night 2nite Will stay at his place c u 2morrow rory x'*. So that took care of Viv, but what about Drew earlier on, wouldn't he think it strange that he hadn't mentioned it to him? Well, too late to worry about it now. The porters came to collect him and take him to theatre, fortunately he didn't know either of them. They were very young and must have been new on the ward. Rory hadn't had time to plan for this and now his mind was full of what ifs and maybe I should haves. He was determined not to back out now though and as he'd said to himself earlier once it was done they couldn't do anything about it. The anaesthetist talked as he filled his syringe.

'I know it's difficult, but try to relax Mr Cunningham.'

It was too late to back out now. What about after the operation? He wouldn't be able to go home straight away and pretend that he was okay. What about the pain and soreness? What if the kids bashed into him in their usual boisterous way? Maybe he could stay at Ted's for a bit longer and make up an excuse as to why he couldn't go home. The surgeon was ready and Rory closed his eyes tightly.

Viv relaxed at the kitchen table with a cup of tea. Justin and Drew had already left for school, which left her to watch over Harry and Jake. They were both at home, while the teachers at their school held a training day. They were quiet to start with, watching TV and drinking their milk. The arguments started when they brought the train track out. Every single piece that they pulled out of the box had the same treatment.

'I want Thomas the Tank.'

'No, it's mine. I had it for my birthday.'

'Well you're not having The Fat Controller, I had that last Christmas.'

Then Harry decided to take matters into his own hands and grabbed a piece of wooden train track and smacked Jake as hard as he could over the head. Jake started to throw the trains back at Harry, but then in one extra hard launch Harry pummelled The Fat Controller into Jake's face. Jake screamed out. He had a cut right next to his eye and blood streamed down his face. Harry panicked at the sight of the blood and Viv came rushing in.

'I didn't mean to hurt him, I didn't mean it,' Harry cowered in the corner of the room with his hands over his face. Viv picked up Jake in her arms and carried him to the kitchen. She gently sponged the excess blood away with wet kitchen roll and compressed the area. It wasn't nearly as bad as it looked and Viv managed to patch it up with antiseptic cream and a plaster. The two brothers were subdued after the fight and took themselves off to their bedroom. Viv washed the blood off The Fat Controller and piled the trains back into the box. She moved to the lounge now that the boys had gone upstairs and made herself more comfortable on the sofa. She must have fallen asleep and it was only the boys calling that woke her an hour later.

'Mummy, come and see what we've done.'

'Yes, come and see Mummy, we're having a jumble sale.'

It didn't sound very good. Viv could hardly bear to go and look. She reached the top of the stairs and saw the beginning of the horrendous mess. The boys had dragged the old coffee table out from her bedroom and there were heaps of clothes everywhere. They'd pulled out all the drawers from their own room and piled their t-shirts, underwear, shorts, trousers, pyjamas in a heap. They'd tipped the bookcase over and emptied all the books into another heap and added to it, two large boxes of cars and other toys. The worse thing was they hadn't stopped at their own room. They'd gone into Justin and Drew's and taken out piles of magazines and books, as well as emptying their brothers' drawers full of clothes. They stood there in shopkeeper mode, displaying excited grins on their faces.

'Come and buy something from our jumble sale Mummy.'

'Come on Mummy, you could find a bargain.'

Viv pretended to buy a selection of clothes, but then told the boys, 'this jumble sale of yours is all very clever and fun for you two, but you've made a lot of work for Mummy. Who do you think is going to put all this away?'

'We will Mummy, later.'

'Yes, we promise to do it later Mummy.'

'I'm sure you do boys.'

Viv wished that she could put it all away that very minute, but perhaps she'd let them keep it out until after lunch.

'Listen boys, I'm going to make your lunch. Play with your jumble sale until then, but after lunch you've got to help me clear it all away before Daddy gets home.'

'Oh Mummy.'

'No Oh Mummy, that's the agreement.'

Viv went downstairs and made sandwiches and cut up fruit to put with yoghurt. She checked her mobile and discovered Rory's message.

'Oh bloody typical,' she said to herself. 'How does he always manage to get the better deal?' She thought about replying to the message, but decided she'd only end up swearing at him. She went upstairs and told the boys to come down, but spotted Adele from her landing window on the way back down. Viv knocked furiously on the window pane, but Adele couldn't hear. The boys sat at the kitchen table eating their sandwiches and Viv dashed outside to attract Adele. She waved at Viv and came over.

'You wouldn't believe the mess Harry and Jake have made upstairs. Go and have a look while I put the kettle on.'

Adele came back down to the kitchen.

'You're right, what a mess. Do you want me to stay and help clear up?'

'No, I'll be okay. I could kill Rory though.' She showed Adele the text message.

'Viv let me take the boys out for a while and give you some time to put away that heap upstairs. I know it's leaving you with the work, but they can burn off some energy. I'm not working this afternoon. I'll take them to the park and buy them an ice-cream.'

'Oh yes please Adele,' Jake jumped up and down and then pushed his yoghurt to one side. Harry leapt up from the table.

'I'll get our coats.'

'Thanks Adele,' Viv smiled at Harry throwing on his coat and helping his brother to speed up before mummy changed her mind.

Viv waved goodbye to the little scoundrels, then quickly cleared up the lunchtime debris before falling asleep on the kitchen table.

Adele waited for Ben to come home. He'd already told her that he didn't need a meal, but she'd made some fajitas and opened a bottle of wine. She hadn't mentioned Bradley wanting to rent the flat yet and couldn't seem to find the right moment. She still wasn't sure of the idea herself. She liked Bradley, enjoyed his company and found him quite funny, but having him on the doorstep, literally would be a different matter.

Adele heard Ben slam the door downstairs. He didn't come up straight away and she heard him walking around the flat for a few minutes.

'Great fajitas, are they chilli chicken?' Ben grabbed a fajita from the plate and sat down with Adele.

'Yes, chilli chicken.' She handed him a glass of white wine with a smile.

'I've just bumped into that boss of yours. Bradley isn't it? He asked me about the flat, said he'd talked about it with you. Why didn't you mention it Adele?'

'He only brought it up within the last few days and anyway I didn't think that you were that keen on renting it.'

'It's extra money isn't it and he seems a decent guy. He's going down the pub now and asked if I'd like to join him to discuss rent.'

Adele decided not to elaborate. Ben could find out what he needed to know for himself. Bradley must be more of a smooth talker than she'd given him credit for. Sheryl had told her that, but to convince someone as superior and self-righteous as Ben had become that was clever stuff.

'Gonna have another pint mate?' Bradley leaned against the bar at The Rose and Crown. He ordered two more pints before Ben could decline. Ben chose to sit on one of the high bar stools as the alcohol kicked in. He wasn't used to the strong beer that Bradley knocked back every weekend. He had the occasional beer, but usually drank wine or champagne at work receptions. Before he knew it Ben was pouring out his worries to Bradley.

'I walked by two women outside your shop the other day. They thought I hadn't heard what they were saying, but ...' Ben slipped off the edge of his stool and hoisted himself back, spilling slops of his beer on the way. 'You will keep this to yourself won't you Brad?'

'Of course, I can't afford to be the instigator of gossip when I run a shop in the middle of the community.'

'Anyway, they were saying things about 'Del, making suggestions about her and that hospital bloke, you know Viv's husband, what's his name, Rodney?'

'Rory.'

'That's it. I could tell that Viv was worried, she kept looking out of her window whenever anyone passed by.'

'And you can tell that you're worried about your wife. She's such a sweet polite girl, but she is naïve isn't she?'

'Yes and if he's messing with her I'll smack the bastard, knock him to the ground.'

'Oh I wouldn't do that mate; you'll only land yourself in the nick. Why don't you let me help?'

'I don't want you to get beaten up 'cause my wife's playing around Brad.'

'That wasn't quite what I meant mate. Let me rent the flat from you and I'll be on the premises to keep an eye on her, make sure she doesn't get bothered by anyone unsavoury. She'd have to walk past my door to go outside the building so apart from the few times when I'm out myself I'd know her every move. And don't worry, I won't come over all heavy, she won't guess that I'm watching over her.'

'That's a brilliant idea Brad, you're on.'

Adele had taken herself to bed for an early night with her latest novel. She'd fallen asleep with her thumb in the book marking the place. It was late when Ben came in and she could feel his freezing cold legs coming through the thin silk of her pyjamas. His breath smelt of beer and his hair of smoke.

'I've had a chat to Bradley about the flat. He couldn't believe that you hadn't mentioned it to me Adele.'

'Mmm,' Adele half grunted from her sleepy stupor.

'So I've sorted it all out Adele. Bradley is going to rent the flat. He's moving in at the end of the week.' Adele turned over. She was still slightly puzzled by Ben's change of tack. She was beginning to wake, but kept her eyes firmly closed. She didn't want to challenge him, he could be really nasty lately when she suggested that he'd done something in haste. She wished that she'd known that he had another side to him before they married, but he'd only painted the picture of a generous and kind man who appreciated her cuddles. She often wondered whether it had anything to do with his parents, particularly his mother. His father was dead now, but his mother was a snob, despite the family being very poorly off. She'd drilled it into him that he should make a success of himself at any cost and that meant financially and influentially.

Ben carried on relating the conversation he'd had with Bradley earlier. Adele wasn't so sure of Bradley and his motives either, there was something about him, something not quite right. Ben gibbered on, ending the story with the sentence she knew had clinched the deal.

'He said it would be useful to live so close to work and besides when I'm away on business he said he'd keep an eye on you for me.'

Viv closed the last drawer full of clothes in Justin and Drew's room. Both of them lay on their beds listening to their music through earpieces. Justin put his thumb up to her and smiled as she left the room. She quietly straightened the book case in the next room where Harry and Jake lay sleeping. The discordant atmosphere between her and Rory lately had made her feel physically sick and quite weak, or perhaps she'd forgotten what the first few months of pregnancy were like. Downstairs, she had to lie down on the sofa and give in to the tiredness. She lay there exhausted, too tired to lift her body up to the bedroom. She looked quite ethereal as she lay with her head supported on a cushion. She slept deeply and peacefully, knowing that although her husband had not come to terms with the prospect of a new child, it was part of her already and an element of fate she had accepted. She was wearing a floaty white muslin top embroidered with blue flowers and it rose and fell in unison with her breathing. The shade of the blue flowers matched the skirt, except for where it had been stained with spots of fresh blood.

Chapter Fourteen

Ben drove down to the post office with his reports and DVDs to head office. He couldn't understand why Adele hadn't been pleased about him arranging for Bradley to stay downstairs in the flat. She was always on at him to have a little more trust in people and he was her boss and she'd never mentioned anything to him about Bradley being a bit dodgy. He looked like he was one for the women, true enough, but Adele didn't go in for cheap obvious guys like him. And he'd know what to look for if she started getting too friendly with that Rodney chap.

Perhaps having Bradley around would get them back on the straight and narrow. Adele was very quiet recently, kind of dull and sullen. Maybe she needed cheering up. He had a lot on at work at the moment, but possibly the answer was to kill two birds with one stone. That was it... he'd make her come to the fashion show with him. Admittedly it wasn't much notice, but that would make it more of a surprise and she'd love it he was sure of it.

Adele gathered her pencils, sketch book and a small stool and made for the peace of the garden. The showers were still holding off and although the sky was black it was very close and humid. She loosened her shirt and positioned her stool close to the old apple tree almost in the centre of all the gardens. The grass was so long now it would probably be easier for the T.V. crew to bulldoze all of the four gardens and start again. She sat facing Eileen's garden with the apple tree in front of her. Just inside her plot she spotted a huge clump of ornamental grass between her and the tree. She remembered buying a similar plant from a school summer fete and planting it in her grandmother's garden. Hers had been a very small specimen, but this plant had taken over the surrounding grass and looked like a whole platoon of pale green beetles abseiling down their darker green stalks to the ground. Adele began by drawing a plan of the garden.

'This seems to be the one place today where I can get some peace and quiet,' she said to herself before Ben came marching up the lane. He spotted her in the garden and walked over towards her, lifting his feet in disgust at the undergrowth.

'Come on,' he said 'I've got a surprise for you.' And he picked up her sketch book and snapped it shut. 'Well come on then,' he said in an agitated voice when she remained on her stool looking surprised. She got up and he picked up the leg of the stool and led the way back inside.

Eileen was working hard as usual. It would take the rest of the morning to finish preparing Claire's room, just in case she did come to visit. The iron expelled fractious steam waiting for its ordeal. The duvet cover was to be ironed inside out first, and then turned the right way, every crease obliterated with another fearful pressing. Eileen had wanted to speak to Adele about the members of the BNG team staying at her house. She'd given them the smaller room at the back of the house with twin beds. She didn't want them to ruin Claire's room with their great big muddy gardening boots. She cursed as she straightened out the pillowcase on one of the single beds. Two cameramen, Colin and Barry had taken up the suggestion of staying with her for the three nights. The director, Crispin had really appreciated Adele's suggestion and Eileen's hospitality.

'Are you quite sure that Eileen doesn't mind Adele?'

'I'm quite sure Crispin. She'll be in her element and besides if there are any questions to ask I can iron them out while your cameramen are under her roof.'

Eileen watched her pretty auburn-haired neighbour, Adele walk with her tall good-looking husband to their car at the bottom of the lane. They loaded up a small amount of luggage into their silver BMW. Why was she going away now, just when the BNG team were due to arrive? They seemed to be going somewhere and with overnight bags. Adele hadn't told her she was going away today and she was sure that she wouldn't let everyone down like that when they'd been so excited about the gardening project. She watched as Ben put the bags into the boot and manhandled Adele by the shoulders into the passenger seat.

Adele watched the array of evening gowns as the models strutted down the catwalk. Spaghetti straps, ruffles, chiffon and slinky LBDs (or little black dresses) all looking their absolute best on the flawless lean bodies.

'You see Adele, I knew you'd enjoy it once you got here.'

84

Adele smiled and said nothing. She didn't want to cause a fuss, well not until the last minute and tonight she planned to get a taxi back to the railway station and catch the night train back home. She'd be there in time to meet Crispin and the rest of the BNG team tomorrow lunchtime as planned. She'd left a message with Viv earlier on her mobile and nothing, not even Ben was going to stop her.

Ben stood at the bar in the interval and ordered two gin and tonics. He stood with her for a few minutes, but she knew it wouldn't be long before he spotted some big name that he had to suck up to. He took his drink with him.

'I'll be back in a jiff sweetheart,' he said patting her on the arm, then he was off chasing the leggy redhead representing FCUK. After fifteen minutes of waiting for him to return, Adele saw this opportunity as her cue to leave. He'd never even notice.

She threw the remaining clothes strewn in the bedroom into her suitcase and filled her toilet bag with makeup and toothbrush. She knew she would not finally find the courage to actually tell him she was leaving early, despite all her recent bravado, so she left him a note on the dressing table.

Ben... Have left early to catch the 11.05 train back to Hexbury. Sorry couldn't pluck up courage to tell you, but I'm sure you'll manage without me. I promised Viv that I'd be at the meeting with the BNG team tomorrow lunchtime. Hope you enjoy the rest of the show and I'll see you in a few days at home...Adele

It was 11.35 before Ben arrived to read the message. He exploded throwing his wallet at the wall and kicking the waste paper bin. The bloody ungrateful selfish bitch, how could she make a fool of him like this? She was probably going back to spend some more time with that good-for-nothing hospital porter, what's his name, Rodney. What a useless waste of space he was. You wouldn't catch him hanging around with people of no beneficial help to his future. Ben sat on the bed and removed his shoes. He threw both of them at the wall and then slumped into a half drunken stupor on the pile of soft pillows at the head of the bed. The room swirled around above his head. He felt slightly sick and stumbled to the bathroom. He was so sick of his wife recently, sick of her new found friends and sick that tonight she'd stopped him from spending more time with that gorgeous redhead from FCUK.

85

Adele arrived back on her doorstep looking and feeling ashen. She prided herself in her escape although she still shook with fear at the repercussions. Ben's flips into anger were only a development in recent years and they accompanied the angst that went with the new job. He'd been full of excitement when he'd urged her to come in from the garden. He'd launched into a detailed account of how she would go with him to the fashion show, stay to watch the displays and socialise with the top buyers. When they were first married she would have jumped at the chance and it would have complimented her job in the department store in Croydon. But now her interests were changing to accompany a more rustic, sedate way of life and Ben found this change difficult to accept. It was when she announced that the Breaking New Ground team were arriving and she had to be there that he'd hit the roof. He'd thrown the suitcases down on the bed and virtually insisted that she came with him instead. She would never have let anyone else treat her in this way, but Ben hadn't always been like this and she kept hoping that his behaviour was just a temporary blip. She told herself that if she went maybe things would return to the way they used to be when she was happy and she wanted her happiness back more than anything.

Crispin hadn't arrived yet and she needed to unwind before he did. She had a few hours yet. She made some warm toast and fresh coffee and wondered what Crispin would be like. His telephone voice was full of character with a resonant yet controlled tone. It was the sort of voice that could be listened to without boredom and the person lived up to the expectations of the voice when he entered her kitchen later that morning.

'Sorry, I'm much earlier than I said I would be in the email. I didn't think I'd be able to find it.'

Adele plunged the filter of the coffee maker down. Crispin's jean clad legs were so long they could almost have touched the floor from the breakfast stool he was sitting on.

'Any sugar?'

'No thanks. I'm trying to wean myself off sweet tastes. Chocoholic, that's my trouble.'

'We must be from the same clan. I can't leave it alone, it's an addiction.'

He nodded his head and smiled sympathetically. It was such a warm hint of his character that any worrying barriers she'd felt earlier dissolved.

'Have you any ideas for the garden from what you've seen on the way to my house.'

'Give me chance Adele', he smiled. 'I didn't even know it was the right house until I found you in it.' He tilted his head in a lilting way, revealing the first signs of grey, annoyingly attractive in a man.'

'Yes, sorry. That was an assumption. You'll get a chance to have a good look when your colleagues arrive.'

'Hey, what are these? Did you draw them?'

He picked up the sketches of Veronica and Hector's garden and delving into his laptop case he located a pair of glasses and put them on. It gave him instant intellectual appeal. Adele opened her mouth to reply, but her larynx had seized up and nothing came out. She coughed and took a sip of her coffee and saved by the doorbell the rest of the team arrived. Crispin was definitely charming, Adele wasn't so sure about his assistant, Ruby though. She'd didn't quite look the part somehow; with her bright red talons, neat coiffured hair and perfect scarlet Cupid's bow on her untouchable lips.

Crispin took control and made all the introductions then allowed Adele to show them to the garden. She watched him in action with his clipboard. There were bodies flying everywhere, some with digital cameras, presenters surveying the scene, cameramen and a team of gardeners who probably did the work that the presenters took the credit for. Eileen managed to sneak into the scene, but thankfully made herself useful.

'Adele would you like me to make tea for the team?'

The whole TV horde went inside for a break, completely missing sight of the ambulance taking Viv away to hospital. Her own doctor accompanied her leaving Viv's friend, a mother she'd met in the school playground, in charge of the boys in case Rory didn't arrive home as planned. They'd tried to tell Rory, but he wasn't answering his mobile.

During the afternoon the crew dispersed until only Crispin and four others remained and Eileen being her usual inquisitive self, delivered more tea accompanied by rock buns offering her an excuse for a snoop around.

She turned to the cameramen.

'I'm the only one who spends any time in this garden you know, so you will let me see the plans before you go ahead.' Then she picked up the tray and marched off.

'Don't take any notice of her. Thinks she owns the place.' Adele laughed and pointed to Eileen's patio.

'I've seen worse and if she's all we've got to worry about then I say we're in business Adele.' Crispin went through the file for Orchard Court.

'I don't suppose you could sketch parts of the garden and get them sent on to me could you Adele? Those other sketches you showed me earlier were first class.'

'Yes, I'd be delighted Crispin.'

Adele left Colin and Barry in Eileen's kitchen and walked down the lane with Crispin and the last two gardeners on the crew.

'Fascinating location you have here.'

'It's very peaceful isn't it?'

'Do you work from home Adele?'

'No, I'm working part-time as a shop assistant at the moment, having only moved into the house six months ago.'

'So you'll be looking for something more fulfilling when you feel more settled?'

Adele didn't answer at first.

'I haven't really looked that far ahead yet Crispin.'

'Well Adele from the work you've produced so far you have a lot to offer.'

He swung his long legs upwards into his silver grey Rav 4. It suited him, a four-wheel drive for his connection with gardening and landscaping. Crispin was staying in Lavender House bed and breakfast with a few other members of the team. The rest were sprinkled around in Bluebell Cottage and The Rose and Crown. One person was booked in at The Hexbury Green Hotel. It was a woman called Ruby Turner, Crispin's assistant.

Adele stood in the same spot for at least five minutes, overwhelmed by a kind of unexplainable drunken excitement. Crispin had turned out to be so pleasant and it was good to meet new and interesting people and break the pattern of everyday events.

Rory lay on the sofa at Ted's house watching morning TV. Ted brought him a cup of tea, 'I'm off now mate, make sure you rest this morning. I'll be back late this afternoon.' Ted pulled up a small table for Rory and put the cup of tea within reach. Rory had been lucky, he'd not been too badly affected by the operation. The pain and soreness was minimal and if he could rest for today he reckoned he'd be well on the way to recovery, even though the hospital suggested 48 hours. Rory picked up his mobile phone from the coffee table. There was one message from Viv late last night, *'c u 2tomorrow.'* No luv from or even x. She must have been annoyed with him. He sent her another message to excuse himself until this evening, *'Hi Viv feelin bad had 2 many beers last night chillin at ted's til 2nite c u luv R x'.* She might reply to that sort of message. If not, he'd ring her later when the kids had gone to school. Rory adjusted the supportive underpants Ted had bought him from one of the hospital shops and got himself comfortable. Morning TV was fairly pleasant to watch – a bit of fashion with some good looking girls, a group of girls talking about diets and a book group discussing the latest best seller. The subject matter was very tasteful until they got onto the medical slot, then of all the operations to choose they had to go and pick a vasectomy. Rory felt sick. He switched off the TV and phoned Viv. The phone rang and rang, then clicked onto answerphone. 'Where was she?' She was nearly always in at this time of day. He rang again, but left no message.

Ted clicked the off switch on the TV and Rory woke immediately.
  'Ted, how long have you been back?'
  'Not long, how are you feeling Rory?'
  'Fine, I think I'll be okay to go home tonight.'
  'How are the …balls mates?'
  'Still there mate,' Rory replied holding himself.
Ted paced up and down the lounge, straightening ornaments and book spines in a casual manner.
  'Sit down Ted.'
Ted ignored him and carried on pacing the floor. He made more tea and brought it in. He sat down with Rory and spilled the news…
  'Rory, Viv's in hospital. She was taken in this morning.'
  'Why?'

Ted hesitated.

'Why?' Rory asked again.

They were interrupted by Rory's mobile. He picked it up. There were four missed calls, all from his home phone number. The most recent bleep indicated a text from Justin.

Dad, come home. Mum's in hospital. Dr thinks she's losing baby.

Rory showed the message to Ted.

'That's what I was trying to tell you.'

'A miscarriage Ted, shit and now I've gone and had this done.'

'You're gonna have to tell her Rory.'

'Yes, I will Ted, but not yet. I'll get her better first and then tell her, when she's better Ted.'

The BNG team met in Adele's kitchen. Crispin gathered the ideas she'd collected from all the neighbours and started a diagram to construct a 3D model of the plans so that Orchard Court could see what they were letting themselves in for. Ruby sat perched on a kitchen stool, her legs crossed at the ankle. She wore pointed brown leather boots with kitten heels, chocolate brown lace patterned tights and a matching cowl-necked soft cotton sweater. Her bright red short woollen skirt contrasted the outfit, as did the perfectly manicured nails, also painted glossy red. She sipped her elderflower tea from the compulsory drinking straw and for each sip pouted her lips to avoid destruction of the lustrous top layer of lipstick.

'Are we going to meet the rest of the residents of Orchard Court soon?'

'Yes Viv Cunningham should be over later today and you'll meet the rest of them tomorrow morning.'

'And Adele, are you married to the man in the fashion industry.'

'Yes, I was in the fashion business myself before we moved from Croydon.'

'But not any more, so where do you work now?'

'I'm a shop assistant at the local store; it's just at the end of this road.'

'And your husband, what's his name?'

'Ben.'

'Ben, nice name, nice manly name.'

Ruby flicked a fragment of dust off her skirt and stared out at the gardens in front of the house. Adele whispered to Crispin, 'Does your assistant ever actually get her hands dirty?'

'You must be joking. All she does is the office work, planning, sketches and makes the models.'

'How can you put up with that? A female garden designer who won't even get into a pair of wellies.'

'She would if they were designer wellies,' Crispin laughed. 'To be honest I don't know how she got past the interview, but she's the kind of woman who will probably move on to something else quite quickly.'

'Well for your sake I hope it's soon.'

Chapter Fifteen

Eileen closed the oven door on the final batch of rock cakes for the BNG team. She wasn't going to let anyone else monopolise the catering arrangements, although she'd made far too many, they'd never eat them all.

'I'll go over to that poor Mr Miles and cheer him up with some home made cooking,' she muttered to herself as she took a plate laden with cakes.

Eileen knocked on Miles's door and stepped back. She caught his shadow on the landing window. Miles tried to hide behind the curtain, but realising that the ever-inquisitive Eileen had seen him he came downstairs and answered the door. He knew she meant well, but there was something about the way she enquired that was intrusive. It encroached on his private thoughts in an antagonistic way. He opened the door to find a plate of warm rock buns thrust under his nose.

'Would you like a nice warm cake to cheer you up Mr Miles?'
Miles took one, said 'thank you Eileen, kind of you to think of me' and then abruptly closed the door leaving his neighbour standing on the doorstep. He knew he'd feel bad as soon as the door was closed, but the woman was infuriating and he was certainly not in the frame of mind to endure one of her mindless chit-chat conversations. Why did she call him 'Mr Miles' for a start? On the other hand though she did live alone as he did now and he knew how painful that could be. No wonder she bustled around baking cakes for everyone and trying to make friends of the neighbours around her. He crept upstairs and peered from behind the curtain to see if she was still on the doorstep. She'd gone and as he glanced up the lane to Adele's house he saw her with a wicker basket full of home baking ringing the bell and knocking the door. She didn't give in easily. In fact it was probably her dogmatic tenacity that kept her going.

Miles went into the bathroom to collect his pills. He was determined to come off them and was now trying the gradual approach. He'd gone from four on Sunday, three Monday, two yesterday and one today. The strange thing was he still felt half dead. It was having the same effect as last time, he was going to be stuck on the wretched pills for ever. He poured a large whiskey to wash down the pill. Perhaps that would make him feel better. He lay down on the sofa and took another whiskey with him. Minutes later he was asleep.

Eileen was still furious as she stood on Adele's step waiting for the door to be answered. Furious with that cheeky teenage brat called Justin who'd helped himself to one of her cakes without even being asked just now on the way over to Adele's. 'Don't mind if I do,' he'd said 'I haven't had breakfast this morning.' Then he slung his rucksack over his back so that it hung low over his baggy trousers and flopped with the long piece of belt dangling alongside.

'Scruffy urchin, just like a gypsy.' Eileen rang the doorbell again. She thought of Justin's hair, jet black and spiked thick with gel. Then of the ear stud in the cartilage of his ear, just like a gypsy, except that they used to wear gold hoops in their lobes in her day.

The BNG team dispersed in the late afternoon back to their accommodation and full to the brim with Eileen's home baking. Colin and Barry both fell asleep in front of the TV and she tidied the kitchen of their debris. Rory cleaned the whole house, did two loads of washing and hung it outside on the line. At least there wouldn't be very much to do when Viv came home in the next few days. He walked over to Adele's to tell her the news.

'She'll need a lot of support when she comes home Rory. She was looking forward to the new baby.'

'And I wasn't?'

'I'm sure you would have got used to the idea. Anyway, it's not the end of the world. You can always try for another one if that's what you both want.'

'Maybe she'll change her mind.'

'I don't know about that Rory. Once a woman gets that maternal feeling again.'

Rory said nothing and sipped his tea in silence. He'd wait until she was better, then he'd tell her.

Rory had only just left when Adele heard another knock on the door and answered it to find Bradley bearing gifts.

'Is your husband in?'

'No, why?'

Bradley didn't reply. He presented her with a huge bunch of pink roses and a bottle of Italian red wine for Ben. Then he asked her again.

'Are you sure your husband's not in?'

'No Bradley and why are you so bothered?'

Adele was determined not to let him over the doorstep. Bradley leaned beside the doorway to the upper part of the house and produced a small package neatly wrapped in tissue and pink ribbon.

'A small present for you for agreeing to have me in your house, but I think you'd be best to keep this to yourself. There's nothing suspicious in it, I just wanted to buy something for you, something nice. Open it later and thanks Adele. Thanks for letting me live in your house.'

He smiled, turned around and walked downstairs to his flat.

Below in the lane of Orchard Court Viv had returned already and recovered sufficiently to have an argument with Rory. Colin and Barry, the two cameramen were wandering around the garden making measurements, pacing out and pointing at various locations. The older dark-haired man looked as if he knew what he was doing, but the younger one was a touch dubious. He was trying to look confident, but as he'd told Adele earlier, it was difficult to appear confident when it's your first job fresh from university. The volume of the argument increased and the two men peered through the undergrowth to enjoy the show.

'Where were you when I needed you Rory? Out boozing it up with your mates again.'

'More fit you paid attention to Justin. He still thinks you don't believe he was innocent over that glue sniffing.'

'And I know you've started smoking again.'

'Well I reckon I deserve the odd fag living with you. Get inside, we've got an audience.'

Viv looked up at the two cameramen and then she rushed inside, pushing passed Rory in tears. The cameramen came down the steps.

'I wonder if they're always like that.'

'I don't know mate, but come on the old lady's made us hot-pot for supper.'

'Has she now, sounds great to me.' The older man turned to his colleague, handing him a five-pound note.

'Here Barry, go and get a bottle to go with supper tonight down at the mini-market.'

The light was fading fast and Colin began to clear the site of measuring tools and camera equipment. Barry had better not be too long, there was more packing away than he'd reckoned here. He'd gathered the paraphernalia into one corner and was just about to start loading it into the van when a gurgling noise distracted him from the task. He glanced down into the lane and saw water bubbling up from a drain. Barry came up the steps carrying two bottles in a carrier.

'Buy one, get second half price,' he exclaimed holding the bag up. Colin didn't reply and Barry followed his gaze to the drain.

'Looks like a blocked drain to me.'

Both men traced the pipe up the wall to the room above, where silhouetted behind the apricot muslin drape was the dark shadow of Adele trying on clothes.

'Shit, are you sure it was only the blocked drain you've been watching all this time Colin?'

Colin said nothing but stared upwards, his jaw almost on his knees. They could see now that it was underwear she modelled as she stood back to examine how it looked.

Adele bent down to light two delicate pink candles on the gothic stand at the foot of the bath. Steam intermingled with the heady scent of musk and sandalwood and she mopped a slight condensation of sweat from her breast bone. She ran her hands over her breasts, down the crimson silk basque to her waist and separating her hands she placed one over the flatness of her stomach and pressed the other at the base of her back compressing her sylph like figure.

In the garden below the two men stood agog, transfixed on the elfin shape in her bath chamber. She discarded the basque, dropping it to the floor, picking up another two small items. She stood naked while she decided which one. The added candlelight highlighted every contour of her slim yet curvaceous figure and the fresh night air from the window open just a chink made her erect nipples visible. Adele leant over a chair near the window and as Barry's head followed the angle of her body he slipped and dropped the extension lead off the wall so that it scuttled noisily into the lane down below. Immediately Adele turned on a light and peered gingerly from behind the curtain. All she saw was blackness and the light behind her did nothing to reveal anything outside. She dropped a thick chintz festoon blind hiding herself behind it.

'Oh well done cloth head. Bloody noisy idiot.' Colin doffed Barry round the head. 'Come on let's finish loading up and get something to eat now the show's over.'

'Sorry boss.' Barry looked sheepish as he followed Colin down the steps to the smell of hot pot and the light went out in the bathroom up above leaving just the flicker of the candlelight.

Chapter Sixteen

Miles sat huddled in the corner of the half landing next to a small coffee table beneath the window. The condensation from the window collected and ran down his arm mingling with the stream of tears dripping onto his dressing gown. He stared out of the window and down to the garden below. His eyes rested on the wooden bench where many a relaxing evening had been spent in conversation with Janet over a glass of wine in the sultry warm weather. The guilt and torment of still being alive while Janet's life had been ripped from her brought a pain to his chest. The relentless unanswered prayer inside his head murmured on… please let it be that it had all happened too quickly and she hadn't suffered. He slowly lowered his right hand to rest on his chest where shallow breathing barely moved it. The sound of a bell in the distance chimed and faded away again. It was replaced by a much louder knocking at the door.

Miles snapped back into today and ran down to answer the door.

'Cameron, is that you? …On my way Cameron.'

Miles unbolted the door to let his close friend and work colleague in.

'Didn't get you up old chap, did I?'

'No, no. Knew you were calling, must have just forgotten the time. Listen, just put the kettle on for me will you and I'll nip upstairs and get myself decent.'

In Miles's bedroom his clothes were neatly laid out on the bed. He pulled on his blue Farah trousers and a white short-sleeved shirt. When he returned downstairs, Cameron had made tea and picked up the paper to read the headlines. He poured a cup of tea for Miles as he entered the room.

'See the Dow Jones is down again.'

'Don't know. That's one thing I haven't been able to get back into yet. The papers are all full of bad news. I have one delivered, but it comes in through the door in the morning and goes straight into the recycling by lunchtime.'

'How are things otherwise? Are you coping with everyday life?'

'Well I get up, eat, drink and struggle through the day. I've only been surviving recently because of all the clearing out I've been doing. It was the doctor's advice; "find something to keep busy" he said. I've cleared all the rooms now, just one more box in the garage.'

'I hope you haven't disposed of anything you might regret later Miles.'

'Oh no, I've kept a few mementoes of all the good times. The only trouble is I keep thinking she's going to walk through the door and I'll be able to tell her about all the hard work I've accomplished.'

'It's early days yet though Miles. Is Viv still coming to see you?'

'Yes, she's been fantastic and Eileen has two of those chaps from the gardening programme staying with her. Can't say I'd go a bundle on them, right little parasites they were with their wires and whatnots snooping around.'

Cameron rinsed out the cups and left them in the sink and lifted the net curtain to wave to Eileen as she picked up Bertie under one arm and went inside. A boy in school uniform walked up the lane kicking a plastic bottle. Cameron paused to knock on the window but instead straightened the net curtain and said his goodbyes to Miles. When he was sure that Miles had gone back inside Cameron crept up to Viv's. He stood just inside her front door to talk to her. Viv told him about the miscarriage.

'I so sorry Viv and I don't want to trouble you under the circumstances but I think he's struggling. He was trying to hide it, but I've known Miles a long while now.'

'Don't worry Cameron, I'll keep an eye on him as long as you realise I can't be watching him all of the time.'

She smiled and showed Cameron out. She probably wouldn't feel like visiting anyone at the moment. He hoped she would remember poor Miles.

Adele hadn't received one text or call from Ben since she'd left him at the fashion show. It was quite usual however for him to sulk like this lately. He sulked first and wouldn't speak to her, and then when she'd forgotten about the argument and spoken to him he would harp on about the indifference and wouldn't let the matter drop. Still, she wasn't going to let it bother her today. He wouldn't be back until at least tomorrow evening anyhow.

Rory had brought Viv back from hospital earlier last night and Adele was rallying around the neighbours for flowers for her. Eileen was quite willing to contribute with the pretty Adele sat in

100

her kitchen. She normally made it quite clear that she disliked Viv's children, especially the eldest, Justin, but today she handed over her contribution with a smile. Miles wouldn't answer the door. Adele went back to his house at several different times during the day trying the door knocker, door bell and tapping on the kitchen window. Each time she received no answer; she thought that she heard a shuffling sound in the kitchen in the morning and she saw him wandering across the landing when she went up to her own garden with the TV crew. Crispin returned to the house with Adele leaving the rest of the team to their planning.

'Adele did you and Viv enjoy visiting the heritage garden I told you about?'

'Yes and Veronica and Hector were delightful. They made us feel very welcome and their garden was so tranquil.'

'I'm glad you liked it.' He fiddled with the hem of his jeans, pulling them down over his ankle. 'I have a few hours spare this afternoon and I was thinking of visiting them myself today.'

He got up and put his empty mug in the sink.

'I don't suppose you'd like to come with me would you?'

Adele sorted her sketches in the folder into order. She pulled out the few rough ideas from Veronica and Hector's garden.

'Yes I would like to Crispin.' She splayed out the sketches on the work surface and picked out one of the contrasting borders.

'I could finish this sketch while I'm there and send it to my mother next week as part of her birthday present.'

Crispin sighed quietly in part relief that Adele hadn't seen him in the wrong light. Colin entered the kitchen and Adele handed him the house keys.

'Colin, please use my kitchen to make tea and coffee for the team. Crispin and I will be back in a few hours. Would tomorrow evening be okay for the meeting for all the owners of garden plots?' She addressed both of them.

'Yes, of course Adele, that'll be fine, 7.30 okay?' Crispin zipped his car keys into his jacket pocket as he sat stood up.

He drove his Rav 4 and Adele sat beside him. He had a warm appealing smile and she couldn't help returning it. He even looked sophisticated in his muddy jeans and walking boots and he was clever all right, but not in a manipulative way. It was refreshing to be with him and relaxing to not have to read between the lines as she had to with other men in her life.

Veronica hadn't minded at all when Crispin phoned earlier and asked if they could come over for an hour of peace. Crispin greeted her with a hug and Veronica brought tea to the conservatory.

'Veronica, is it okay if Adele finishes her sketch while you show me how the garden has developed?'

'Yes, of course Crispin. Does that mean I get you all to myself?'

'Yes it does Lady Chatterley.'

Veronica turned to Adele in a fit of giggles.

'You see, what did I tell you my dear. We'll leave you to it and if you need me for anything I'll be on tour in the garden. Hector is out on his Bridge afternoon so he won't be around for a few hours.'

'Thank you Veronica,' Adele settled herself pulling out the sketch and her pencils. By the time that they returned she'd almost finished.

'That's wonderful my dear. You ought to be doing this for a living.'

'I'd love to Veronica, but unfortunately beautiful sketches of other people's gardens won't pay the electricity bill.'

They stopped off in the town of Saltash, just before the Tamar Bridge back into Devon to buy a card for Adele's mother and she put the dreamy idea of a job sketching gardens out of her head.

Adele handed the large bouquet of flowers and the card over to Rory. In the shadow of the lane someone watched her and as she moved away from Rory and Viv's doorstep the person quickly moved and hid. Adele rushed home to change for the meeting. Ben should have been home by now, but she couldn't really say that she'd been looking forward to his return. She left a note on the front door to tell him that the BNG team were there for the meeting in the garden and would he join them.

Crispin offered Adele a glass of red wine while Colin and Barry's eyes were all on her. Ruby sipped her white wine through her own personalised drinking straw nodding disdainfully at Adele. Ben still wore his smart suit when he joined the party later.

'Aren't you going to introduce me to your new found friends Adele?' he smiled. Ruby swivelled round immediately. Ben manoeuvred himself behind Adele so that he could grab her arm roughly without anyone noticing. He forced her forward, making her spill her wine down the front of her burgundy cords.

'Oh trust you, you silly girl,' he patronised as he brushed the droplets off with his hand. Crispin handed her a serviette.

'At least you chose the right colour Adele.'

Ben sneered at him and turned towards Ruby.

'Hi, are you Ben? I'm Ruby, assistant director.' She shook his hand.

'Yes, I'm Ben and I'm sorry I had to arrive late for the party.' She didn't look the part for an assistant director on a TV gardening team, but she did look the part. Wow did she look the part. He recognised all the designer labels she displayed and she was an ad for all of them.

'I hear you're in the fashion industry Ben.'

'That's right and I take it you're interested in clothes design as well as gardens,' he said as he lifted her well-matched silk fringed scarf. She took a seat on one of the plastic patio chairs placed in the garden temporarily by the team. The chair next to her was free and ignoring Adele, Ben slid into the seat next to Ruby

'I've just got back from a show tonight, a three day event, all the top names.'

'Wow, tell me all about it Ben.'

Adele gasped as Ben pushed her through the hall way of their house and onto the sofa.

'Don't you ever dare embarrass me like that again you bitch. I had to make out to my colleagues that you'd been taken ill, but then they asked why I hadn't gone with you to look after you. So I told them you were mentally ill.' He laughed mockingly. 'That made them all feel sorry for me and anyway I'm not really lying, you are sick in the head. No other normal wife would take up and leave like that.'

Adele went to get up from the sofa and Ben pushed her back down again.

'Ben, you knew I'd made arrangements to meet the BNG team for the garden project and you still insisted that I went with you.'

'That's what you told all your new friends is it? That I made you go. Most women would love to go to a fashion show. Take that

Ruby tonight for instance, she was enthralled by everything I said about it.'

'You're being unreasonable Ben.'

'Oh am I indeed, she wouldn't have thought so. It's you that's got it wrong Adele. It's all a case of duty, that's what's lacking in your head, duty.'

Ben went to the kitchen and poured himself a glass of water. He was holding the flower receipt when he came back in.

'So what's this?'

'Flowers for Viv, she's just had a miscarriage. The flowers are from all of us.'

'And you had to organise it, just for poor old Rodney.'

'You mean Rory?'

'Well you would know his name and don't you dare say that you didn't go up there and deliver them personally, because I know.'

'Why would I deny it?'

Ben grabbed Adele's jumper and then released her dropping her back on the sofa.

'I came back earlier today. You weren't here, but don't you deny it, because I know, I saw you.'

Ben starred at her with an evil look of contempt, and then he picked up the glass and threw the water into his wife's face in an outburst of rage.

Chapter Seventeen

Adele tried to get comfortable on the sofa. She'd calmly dried her face with the kitchen tea towel and pulled a sleeping bag out from the cupboard. If anyone was mentally deranged it was him, not her. Perhaps she should go and see her doctor about his behaviour, just for advice and maybe eventually she could persuade him to go and face up to the fact that he had changed. If her mother knew about Ben's behaviour lately she'd kill her for letting him get away with it. 'If you let him get away with it this time Adele you'll pay for it,' she'd tell her.

'He'll think it's his God given right to push you around.' It was all very well for her mother to preach to her; dad had been scared of mum and that's the way it had always been.

Ben left the house earlier, slamming the door behind him. Adele huddled into the sleeping bag. Perhaps he'd simmer down, although she still chose to sleep on the sofa in case his temper still flared when he returned. Where had he gone anyway? More than likely it would be his mother's. He was her little angel and could do no wrong. Bet she's tucking him up in his old room with a mug of hot chocolate, sitting on the edge of his bed while he pours out his problems to her. Poor old Ben.

Ben took his wallet, mobile phone and jacket when he walked out into the night. He met Bradley in the corridor, but pushed past saying a quick 'Hi', not wanting to engage in a conversation. Outside, standing on the pavement he wracked his brain for the name of the hotel. That was it... The Hexbury Green Hotel. He called a cab and went straight there. It was a stroke of luck as he got there, the doorman was chatting to a woman and Ben managed to sneak past. It was getting late and there were hardly any staff around the lobby to ask. He wandered into the bar where there were a few guests lingering on last drinks. Ben ordered a red wine and sat at a table. He harboured no remorse over his eruption of rage with Adele earlier; she deserved it, the bitch. He sat still fuming, gulping down the wine. Two more guests left the bar area, leaving a couple of sergeant major types on a table near the ladies' powder room. Ben watched the two old guys chatting over their whiskies. Then the ladies' door opened and a refurbished Ruby emerged. Her crimson lips broke into a smile when she spotted Ben.

'What on earth are you doing here and so late?'

'Fancy a nightcap Ruby?'

She sat down at Ben's table and put her hand on his.

'I'll have a Tia Maria, no ice.'

Ben ordered the drink and brought it to her. She took out a miniature straw from her handbag and placed it in the liqueur glass. Ben ran his hand up and down her back.

'I thought I'd see what The Hexbury Green Hotel was really like.'

'Have you never been here before?'

'No, I haven't lived here for long.'

'I'll show you round. That's if you've got time, it's getting late.'

'I've got the time Ruby. I've got lots of time.'

The tour didn't take long and Ruby tried to get Ben to hold her hand, just to make it look good for anyone that saw them.

'They'll think that you're staying here as my partner and they won't bother to check.'

Her own room was very dark as they entered and Ruby fumbled for the light. A terrible crash followed and Ben fell headlong onto the plush double bed.

'What have you rigged up there, a man trap?'

Ruby found the light and gasped at Ben lying sprawled out on the bed. She laughed and so did he, then he put his hand down by the side of the bed to see what it was that he'd tripped on. He pulled up an electrical cord. It was plugged in next to the bed and fed an extension lead placed on the dressing table.

'That's a dangerous system for a hotel to have installed in a bedroom.'

'It's not their system Ben, it's mine. These wretched hotels never have the plugs placed near enough to the mirrors. I must be able to see my hair from all angles when I dry each section and use my straighteners. Then I have to have an extra plug for my spotlight, so I can examine the contours of my make-up. Light makes a difference you know, to the shadows on one's face and how it makes you look.'

'Oh, I see,' Ben looked in amazement. 'So how long does it take for you to carry out the whole session of hair and make-up?'

Ruby sat on the bed and stroked her cherry red talons.

106

'It depends on whether I'm touching up these or whether I've just been to the hairdressers or beautician. On average it takes me about two hours. Oh and it takes about forty minutes to lay out my clothes, jewellery and accessories.'

Ben winced, it looked as if she looked after herself, but nearly three hours to get ready to go out somewhere was a joke. He couldn't handle a woman like that long term. Ruby got up and picked up the spotlight Ben had knocked off the dressing table. He'd broken the bulb. She unscrewed the bulb and threw it into the waste paper bin. Then she opened a packet from one of her suitcases and screwed a new one back in.

'You even carry spare bulbs?'

'You never know Ben. You never know when an emergency is going to occur.'

'Well I wouldn't exactly call it an emergency Ruby.' He patted the bed by his side.

'Come and sit down again Ruby.'

Ruby sat down and Ben began kissing her neck. He forced her top down.

'Hang on, you'll snap the elastic. It has to be unfastened first.'

Ben waited patiently while Ruby removed all her clothing and meticulously hung some items up and folded others away into tissue paper. He in turn removed his clothing leaving it in a heap by the doorway. He gently pushed her back onto the middle of the bed and began kissing her on the lips, but she immediately jumped up. She grabbed Ben by the arm and forced him to lie down. She threw a condom at him from her handbag, checked her hair in the mirror and reapplied the lip gloss Ben had wiped off. Only when she was ready, she carefully got back onto the bed astride Ben.

Rory watched every move of the tall gangly looking dark haired boy on the football field. He held the onyx coloured ear stud in his hand and twiddled with the bar. Justin tried so hard to be one of the lads and playing football was just part of it. Having his ear pierced was another trend he'd begged his mother to allow him to have done. She hadn't liked the idea but Rory had won her over by saying there could be hundreds of worse situations he could be getting involved with behind her back. At least he was out in the open asking for their approval.

He played better when Rory was there to cheer him on. He needed something to make him appear better. The team manager placed him in a defence position but as far as Rory could see he couldn't defend to save his life. Every time the ball came anywhere near him he chased after it more in the manner of a ballet dancer than a skilled player and he left all the hard work completely in the goalie's hands. Rory bellowing tactics encouraged him to go for the ball slightly harder but it didn't stop the opposition's strikers from breaking down the wall. Rory was quieter on the field, just as he had been at home. His usual 'Get stuck in lad' and 'Go for it mate' were absent today as imaginary sperm cells swarmed through the hive of his thoughts. If only he'd had the courage to tell Viv that he'd had the vasectomy. He couldn't tell her, she'd kill him. He went over it every day, what he'd planned to say to her, how he would break it to her, but he couldn't bring himself to come out with it.

'Hang on to it Justin.'

Rory looked up to see Justin in the distance belting the ball up towards his end. Mark in midfield took it on and passed to the team's best striker. Bill slammed the ball into the corner of the net. They were 2-0 up and Rory was at the wrong end of the pitch for watching Justin. He'd been so immersed in his thoughts that he'd forgotten to change ends at half time. He ran down to the other end and hoped that Justin hadn't noticed. He'd never lost interest like that before.

Rory and Justin walked home together after the game calling in at the fish and chip shop on the way. They talked the game through and Rory found himself fabricating the bits he'd missed.

'Where were you Dad? You know just before we scored the second time. I slammed the ball and when I looked for you, you were right up the other end.'

'Talking to Tony, the coach for the trials next month.'

'So you missed my best move of the whole game.'

'No, no I saw it. I was just about to run back down anyway.'

Justin took a handful of chips and filled his mouth. He didn't say another word about the game.

It was a glorious morning in Orchard Court and everywhere else in Hexbury. Eileen put the hard broom back in the cupboard and stepped outside to watch the sun's rays dry her steps and path.

She'd bleached them early today in her excitement. Robert telephoned late last night to tell her that he, Carmel and Claire had spent a few days away in Cornwall. 'Could we visit you for a cup of tea, we can't stay long, just passing through, is that okay Eileen?' Was it okay? Did he really need to ask? She hadn't slept for more than half an hour at a time last night, but everything was ready, pristine and sparkling. Even Bertie had been sprinkled with talcum powder and brushed well. All she had left to do was to pop an apple cake in the oven to bake slowly, make a fresh batch of scones to go with the Devon clotted cream and home-made raspberry jam and cut some cucumber sandwiches. Surely they'll stay for a while longer with all that on offer.

The best china was set on the scrubbed pine and she'd managed to find the antique sugar tongs that had once belonged to her grandmother. It was 11.30 a.m.; they should at least be peckish by now. She kept Bertie upstairs in his basket, he always slept in the morning anyway and the last thing that she needed was Carmel turning up her nose at a few cat hairs floating near the clotted cream. Robert's face appeared at the kitchen window. Eileen flew to the door.

'Come in my darlings,' she squeaked in excitement. She kissed Claire first and then felt Carmel wince as she offered her cheek. She threw her arms around Robert kissing and hugging him.

'Sit down and I'll get the kettle on.' Eileen added more water. It had been boiled so many times in anticipation that morning much of it had evaporated. She put the teapot on the table and took the cling film off the cucumber sandwiches.

'Sandwich Carmel?'

'No thank you Eileen, cucumber gives me indigestion.'

Claire put some on her plate and glanced at her auntie. Robert had his eye on the scones.

'Do you mind if I skip the sandwiches?' Eileen passed the plate of scones to her brother.

'Always had a sweet tooth Robert, didn't you?'

'Will you have anything Carmel? Just a sliver of apple cake perhaps?'

'No thank you Eileen, honestly I couldn't eat another thing. I've been eating rubbish in the last few days while we've been away. Can't wait to get back to the gym and some healthy eating. I'll have a tea, black, no sugar.'

The BNG team were outside in the lane measuring up and filling out forms. Someone had come to examine the stone wall. They'd talked about keeping the wall, as it was a character feature and the guy looking at it now built dry stone walls.

'I don't know Crispin. This is a retaining wall; it's going to have to be strong. The type of walls I generally build are to mark boundaries and trick the sheep into thinking they have to stay there. Fortunately most sheep are pretty dim and believe it, but you do get a few that barge the walls and knock them down.'

'Don't worry we have some builders on the team. They'll be building the patio. We can ask them about reinforcing the lower section of the wall and you can build your more decorative part on top.'

'What about that woman's kids. You know Crispin the teenagers on their way to school this morning. If they lean on it too heavily, it'll collapse. It could cause a nasty accident dropping into the lane.'

'You've got a point there. Listen I'll have a rethink, talk with health and safety back at the studio and call you again. Come and have a look at the rest of the garden while you're here.'

The two men walked up the steps to the garden and over to Eileen's patio. They watched as Eileen's cottage door flew open and a smartly dressed slim woman came striding out.

'I'm not staying any longer Robert. We have to get back, you said we'd only be calling for a cup of tea, not all this rigmarole. Claire, Claire are you ready?'

Claire came outside without her coat and bag. Her mother stood with folded arms.

'Well Claire get your bag and coat, we're going.'

'I'm not,' Claire replied staring her mother straight in the eye. 'I'm staying with Auntie Eileen for a week or so. I have the time and it would be quite restful down here. So Dad, could I have my suitcase from the car?'

'Well after all that you said Claire,' Carmel stormed off muttering goodbye to Eileen under her breath.

'What exactly was I supposed to have said Dad?'

'I don't know Claire, but I'll get your suitcase and don't fret, I'll deal with your mum.'

Robert was soon back with the bag. He kissed Claire and hugged his sister.

'I'll be back as soon as you say to pick you up and thanks Eileen.'

'No, thank you Robert.'

Colin and Barry had joined Crispin and the dry stone wall guy up in the garden. They kept quiet while the argument fermented down below before continuing their conversation about their plans. No sooner had they struck up conversation again when Barry piped up with, 'Hang on boss, who's that up there in that window?'

The men looked up to see Miles standing in the picture window overlooking the garden. He was completely naked as he leaned against the glass looking into the garden.

'He obviously hasn't noticed us.'

'I wonder if he normally exposes himself to the neighbours like this. Perhaps what they really want for the garden is a naturists' paradise. Can you imagine, big wall all the way round so they can all get together in the buff for the annual barbecue.'

'Well bags I sit next to that girl we saw the other night.' Barry stood up and made some rude gestures with his hands and Colin joined him adding: 'Not if I get there first you won't.'

The men had brought notice to themselves and Miles was frowning down on them.

'He's seen us.'

'And he's still not covering up.'

The men were directly beneath the window as Miles opened it snarling.

'Why don't you just bugger off and give us all a bit of privacy. You're supposed to be working, not snooping around. If you don't bugger off and stop meddling with this land, I'll...I'll...' Miles picked up a book from the window sill and threw it at them. The pages flew everywhere and they both cried out bringing Adele out to the garden.

'What's happened, and what's all this paper?'

'It's him up there.' Colin pointed up to Miles's window, but Miles had disappeared back to his bedroom.

Chapter Eighteen

Ben towelled his hair dry in a hurry to answer the door. She was early and he definitely did not want her standing on the doorstep. He threw a bathrobe on and ran downstairs.

'Come in Ruby.' Ben pulled her inside and up the stairs past Bradley's ground floor flat, although if Bradley had come out he guessed he would have understood, he was his mate and a man after his own heart.

'Sorry I'm not quite ready Ruby.'

She dumped the bottle of Chardonnay on the kitchen table and slipped her hands inside his robe.

'You're ready enough Ben.'

'Shall we eat later Ruby? I'm afraid I've only ordered a Chinese takeaway. It's keeping warm in the oven, it's not my forté cooking.'

'Where's your bedroom Ben?'

She picked up his hand. Usually he never would have allowed a woman to take the lead. He would have been the one to lay down the conditions, although with Ruby it was strangely exciting. It was almost as if it turned him on to be forced into situations by this harsh demanding woman. She guided him to a chair in the bedroom.

'Sit there,' Ben did as he was told. Ruby sat on the edge of the bed and removed her clothes slowly and carefully. When she was completely naked and her clothes folded into a neat pile she got up and pulled him towards her. She flipped him over and lay on top of him. She kissed him and he tasted her lip gloss. It was like wild ripe cherries and rubbed off on his lips readily. He noticed that she'd laid out her usual crimson colour, a lip brush and a lip liner on the dressing table, alongside her hairbrush and powder compact. She passed him a condom and waited in clinical anticipation. She asked him to hold his hands up to hers and leaning on him she moved rhythmically until Ben's glazed pleasure culminated simultaneously with her ecstatic cries and held breath. He lay back flushed with perspiration on the soft pillows, inhaling the aroma of his wife's perfume. Ruby didn't make any move to lie in his arms afterwards and as thick-skinned as Ben was, even he felt a twinge of disappointment. She left him lying there discarded like a pile of dirty washing. She sat naked at the dressing table, brushing her hair neatly back into place and reapplying her make-up.

'Where did you say your wife was Ben?'

'At her mother's, she'll stay the night so no need to worry.'

Ruby sprayed her settled hair with a mini aerosol from her bag. Why should she be bothered anyway, he was the married one, it wasn't her problem. Ben moved from the bed.

'I'll go and check on the food.'

Ruby, still naked at the dressing table continued to apply her make-up.

Ben stopped dead at the bedroom doorway. Adele stood there, eyes wide and mouth gaping. Why hadn't he heard her come in?

'I thought you said you were staying at your mother's.'

'Obviously,' she choked, tears already appearing.

Ruby looked round, picked up her pile of clothes and pushed past them to the bathroom. She was not going to be compromised even under these circumstances. Neither was Ben and he stood defiant glaring at his wife with just the tinge of a smirk.

'You brought all this upon yourself Adele.' Ben fastened his bathrobe. 'You can't say I'm to blame.' Adele couldn't believe she was hearing this. An inner voice shouted out inside her body, 'Stand up for yourself. It's not your fault.' Instead she stood there intimidated and shamed while he twisted his words into an abusive noose, pulling them tighter and tighter around her neck. He threw the guilt into her court. She was the wronged one and yet he made her stand there while he judged her. She opened her mouth to speak and he beat her down again.

'You were the one messing around with that Rodney.'

'Rory,' she whispered. 'And I'm not remotely interested in Rory,' she said inside, but the words wouldn't come out, she couldn't speak, it sounded so feeble. The longer she stood in the room, the more worthless and wretched he made her feel. Her voice became frail and pathetic with the continued stream of false accusations that he fired at her. She did the only thing she felt able to; she ran out of the room.

'That's it run away. That proves you're guilty Adele.'

She hadn't a clue where she would go, anywhere away from his sharp, bullying words. She still had her overnight bag and the keys to her blue Renault Clio, parked opposite the house.

An arm came around her as she stood waiting to cross the road. She jumped and gasped at the same time.

'It's okay, it's okay,' Bradley soothed her. 'I heard everything Adele and she's gone now, the woman with the huge red lips. I saw her leave.' Bradley stood holding her hands, but she shook with fear. He looked into her frightened eyes and instead of looking back at him she peered over his shoulder Then she flinched and looked over her own shoulder, watching all around her in trepidation.

'He scares you, doesn't he?'

'I haven't done anything Bradley.'

'I know you haven't sweetheart.'

He put his arm around her again. 'Come with me. You can sleep on my sofa.'

'I don't know whether that's such a good idea Bradley.'

'Do you want to go back to your mother's tonight Adele? Do you?'

'No,' she replied as she allowed him to ease the hurt.

'Come on sweetheart, I'll look after you. Then tomorrow morning you can go back home. You don't have to say that you stayed with me, probably best that you don't. And I'll come upstairs with you if you're scared of him.'

He carried her bag and she allowed him to escort her into his flat. She was scared of the man Ben had become, but he couldn't help it. She vowed that this time she would go and see their doctor and see if she could alter anything, but for the time being she'd let Bradley look after her. So as Ben sat upstairs on the sofa with his head in his hands and his wife gone, she sat downstairs sipping hot tea in Bradley's kitchen. He poured her another and she looked up at him comfortably.

Crispin had been trying unsuccessfully to get hold of Ruby all night. They had a few details to arrange then they could organise when to return to do the work and the filming of the garden transformation. He went outside to join Colin and Barry sitting on the garden steps enjoying the sunshine. Crispin was convinced that he would go ahead with the plans. He'd seen a few minor upsets with the neighbours. Eileen's family crisis and Miles's naked appearance at the window, but he didn't think that it was anything major to worry about.

'Where's Ruby today guys, I've been trying to get hold of her all last night.'

Colin and Barry looked at each other and started laughing.

'Is there something I should know?'

'No nothing boss.'

They tittered amongst themselves and Crispin merely tutted to himself. They were like a couple of washer women, Colin and Barry, always the same. He ignored them and started to write up some plans. At the precise same moment Ruby walked up the path. Colin and Barry couldn't contain themselves, they went indoors giggling.

'Where have you been and where were you last night?'

'Alright, calm down Cris. It was only one night and it was worth it for my cosy little rendezvous with delicious Ben. He might even take me to one of those fashion shows soon.'

'Oh you haven't Ruby. You can't leave it alone can you?'

'I can't help it. I don't ask for it, they come to me.'

Cris spotted Ben at the bottom of the lane, then Adele. Ben stood with his hands on his hips, while Adele cowered from him. Bradley was standing next to Ben trying to calm him, but Ben took no notice of his composure. He lunged at Adele, Bradley stepped in front of him. Ben stared at Adele and then drove off in his BMW.

'Now look what you've done Ruby.'

'Me Cris! Why should I have anything to do with their marital problems?

'You are the limit Ruby, it's just as well we're nearly finished here.'

Rory made tea for Viv when she returned from delivering the boys to school.

'I've been thinking Rory. Perhaps we should try for another baby straight away. I mean you had become used to the idea of having just one more hadn't you?'

'Well, yes but…'

'But what Rory?'

Rory started cleaning the kitchen furiously. Spraying the work surfaces with antibacterial spray and wiping the sink out with paper towels.

'Rory, answer me.'

He still didn't answer. He polished the kettle and wiped the inside of the cupboard. He sprayed the work surfaces again and started wiping.

'You've already done that.'

'What?'

'I said you've already done that.'

'I've had the vasectomy.'

'You missed a bit.' Viv pointed to a sticky bit of work surface by the kettle.

'I've had the vasectomy.'

Viv didn't say anything at first. She stood and stared at Rory. Then she picked up Harry and Jake's marbles and started throwing them at him. Once she'd thrown all the marbles she started on the Lego in great handfuls. She raged incoherently at him, 'Bastard, you bastard. Why didn't you tell me?' After the Lego came a metal colander and a sieve. Rory dodged all the items thrown and finally resorted to running outside. Viv grabbed a saucepan and followed him seething and expelling swear words as she chased him. Rory pushed past Cris and Adele on the steps to the garden, pursued swiftly by Viv. The string of swear words persisted and Viv finally threw the saucepan at Rory's head and ran back down the steps awash with tears. She flung herself through the door, slammed it shut and locked it. Rory picked up the saucepan and rubbed his head. He glanced at the onlookers and shrugged his shoulders. Adele went over to him.

'You'd better come inside with us until she calms down.'

'It'll be a long time before she calms down this time Adele.'

'Well there's always a pillow and a sleeping bag in our small lock up shed if she won't let you in.'

That night Rory tried to keep warm on a camp bed in Adele's shed. It was only one step better than sleeping out in the open air. Eileen's cat scratched at the door and meowed. He could hear a pattering sound on the roof, like something running up and down. Eileen's niece had her window open and he could hear her music and Colin and Barry had their window open emitting the faint sound of snoring. It was only when the street lights went out in the lane that Rory finally drifted off and it wasn't until the next morning that Rory and everybody else in Orchard Court discovered the roped off apple tree.

The old apple tree, which was near enough in the middle of all the plots was destined to be chopped down. It took up a lot of space and it was space that could be utilised in a much more resourceful way. The neighbours and the TV team had planned to put a pond there and either a fountain or a water feature.

Rory wrapped his sleeping bag around himself and walked closer to the tree. Someone had placed a temporary fence around it and there was a notice tied on to the trunk, *'Preservation Order'*. Rory couldn't read the rest of the blurb, the fence prevented him from getting closer and the print was incredibly tiny. Adele appeared in her dressing gown. She walked sleepily towards the tree clutching a letter.

'Didn't you hear anything Rory?'

'Last night I heard plenty, but this morning I must have been sound asleep. I didn't hear a thing, although I reckon it was done first thing this morning. I'd have certainly heard someone putting up a fence last night.'

'What does it say Adele?'

'That the tree has to stay. It's a protected species.'

'Why didn't they tell you this before?'

'They said they did. As soon as they had the application forms from the BNG team they posted out four replies to tell us about the tree. Normally fruit trees are exempt from tree preservation orders, but it's a rare variety and we need to get permission before we do anything to it.'

'We didn't get anything like that in the post.'

'Neither did we, it's a complete mystery.'

Adele slumped down on the grass next to the officious fence.

'Crispin must have known how to check up on trees like that. He must have come across it in other gardens. What a mistake for him to make,' Rory said sarcastically.

'What, nearly as bad as having a vasectomy at the same time as your wife miscarries.'

'Adele, I didn't know you could be such a cruel woman.'

Rory stared at Adele, but with a glint in his eye.

'You could always have it reversed.'

'Yes, I know I could have it reversed. But somehow it's as though it was meant to be. Do you believe in fate? It's like fate intervening.'

'Perhaps you're right, so is this flaming tree fate intervening?'

'Maybe, but I'm sure that if you get the right advice you can get round it.'

The BNG team's decision to leave tomorrow was brought forward when they received the news about the tree. Crispin and the team walked down the steps laden with equipment. Ruby wheeled her designer suitcase and Colin and Barry were weighed down with leads and contraptions. They took no notice of Rory and Adele still draped on the grass by the forlorn apple tree. They loaded the white vans and within half an hour they were all set to go. Adele, still in dressing gown met Crispin on the path.

'I'm sorry Adele. We're off earlier than expected. I don't know what to say really.'

'So you'll be in contact soon?'

'I'm not sure about anything at the moment; it's all become so complicated, I'm sorry.'

'You haven't changed your mind about us have you?'

'As I said, I can't say anything for sure. Let's wait and see shall we? I'll be in touch.'

Rory and Adele watched them drive off. Adele sniffed and Rory put his arm around her shoulders.

'Fate Adele. That's all it is and there's nothing you or I can do about it.'

Adele wrapped her gown around herself and replied determinedly.

'Oh isn't there? Isn't there?'

Chapter Nineteen

Cameron poured another tea for the agitated Adele pacing up and down in her kitchen. He'd found the four letters from the council in Miles's pile of unanswered mail when he'd visited him a few days' ago. They all been posted to the wrong house by mistake and been buried in one of the heaps of junk to be dealt with. Neither of the two blamed Miles. It wasn't his fault that the letters had all been sent to him and he was finding it difficult to get through the day at the moment let alone consider tree preservation orders.

The window where they sat overlooked the garden and as Adele stacked the papers into order the two tried hard not to look down on the forlorn looking apple tree with its makeshift fence. The grass beneath the tree had been roughly shaved by an industrial strimmer so that a green circle could be painted around the ground. This served as a warning from the local tree warden – 'don't touch me I'm sacred.'

Cameron was at Adele's on two counts this morning, the first being the welfare of his friend and colleague, Miles.

'He's been signed off for another two months Adele. I assume he has to go and see his GP periodically. I rang him yesterday. He answered after about ten rings, but he didn't have an awful lot to say. And there was no lilt to his voice like there usually is.'

Adele helped herself to another Rich Tea biscuit while Cameron continued.

'I saw him this morning on my way to your house. He was cleaning an upstairs window. I waved to him, but I don't think he saw me.'

Adele thought deeper about the location of the window. It was the one next to the picture window where Colin and Barry had spotted him from the garden. She visualised going up the staircase in Miles's house and turning left at the top. It would have been the room she ventured into by accident when she visited Miles. Did it need mentioning or was she delving too deep? It was only a window and it was probably part of his cleaning out therapy. There was no harm in that was there?

'At least you've seen him Cameron even if he won't speak to anyone.'

'I think we should still keep watching out for him and if we don't get any joy within the next few weeks maybe we could contact the surgery and speak to his counsellor.'

'Yes, I think you're right and you're right about leaving it a few weeks. We have to give him time to get his thoughts sorted out.'

Adele checked her mobile phone in her bag. Still no message from Ben. He'd been gone now for two days. She knew he'd be away for at least one night and the company briefing for the new season's fashions always dragged itself out, but he could have let her know. She didn't deserve this sort of treatment. Although perhaps he might have emailed her or tried to ring on the land line and she'd already been with Cameron for over an hour.

'Right Adele, let's get down to business on this apple tree. We'll look at the letter from the council.'

Adele handed it to Cameron and he began to read it out aloud.

Copies sent to Mr and Mrs Parker, Mr and Mrs Cunningham, Mr Harper and Miss Dolce.

Dear Residents of Orchard Court

Hexbury Borough Council would like to bring to your notice the Tree Preservation Order placed on the central apple tree in the gardens of Orchard Court. The order is legalised under The Town and Country Planning Act of 1990, which protects trees in the interests of the amenity by enforcing TPOs. The value of the tree in question is enhanced by its scarcity and its relationship to the ancient variety 'Great Alexander' introduced to Britain in 1805. The felling of such rare trees is under the control of the Authority and it is felt that the destruction of the tree would have a significant impact on the environment and its enjoyment by the public, particularly as the tree in question is clearly visible from the main road and the public footpath adjoining your houses. We also perceive that the tree is under considerable threat by the development of the gardens in Orchard Court and we therefore deem a TPO to be expedient, not only for the tree in question, but for the whole area to include all residents' gardens.

Yours sincerely

Emanuel Fitzsimmons

Tree Warden, Hexbury Borough Council

Adele picked up the letter

'Does that mean what I think it means?'

Cameron nodded.

'That we cannot under any circumstances cut the tree down, but in addition we can't make any undue alterations to its surroundings.'

'Yes, so even if Crispin does want to carry on with the project the wretched local council will stop us anyway!'

'That's about it Adele.'

Adele flattened the letter out and put it back with the rest of the correspondence.

'They can't do this to us. We must be able to do something to unravel this loophole.'

Cameron picked up another sheet of paper.

'That's not the whole story yet. I've been in contact with Crispin on behalf of all the residents. I know you think that he and the team might have been put off by all your neighbours and their behaviour, but he's our strongest link. He relished the idea of transforming the gardens in the first place and they must have come face to face with similar issues in previous projects. Anyway, this is what he came back with.'

Cameron laid the copy of Crispin's returned email on the coffee table.

Dear Adele and Orchard Court residents
Sorry to hear the details on the Tree Preservation Order for the old apple tree. However, I have always understood that fruit trees were exempt from this type of order. Perhaps you'd like to check it out with your local council.
Best Wishes
Crispin (BNG)

'Well Cameron, don't keep me in suspense. What did they have to say to that?'

'I telephoned and spoke to the tree warden himself.'

'And?'

'And he took great delight in telling me that fruit trees were exempt, but only if they are used for commercial production of fruit. The tree in Orchard Court is a sole specimen, enhanced by its scarcity and indeed by its local value.'

Adele frowned and holding the chair she took long deep breaths.

'They'd do anything to stamp their authority. It's ridiculous, you can hardly see the tree from the road and it's a gnarled ugly old specimen of a tree anyway.'

'I know Adele, so here's round 3.'

'You mean you've managed to think of something else to abate them?'

'I thought it might be worth a try.'

Cameron grinned and carried on with the saga.

'I thought long and hard about what they meant by "used for commercial production" and wondered if that might be a way around it.'

'What do you mean?'

'You know that Eileen makes preserves and baked goods for the W. I. sometimes?'

'Yes?'

'Once she made some delicious apple chutney. She gave me a jar before she took it for sale down at the local market.'

'I'd hardly call the W.I. stall commercial production though Cameron if you don't mind me saying.'

'Neither would I at face value, but I felt that if they wanted to be small-minded and bureaucratic then we could have a go at this game of rule-mongering just as well as they could.'

Adele sat down and mused at his attempts to bend authority.

'Unfortunately, Mr Emmanuel Fitzsimmons came back with "To be considered commercial, it has to be within a large orchard and therefore a large scale of production." But this is where it gets better.'

Adele sat forward on her seat and clasped her hands together waiting for the next instalment.

'We could try the DDD rule.'

'What on earth is that?'

'It stands for Dead, Dying or Dangerous. Here read this.'

Cameron handed her a booklet on tree preservation from the Forestry Commission.

'If a tree is dead, dying or dangerous (DDD rule) then you only need to give the Authority 5 days notice that you intend to carry out works to the tree. However, you must provide evidence that this is the case e.g. relevant photographs or a report by a qualified

and experienced arboriculturist. The onus is on you to prove that the tree is dead, dying or dangerous and if you cannot do so, a court may find you guilty of an offence.'

'That's fantastic, so all we need to do now is find ourselves a reliable arbo...what his name?'

'Arboriculturist.'

'And please tell me that the bureaucratic band couldn't dispute that.'

'No, he couldn't. I spoke to the tree warden again and he said, "If you can prove it then yes, you have the authority." That means if we can prove the DDD rule we can do what we damned well like with the rotten old tree.'

'Any idea where we'll be able to find one of these Arbotreefellows?'

'No, but we both know a man that does,' Cameron smiled and pointed to a hard copy of the home page for Breaking New Ground, where a photo shot of Crispin filled the top right hand corner.

Chapter Twenty

Viv allowed Rory back inside the house, eventually, but she hadn't come to terms with what he'd done. They'd finally settled that evening silent, exhausted and slumped on the sofa with a hot chocolate each, watching a TV soap.

Justin crept past the living room with his rucksack and his rolled up sleeping bag over his shoulder. He held the front door latch in with his thumb to stifle the noise of its closing. Craig was waiting for him outside. It was 7.00 p.m. They'd iron out their final plans for tonight then they'd be ready for one hell of a night. He'd already told his dad earlier that he was staying at Craig's, and now he couldn't be bothered to speak to either dad or mum, so he left without saying goodbye.

Craig had his board stuffed into the elastic thongs on the back of his rucksack, Justin carried his under his arm. Neither of the boys attempted to ride them. It was as though their plans demanded silence; the silence necessary to think it through and the calm to build their courage. At the end of the lane they lit up their joints and walked in stubborn fashion down to the park.

Safe in the haven of the old bandstand Craig crumbled hash into a fresh packet of Old Holborn. They hid their boards behind a dense privet hedge near the bandstand and wrapping their legs in the sleeping bags they settled into the harsh darkness of the night, sweetened by the intoxicating cloud of cannabis. The park was fairly quiet tonight and they shared the steady thumping base beat of the iPod with one earpiece each. Neither of the two boys had managed to smuggle any alcohol from their houses, but Craig had nicked a tenner from his dad's wallet. Half an hour later they signalled to each other. It was time to move on and hang out elsewhere. They stubbed their joints out on the wall and pulled the wires out of their ears. Coming out of the bandstand they heard giggling and sharp clicking of high heels.

'See those birds over there?' Craig leaned on the wall trying to look cool.

'Yeah, do you know them?'

'They're in the year below us at school. The blonde one's Lynch's cousin.'

'She's well fit.'

'And she's got massive tits.'

'Come on let's go over and hang out with them. They look like they're pissed already.'

Justin and Craig left their sleeping bags in the bandstand and made their way over to the girls. There were four of them and no other blokes hanging around. Craig whispered to Justin' 'Hey, two each mate.' They staggered slightly as they reached the girls and Justin beamed stupidly in Craig's direction.

'That's good shit you got tonight, makes me feel like I'm walking on air.'

The tallest and more mature looking girls were sent into the minimarket to buy the booze. They both wore short black skirts and calf length suede boots. One had a pink, fur-edged corduroy jacket and her friend had a similar jacket in cream. They looked decent girls, the sort Justin would bring home for tea with his mum and they looked older then they really were. They could easily pass for two nineteen year olds on their way out to a house party. Justin and Craig waited a hundred yards or so up the road from the shop with the other two girls.

'Twenty two quid between us, that's not bad is it,' Craig said with his arm round Lynch's cousin.

'And don't forget this,' Justin bent down and kissed the full bottle of vodka sticking out of the other girl's bag.

The girls were in the shop for what seemed like ages and when they finally came out they ran up the road to the others panting and giggling like the school girls that they really were.

'Come on let's get back to camp before our place is nicked.'

Justin and Craig opened up their sleeping bags and spread them out so that the girls could sit down. Natalie (Lynch's cousin) and Becks were well gone already and they'd smoked a joint each while they waited for the other two outside the shop. Laura and Linette perched on the edge of the skateboards, covered with a bit of sleeping bag. They refused to get dirty and sit on the floor. They sipped cider from plastic cups, which they'd brought with them and burst into fits of giggles, spilling their drinks every time the skate boards moved. The group finished drinking and left their stuff in the bandstand while they ran down to go on the swings further down the park. The girls climbed on the roundabout and the boys stood by the side whizzing it around. They spun it so fast

128

it almost came off its hinges. Natalie and Becks were cheering for it to go faster, Laura clung on, her nails gripping into the wooden struts and Linette turned pallid. It gradually stopped and Linette couldn't move or speak.

'Look what you've done to her,' Laura cried out. She helped her friend off the roundabout. Linette collapsed onto her knees and vomited on the grass. Laura helped her up and gave her a tissue from her pocket. She clung on to her friend's arm for support.

'I'm okay now,' she croaked wiping her mouth. 'Take me home.' Laura gave the boys a filthy look and the two of them left the park.

Natalie and Becks took off their shoes and skirts and climbed into the sleeping bags.

'Come and keep us warm boys,' Natalie tempted. Craig took off his jeans and climbed in with her, zipping them close together. Justin lay down with Becks.

'Come on big boy,' she said.

'What,' Justin said, trying to hide his shyness.

'Take your jeans off and get in, I'm cold.'

Justin did as he was told and quickly forgot about his shyness. The girls rapidly shed the rest of their clothes and they didn't seem to mind the close proximity they had with each other whilst intimate liaisons were taking place.

Craig unzipped the sleeping bag slightly, revealing Natalie's bare breasts. She shivered, then looked over to Becks grinning.

'Need a fag,' Craig said. 'Coming Justin?' He beckoned to his friend. Justin followed leaving the girls to chat.

They walked down to the river a few hundred yards from the bandstand and exchanged info on the girls. Craig suggested that when they went back that they swap girls. Justin wasn't keen, but he didn't want to say too much and he held back his natural inborn disgust. This wasn't how he'd intended it to be when he finally got off with a girl.

'Won't they mind if we swap,' he said.

'Nah, course they won't. They're right little scrubbers, it was a race for them two to lose their virginity and they didn't keep it a secret either.'

That scared Justin even more if they were going to tell all their friends about his performance.

'Come on Justin, you're not gonna chicken out now are you?'

Justin shook his head and walked back to the bandstand with his mate. They could see the crumpled sleeping bags from a distance and when they got closer the half full bottle of vodka on the bandstand steps. Mounting the steps and entering the bandstand again Justin stifled his sigh of relief. The girls had gone. He pretended to be as pissed off as his mate as they sat on the steps swigging the vodka.

'Looks like it's just me and you,' Craig said passing the bottle to Justin.

'You still up for staying out for the whole night?'

Justin nodded, took a swig of vodka and tried not to gag on the bitter taste. He shivered with the cold, and looked at his phone to check the time -1.00 a.m. His dad would have been home from the pub long ago. He'd be tucked up in his warm cosy bed by now. It started to rain; great heavy drops at first, then the wind picked up and showered the two friends huddled on the steps. They picked up the bottle, zipped themselves into their sleeping bags and nestled together like a couple of field mice on a cold stormy night.

Rory unfastened the chain and unlocked the front door to collect his motor bike boots from the porch. He tripped and landed right on top of the padded lump in front of him.

'Ow, shit that hurt,' Craig cried out. Justin woke immediately and stared in a look of utter panic at his father.

'What the hell are you two doing here? It's six in the morning. Have you been here all night?'

The two boys stared blankly at him. Rory turned to Justin.

'I thought you were staying at Craig's.'

The boys said nothing.

'I think you've got some explaining to do lad.'

Justin's biggest fear drove him to speak.

'You're not gonna tell mum are you dad? Please don't tell mum. Me and Craig'll creep up to bed now, she'll never know.'

'Are you going to tell me what happened, both of you?'

'Later dad, please. Let us go upstairs and grab some sleep.' Justin picked up his sleeping bag and beckoned to Craig, just as Viv appeared in the doorway.

Adele's phone beeped loudly in her bag under the counter. She pounced on it and opened the text envelope.

130

'Might be bk thurs but dnt hold out hope.'

Sheryl looked over her shoulder.

'The bastard,' she said.

Adele put the phone back in her bag before Bradley came out from the stockroom. He didn't need any encouragement he'd been asking enough questions about Ben's whereabouts in the past two days. He came out, all smiles with coffee for the three of them.

'You can go home early if you want to Adele,' he said. 'You'll probably want to be getting yourself all fresh for that husband of yours.'

'No she won't, the sod's not coming home until Thursday if she's lucky,' Sheryl piped up.

'You can still go home early if you want to,' Bradley said with a smirk.

Adele made the most of her time alone. She had a simple jacket potato with tuna and salad for dinner and an individual tiramisu while she watched a garden design programme similar to Breaking New Ground. She read Woman and Home with a cup of coffee and then prepared for a long lengthy soak in the bath. She'd had no more messages or calls from Ben, so she shut him out completely and turned off her phone and the computer.

Adele pulled the lead of the portable CD player so that she could hear it from the bathroom. She inserted the new disc received that morning, 'Romantic Adagios', a classical mix of slow sultry numbers from Bach to Schumann. She dropped the blind and filled the room with candles. The oil burner glimmered and the aroma of musk crept into every corner of the room, like a scented sprite on a mission of persuasion. Adele sprinkled in the bath oils and the bubbles erupted into a soft mound with a trickling stream creeping into it from the tap of hot steamy water. She collected her glass of Chianti and her copy of Wuthering Heights and sunk into warm bliss.

Bliss was interrupted twenty five minutes later by the phone ringing. Adele let the answer phone collect the message, but the caller left nothing but a long beep. The number was withheld so she couldn't even call back. She pulled the plug on the bathwater and blew out the candles. The phone rang again and she answered.

'Hi Adele, are you okay? It's Bradley. You didn't pick up a few minutes ago.'

'I'm fine Bradley. I was in the bath.'

'Wondered whether you'd like to share a bottle of wine with me. You must be lonely up there by yourself.'

Adele hesitated. She remembered what Sheryl had said about Ben earlier. She'd agreed, he was a bastard, but it didn't give her an excuse to have a secret liaison with a man like Bradley.

'Well...Adele?'

She wasn't doing anything tonight and she could do with a chat to someone, even Bradley. She had to give him an answer and on the spur of the moment she relented and allowed him in. It was only a glass of wine after all.

'Give me a chance to get some clothes on and come up Bradley.'

Bradley gave her ten minutes and knocked bearing a bottle. She showed him into the lounge and brought two glasses in. It was Californian red, an intoxicating mix with the Chianti. Adele shivered with her still wet hair and Bradley wasted no time.

'Wait there Adele.'

'Where are you going Bradley?'

He disappeared and returned a few minutes later with a basket full of logs and some chopsticks to light a fire.

'Don't tell me you haven't lit it since you've been here?'

'No, Ben always says it's too messy.'

The fire was very quickly roaring away and Adele and Bradley sat on the mat in front of it. They talked and drank wine until the log basket was empty and the flames had died down into glowing embers. They lay in front of the shimmering ashes, their cheeks radiant from the heat. It seared the innermost parts of their bodies, dissolving their inhibitions and melting their hearts. They stayed there, bodies snug and entwined eking the very last drop of warmth until the cold early morning dawned.

Chapter Twenty One

Claire walked through the garden with her auntie to see what all the fuss was about. The apple tree swayed pitifully in the slight breeze, all alone in the middle of the gardens. It didn't take an expert to affirm that it was dying.

'I do hope that they get it sorted out with the old tree. You could make so much of this garden.' Claire reached out to touch the tree.

'As long as it's clean and tidy, that's why I like my pink and white slabs.'

'Don't you think that your pink and white slabs are just a tad old-fashioned?' Claire smiled at her auntie.

'Clean and tidy my girl that's....'

She stopped short when she saw Adele walk up the lane towards them.

'This is my lovely niece, Claire.' Eileen said to Adele.

'Hello Claire, good to see that you're keeping your auntie company.'

Adele turned to Eileen and handed her a brown envelope.

'This is an update on the Tree Preservation Order Eileen. I called Cameron, he's a solicitor and Miles's colleague at work. We're waiting for Crispin to make a recommendation at the moment, but it'll tell you all the details in my letter.'

'Thank you Adele, very kind of you to keep me informed.'

'That's okay Eileen,' Adele replied and she waved her hand to both of them as she turned and returned to her house.

'She seemed nice,' Claire said. 'She looked as if she was sad about something though. I guess it was the garden.' Claire linked arms with her auntie and they returned to Eileen's kitchen.

'What are these small orange fruits?' Claire examined the Kilner jars on the kitchen table.

'They're kumquats, they're pretty aren't they? They look too good to eat. If you buy them fresh they're quite bitter, but preserved in syrup like those they're delicious.'

Eileen had nobody nearby to take an interest in her baking and preserving, apart from the competitive W.I. group. It was so refreshing to be able to show Claire some of her skills, especially since they were becoming fast forgotten in this day and age. This afternoon she was showing Claire how to make brandy snaps. Eileen opened the oven door.

'Yes, they're just about ready.' Eileen passed her the oven glove and continued to deliver the instructions.

'Now you have to ready with the palette knife. Wait until the mixture stops bubbling and slide the knife underneath. That's it. Now the wooden spoon and wrap it carefully around the handle.'

'That's magic, I would never have thought that's how you made them.'

'I don't suppose it is on a commercial scale dear.'

'I'd like to know more about preserving fruit in jars like this. Have you got any spare jars Auntie Eileen?'

Eileen opened a few cupboard doors near the sink and then pondered with her hand on her chin. She remembered.

'Yes, I think there are some in the attic. We can go and look after lunch if you like; you can take some home with the recipe book and try it out.' *That's providing Carmel didn't find an excuse for not allowing Claire to experiment. Eileen didn't want to overpower Claire with too much about her life. She wanted her mildly intrigued, intrigued enough to return and pay her another visit.*

Eileen handed Claire the torch to find her way around the loft.

'There's a cardboard box if I remember rightly by the water tank, but be careful. Try to stand on the wooden struts or you'll go through the plasterboard on the ceiling.'

'I think I've found it. Is it the old apple box?'

'That's the one; if you could just pass it through the hatch to me.'

'There's another one right next to it, with some newspapers keeping the dust out. Shall I bring that one as well?'

'If you like dear. Can you manage that one by yourself?'

'Yes.'

Claire carefully carried the other box down and closed the trapdoor to the attic. They took the boxes down to the kitchen to wash the jars.

'It's a shame that more young ladies like you aren't interested in the old skills and traditions. It's all fast foods and convenience these days. There's no respectability in the world any more.'

Eileen ran a bowl of hot soapy water and began washing the jars. They weren't really dirty, only dusty. They ran some more clear hot water to rinse them and then left them to drain. Claire towelled them dry with a clean towel. She dusted the box and put fresh newspaper in it, then carefully selected six of the best jars for Claire to take home.

'Don't forget dear to heat the oven to 75°C and leave the jars in there for a while so that the heat sterilises them.'

Eileen picked up one of the brandy snaps and snapped the end off.

'These are excellent, especially for a first attempt. They're really crunchy. I've got bottled peaches in the larder, but I'm going to walk down to the mini-market and buy some fresh cream to go inside the snaps. Perhaps you could wash those other jars while I'm gone dear.'

Claire found the bottled peaches in the larder. The larder was an emporium of goodies; the sort of foods that you might find at local fairs or W.I. stalls. The walls were lined with jars of marmalade, runner bean chutney, jams of all sorts and a silky velvet lemon curd. Auntie Eileen had told Claire about the W.I. and the way that they shared the stall at the market and other stalls at events throughout the year. It sounded like a cooperative system and it worked, although Eileen had also told her about some of the competitive bitchiness between a few of the women. 'There's those you get on with and those you don't,' she'd told her. Claire studied food at school and was genuinely interested in the old crafts, but some of Auntie Eileen's recipes sounded as if they were straight out of Mrs Beeton. She wondered whether her auntie would approve of her body piercings or her swan tattoo on her left buttock. Claire's mother had gone mad when she came back from a trip to the town one day and proudly showed off her navel piercing. Claire thought it was so 'cool' and pretty to look at, but Carmel hadn't stopped ranting and raving for days. That's why she'd chosen not to tell her mother about the tattoo or the nipple piercings. As long as she kept her bra and knickers on all the time that her mother was around she'd probably never get to find out.

She ran another bowl of hot soapy water and put the rubber gloves back on to wash the jars. She removed the newspaper from the top of the box. There were no jars in this box; instead it was full of some sort of memorabilia. She took the gloves off again. Perhaps she should wait until Auntie Eileen returned so that she could ask her permission to look through the box, but then she couldn't imagine that staid old Auntie Eileen could have anything revelatory to hide. She carefully tipped the contents out, placing them carefully on the kitchen table. Slowly Claire examined each item and made a pile of the items looked at. The more she discovered the more she felt that she shouldn't be doing this, but as she found out further details she felt compelled to carry on. She went through everything in the box, trying to be swift and take it all in at the same time. Perhaps she should hide the box back in the attic; she should at least put it all back and pretend that she'd not ventured as far as rifling through the contents. Yes, she'd quickly do that. She picked up the pile to put it back in the box and Auntie Eileen entered the kitchen with the cream.

Claire packed her bag to go home. Her dad had arranged to pick her up at eleven this morning. They'd eaten the brandy snaps, cream and peaches last night and enjoyed the last evening together, but it was blighted by Claire's discovery of the box. The box that Eileen had forgotten existed; she'd put it to the far corner of her mind, compartmentalised into her own emotional box with the lid firmly closed. Now Claire had opened it and all the memories and reasons that went with it. Perhaps Claire would understand her feelings now that she knew the truth and she'd asked her to keep it to herself if she could manage it. Eileen had worried before all this that Claire might not return to visit again. Now her visions of a good sustainable relationship were all on the brink. And if Claire decided to reveal the truth everything, yes absolutely everything could be shattered into oblivion.

Chapter Twenty Two

Crispin emailed Adele a list of five arboriculturists. She selected three names and by 11.00 a.m. had quotes from all of them. They were all from nearby villages and sounded intrigued when they heard about the TV programme. She chose the middle price and fixed up a definite appointment with a Mr Beazley. She was so excited that she felt she had to tell somebody. Crispin's name sprang to mind first, but she wanted to have more concrete evidence before reporting back to him. She was determined to show that they really wanted the garden refurbishment and that they were prepared to put themselves out.

She brushed her hair, slipped her feet into a pair of flat shoes and walked around to Viv's house. It was the first time that she'd seen her since her return from hospital and Rory had told her that it was all out regarding the vasectomy. She knocked gently on the front door. Viv answered almost immediately and threw her arms around Adele.

'Come in Adele.'

Adele waited for Viv to release her from the tight hug before asking if she was any better.

'Physically I'm fine,' she told Adele, 'but it's a lot to get my head around at the moment. First of all I have four children and I'm happy to stick at four and then the unexpected pregnancy and then just when I'm accustomed to the idea it's taken away again. The vasectomy was the last straw. Rory said he'd mentioned it to you.'

'How about Rory?'

'He's really sorry he didn't tell me that the appointment had come up and he'd made the choice alone to go ahead with it, but he's trying to get me to believe that it's fate that has got us into the situation we're in now. I keep telling him that he chose to have the vasectomy not fate.'

'I think he's referring to the whole scenario Viv, not just one slice of the pie. Maybe you could think about what he means.'

'Well maybe I could, but I'd rather not at the moment. Have you got any other news?' Viv remarked eyeing up Adele's envelope.

Adele gave Viv the envelope with the updated information about the garden and the tree.

'So now all we need to do is wait for the examination of the tree and the reports.'

The two women walked outside to the garden to take another look at the apple tree impostor. They took their mugs of coffee and a packet of ginger snaps and sat on the grass in front of it.

'Have you seen Miles in the last few days Adele?'

'I haven't seen him for at least a week.'

'I knocked on the door yesterday, but there was no reply. I think we should ring the surgery and get somebody to check on him. We've left it long enough.'

'You're right. He'll probably be fine, but at least we've acted in his interests haven't we?'

'And what about your interests with that bully of a husband of yours? Is he back from his business trip after his last outburst?'

'He's due back tonight. He sent me one curt message while he was away for three days.'

'I suppose he'll expect you to be all sweet and caring when he gets back and for you to wait on him hand and foot.'

'I can stand up for myself Viv. I'm getting braver by the day,' she laughed.

'That's good, you're settling in that's what it is. Moving house, and to a new area can be a very stressful event Adele. You make sure you stand up for yourself.'

Adele had a rosy glow on her cheeks in the last few days. Her recent feeling of bravado made her feel two inches taller with her head held high, but with bravado came his partner in crime, guilt. Whatever bravado said and however many times he told her to be bold, guilt ran in and kicked him in the shins. Bravado pushed her forwards and guilt slapped her back down with his knowledge that she'd allowed Bradley to be become too familiar. Bravado said it wasn't her fault, but guilt stepped in to throttle her with his silken scarf of remorse, reminding her that she'd let Bradley go too far.

Drew skipped brushing his teeth properly, spitting goo on the taps and throwing his brush into the sink.

'Wait for me Justin.'

He pulled his rucksack from the pile of shoes by the door and ran after his brother.

'You're not walking with me today shrimp,' Justin told him. 'I'm meeting Laura at the end of the lane. She won't want you tagging along.'

'Oh please Just, please let me walk with you.'

'No,' and Justin held his shoulders firmly. 'Stay back.'

Laura waited by the lamp post, looking up and down the road for him. Justin's gait slipped into a lilt and he put his arm around her waist. They kissed and Justin picked up her bag and offered to carry it for her. Drew held back behind them. Justin glared at him. Laura spotted the frail skinny boy just a few yards behind.

'Who's that?'

'That's my shrimp of a brother, Drew.'

'He looks scared, have you been shouting at him?'

'No,' Justin looked indignant. 'He wanted to walk with me that was all and I said no. You don't want him with us do you?'

'But Justin he's sweet and he looks so timid.'

Laura turned around to speak to Drew.

'Do you want to walk with us Drew?'

Drew's face lit up immediately, but he looked to his brother for confirmation. Justin waited for Drew to catch up with them. He put his arm around his brother's shoulders. Drew blinked; he had a habit of blinking and he did it more frequently when he was nervous.

'Come on then shrimp.'

Drew walked behind Justin and Laura through the school gates. The bell rang and he just about managed to get into his tutor room before Eric Bullen could get hold of him.

At lunchtime Drew hadn't managed to collect a detention today. He usually climbed the fence to bunk off home for lunch, but today Mr Valcheva was on smoking patrol. He hung around the side door to the tennis courts talking to one of the lunchtime assistants until she was called away for trouble at the PE block. Drew walked by the tennis courts looking over his shoulder the whole time. He kept close to the shrubs on his left hand side and walked steadily onwards. He kept listening hard. He could hear the voices around him and the wind blowing the leaves. There were groups of girls huddled together nearby and the wire fence they were leaning on made a tinny jingling sound. In front of the girls were some of the kids from Drew's tutor group. They were nice to him at registration time, but now when he needed someone to be

139

with they looked the other way, pretending that they hadn't seen him. Drew glanced over his shoulder...no one there. He took a deep breath, easing the queasiness in his stomach. Perhaps he'd manage to get through lunchtime today, maybe things were on the up. He continued to look all around him and listen hard. He was aware of everything, the groups of kids, the noises, the sharpness of the wind, even the smell of fresh coffee wafting from one of the windows where teachers took their lunch. He was ever on the alert, but still not prepared enough for Eric Bullen leaping from his hiding place in the bushes and pinning him to the ground. Bullen pulled Drew up by his collar, choking him. A group of Bullen's mates stood around looking casual to obscure the scene from the teacher on duty, then Bullen gave the order.

'Fryman and Mitch, get the skinny little weasel.'

Fryman was an enormous guy. His mum and dad owned the local fish and chip shop in the town. You could fit four of Drew into one Fryman. Mitch was equally tall, though not as thick set. They both played for the local rugby team and neither one of them was used to holding back. Fryman put his foot on Drew's chest and kept him down while Mitch kicked him in the shins. Another boy in the group sprayed his face with water from a drinking bottle. Cheering broke out in the group and they made a close knit circle around Drew. Fryman dragged him to his feet and smacked him around the head. They would have carried on if it hadn't been for two older boys breaking the group up.

'Hey, what do you think you're doing?'

Another girl ran to get help and Drew managed to crawl free and escape. He ran and ran to the other end of the school, no one on duty. He climbed the wire fence throwing all his energy into scaling it before he was caught. He slid over the top and heard a ripping sound as his trousers got stuck on a jagged wire. Half his pocket remained on the fence as he dropped to the concrete on the other side. He landed on his knees and winced at the crunching cartilage on the hard ground. He quickly picked himself up and ran again until he landed exhausted and weeping on the kitchen floor in front of his mother and father.

Ben paid for his coffee at the service station and sat down to check his mobile. No messages. He was an hour and a half from home now, but he tried the number one more time. He unfolded the piece of paper that Ruby had given to him before the BNG team left and started to type in the number. He pressed call and it started to ring. Seven rings later and it clicked onto the Vodafone answering service. He didn't leave a message. He couldn't understand it; she said she was available when he'd mentioned the dates before she left to return to London. Well it was too late now, maybe some other time. He'd send her a text later.

Wired Gerberas stood proudly in a glass vase. Adele was on auto pilot for the return of her husband, doing what she always did and making it nice for him. She made even more of an effort this time. Not because of renewed enthusiasm, but because of the ever increasing burden of guilt weighing on her shoulders. She'd kept away from Bradley ever since that night a few days ago, but it was so difficult, not only for the obvious reasons of him living in the same building and having to work with him, but because she yearned to see him again and to be with him alone She wished that the ache of her desire would leave her, but every moment of the day she relived a moment from that night. She remembered the soft way that Bradley had touched her, his silken kisses and the heat of the fire on their molten bodies. She smiled to herself when she recalled the thoughtful gifts he'd given her, only small things, but caring all the same.

Adele arranged the candles on the mantelpiece and pulled the clean sheets from the pile in the airing cupboard. She'd been at work that afternoon and Bradley had been away. She'd convinced herself that she could manage to work there with him as her boss. That was until he walked in at 4.30 p.m. She felt her heart beating and she couldn't take her eyes off him. She was glad to escape at 5.00 p.m. He, on the other hand remained exactly the same Bradley that he'd always been. So he'd had a romantic liaison which had turned into a sexual encounter, well so what! The price of Cheerios remained the same today as it was before he'd had sex with Adele and the stock room door still stuck with the swelling of the wood. Life went on. He made Adele and Sheryl coffees served with his usual cheeky grin and chatted in his usual casual way. Adele resented Sheryl being there. She was jealous of the affectionate way Bradley spoke to her, even though nothing had changed. Bradley and Sheryl spoke and reacted towards each other in the same way that they had ever since Adele had joined the staff. Adele watched Sheryl and her closeness to Bradley. She even began to wonder if Bradley was physically attracted to Sheryl and whether anything had gone on between the two of them before she arrived on the scene.

The Egyptian cotton sheets lay crumpled on the bed and Adele held the corner of a sheet, staring into space. Her mother would say, 'snap out of it Adele', but her mother would also disapprove deeply. She finished making the bed with dogmatic determination and she forced herself to adopt that attitude in order to get the rest of the tasks finished before Ben came home.

Rory picked his son up off the floor and carried him whimpering to his bedroom. Viv brought up a bowl of warm disinfected water and some cotton wool. They stripped his clothes so that they could see the full extent of Drew's injuries. His trousers were muddy and ripped. His right knee was badly grazed and his shins were covered in red marks which would inevitably turn into bruises. His ribs had a few red bruises and his neck had marks signifying throttling by rough handling. The worst mark was the one near his left eye. It was a red bruise and a cut and it was quite obvious that this had been caused by a punch from someone's fist. The poor child was still shaking and in no fit state to tell them what had happened. Viv bathed his knee and eye wounds and then tucked him up into bed. She stayed with him comforting him while Rory rang the doctor and the school. Rory had to contain his anger when it came to the school. He'd kill the little runt who'd done this to his son. The school were deeply concerned and said that they would send someone to see Drew and in the meantime investigations would take place to try and find the culprit.

The doctor came within fifteen minutes and sedated Drew. He said that he'd been lucky that the cut on his head hadn't gone any closer to his eye and that it looked to him like an obvious case of bullying. He told Rory and Viv to let him get some rest and keep him off school until it was resolved. He would need to stay off until the end of the week in any case in order to recover from his injuries. Viv slept next to Drew that night just in case he woke up traumatised. Rory came to look at the two of them sleeping before he left for his night shift. Viv had her arm across Drew holding his hand. She'd only just got over Justin's secret night time escapade and the earlier glue-sniffing episode. Justin tried to tell her that he and Craig had made a mistake about whose house they were meant to be staying at and then when the arrangements had gone wrong they had to stay out for the night because they couldn't go back to either of their houses at 2.30 in the morning. Viv didn't really believe them, but she told Rory later that they looked like they had learned a lesson and it had probably scared them so much that they wouldn't be planning on doing it again.

Drew's eye was beginning to swell up. Viv moved and he snuggled into her. Rory watched them for a few more minutes. He would never have wished for his two eldest sons to get into any sort of danger, or to be hurt in any way, but the facts were plain to see. Justin and Drew's recent troubles had taken Viv's mind away from her own recent loss. Their needs could be the beginning of Viv's recovery.

Chapter Twenty Three

Ben put his suits away in the wardrobe and flung himself onto the newly made bed. The house was spotlessly tidy and Adele had flowers or candles in each room. She walked into the bedroom to tell him how long it would be before the meal was served. He patted the bed for her to lie down next to him. It reminded her of the way her father used to pat the sofa when he wanted their pet sheepdog to sit next to him. She hesitated and turned away, unable to look him in the face.

'Well come on then.' He patted the bed again and she lay down to begin the ritual of his return. She looked at the clock and subconsciously made a mental note of the time so that she could see how long it took. She'd got into the habit of measuring tasks by time and now the wily figure of guilt threw cold calculating spears telling her that what should have been an act of desire had been thrashed to a mere job to do. Guilt crawled into every crack in the woodwork, not just for the love she didn't seem to be able to find for Ben, but for the yearning to feel Bradley's body next to hers again and taste his wine flavoured kisses. She tried to imagine that it was Bradley, for she knew that her heart and soul had been reserved for the cravings and the longings that she offered to him. It was since he'd shown a physical interest in her that things had really changed. The newness of a fresh body and a different character sparked the fire in her; it was a fire deep within her that could not now be dampened.

In the kitchen she poured two glasses of wine and reheated new potatoes. Guilt followed her in and changed his tack. She shouldn't be doing this to Ben. It was true that he'd had a fling with Ruby from the BNG team, but that was over now and she was sure that he was sorry. Ben was an overbearing man, but he didn't deserve this. She called him to come downstairs for the meal, but he didn't appear to have heard her. She ran upstairs and into their bedroom. Ben flew off the bed, like a startled rabbit, throwing his phone into his briefcase and zipping it up.

'Good God woman you scared me. Can't you come in quietly? I'll be down soon. I need to go to the loo first.'

Adele sighed, left the room and ran downstairs to save the potatoes. Ben unzipped his briefcase, grabbed his mobile phone and sat on the closed toilet seat with the door locked. He started the text message to Ruby again.

'*Sorry I missed u can I meet u on my next trip away?*'

He deleted it and turned his phone off. Then throwing his phone back into his briefcase he joined his wife for dinner.

Adele had gone to great lengths to make it a special meal tonight. The starter was something she'd found in a magazine at work. A pastry case filled with slices of avocado and sun-dried tomatoes, then topped with cheese and baked in the oven until the cheese melted. She served it on a delicate bed of mixed leaves with a drizzle of balsamic vinegar. Ben didn't talk very much at first, slugging the white chardonnay back and twiddling the stem of his glass.

'Interesting,' he said.

'What is?'

'The food.'

'You liked it then?'

He didn't bother to reply, but nodded his head and murmured mmm. Half way through the steak course he got up to open another bottle of wine.

'I'm opening a bottle of Shiraz; you know the one with the red kangaroo on it.' He ran upstairs to their wine store in the spare bedroom and checked his phone for messages at the same time. '*1 new message*'

'*Can u make it 2moro? Confused over d8s.*'

Ben replied immediately.

'*Will c if I can. Text u 2moro early.*'

Ben couldn't quell his excitement, even though he hadn't planned on driving long distances again so soon. He was tired, but it wouldn't stop him seeking out a screw with Ruby. It gave him a thrill to recall her domineering temperament, but he'd have to think of an excuse and that meant scoring a few Brownie points with Adele first.

Ben opened the wine and offered a glass to Adele.

'Superb meal,' he said, patting her hair.

'There's a pudding as well, pear and ginger comfit with vanilla sauce.'

'Well, I've always been partial to a nice pair,' he said laughing. This wasn't going well, he'd had too much to drink and he was saying all the wrong things.

146

Adele got up and served the pudding, bringing the two bowls back to the table. Ben had by now drunk nearly two bottles of wine and he slouched over his bowl with his elbows all over the table. He tried to prop himself up and conduct a conversation.

'How's the job? Is my old mate Bradley treating you well?'

Adele could feel the colour coming up in her cheeks. Act normal, act normal.

'Fine, absolutely fine.'

She didn't expand on anything and got up to make coffee. While waiting for the kettle to boil Ben brought the pudding dishes into the kitchen. He dropped them both and smashed them on the kitchen floor.

'Zorry, zorry,' he slurred. 'Zorry gotta go bed 'Del.'

He helped Adele to pick up the main pieces of the bowls and while they were scrabbling around on the kitchen floor he added, 'Zorry bout Ruby as well 'Del. Really, really zorry.' He held her arm and then got up and took himself to bed. She swept the kitchen floor and sat down in the dark on the sofa. He was really sorry about his fling with Ruby and now she'd gone and thrown it all away. Just like the broken crockery in the rubbish bin; she'd rubbished their marriage and thrown it all away. It was all her fault. Adele fell asleep on the sofa in the dark. Ben lay sprawled diagonally across the double bed, snoring loudly while his phone beeped *'two new messages'*.

Adele woke early the next morning, partly because of the cold. She hadn't bothered to pull the sleeping bag from the cupboard and had been waking constantly during the night. Ben still lay flat out diagonally in the same position as she'd left him last night. She grabbed some clothes from the bedroom and washed and dressed quickly and quietly. Then leaving Ben to sleep she walked up the lane to visit Viv. Rory hadn't left for work yet.

'Coffee Adele?'

He handed her a mug of coffee and the sugar bowl then he picked up his bike helmet and left for work. Adele caught him smiling at Viv on the way out and hoped that this would be an opening for them. Viv sat down with her at the table.

'Is Ben back?'

'Yes, I left him sleeping off the drink. He arrived back fairly late last night. He managed to get himself plastered; he drank nearly two bottles of wine. Then he broke two china bowls before collapsing on the kitchen floor. He couldn't stop apologizing about his fling with Ruby. He said he was really really sorry.'

'Did he?' Viv frowned at her. 'And that makes it alright does it?'

'It's a start isn't it?'

'I think he's going to have to do a lot more than mere apologizing to make it up to you. He's not only treated you badly, but he's had sex with another woman. You've done nothing to be ashamed of Adele and I wouldn't blame you if you had with his temperament.'

Viv poured herself an orange juice and sat down. Adele shifted her bottom nervously on the kitchen stool; maybe she could confide in her friend.

'So you're going to let him get away with it Adele?'

Viv waited for a reply.

'It's just...just that I'm not whiter than white.'

'What do you mean? You're not talking about chatting with Rory are you? You're allowed a conversation with a man for God's sake.'

'No, not Rory, but I have become more friendly with Bradley recently.' Adele didn't expand initially, waiting for Viv's reaction.

'Go on Adele.'

'He started to become friendly towards me at work and then he invited me to lunch when one of the reps visited. We began to chat when I stayed late and Sheryl had gone home early and he invited himself round for a glass of wine while Ben was away.'

'Oh Adele, please tell me that it's gone no further than that. Has anything else happened, tell me?'

Adele hadn't expected Viv to react so ferociously. What did she know about Bradley that she had overlooked? She wasn't aware that Viv knew him for any more than what he was, the manager at the mini-market.

'He's given me a few freebies from the shop, that's all. You know magazines, chocolate, that sort of thing, but that's pretty harmless isn't it?'

Viv looked awkward, but before she had chance to explain they could hear somebody knocking loudly on the door and shouting. Viv went to answer it and Eileen burst in.

'Come quickly, it's Mr Miles. I can see him lying on the floor, but I can't get in.'

Viv and Adele followed the frantic woman to Miles's house. They could see him lying on the hall floor, face down, motionless. The front door was firmly locked. Viv pulled her mobile phone from her pocket and called the emergency services.

'We can't wait around Viv,' Adele threw her weight against the door. 'He could be dead by the time the ambulance gets here.'

None of the three women could budge the door. They sat in the porch and waited, not one of them daring to say the worst. They listened for the ambulance siren in the silence and all that came was a deep rumbling sound. It was the sound of an engine just ticking over, grumbling along the lane.

'It's Rory. I'll stop him.'

Viv ran out in front of the startled Rory.

'Rory, it's Miles. Come quick.'

Rory turned the engine off and jumped off his bike. They managed with the extra strength to break the lock on the door and force their way in. Rory, although not a qualified doctor was up-to-date with first aid and he tended to Miles's needs.

'He's just about breathing and his pulse is weak.'

Adele ran into the hall from the kitchen holding the empty bottles, a concoction of pills, sleeping pills, anti-depressants and paracetamol. Miles moved slightly and groaned.

'Get him up and moving,' Rory shouted out. 'Everyone help to get him sitting and then standing.'

The four neighbours took a part of Miles's body each and had him standing, albeit droopily before the ambulance came. Paramedics took over helped by a commentary by Rory. Adele and Viv looked on helplessly and Eileen was surprisingly and thankfully quiet for once, until they helped Miles into the ambulance.

'Does he need someone to go with him,' Eileen offered. The four neighbours waited in trepidation. Were they going to be told the worst now? The paramedics said that it was probably best that nobody came with them since they had to get Miles to the main hospital as quickly as possible. They could ring later to find out about his condition, but the odds looked good. The ambulance closed its doors and sped off.

Eileen started to cry as they all walked back up the lane together. Adele comforted her.

'You did all you could Eileen. Don't upset yourself.'

Eileen sobbed and could hardly speak for sniffing.

'I know what it's like to live by yourself and he didn't ask to be by himself all lonely without his wife.'

Adele tried to console her. 'We all wish we could have prevented this. I talked of Miles to Viv on many occasions, but did nothing. I feel responsible for not acting sooner Eileen.'

Viv agreed, 'The paramedics seemed optimistic though didn't they Rory?'

Rory answered a short 'yes'. He of all people didn't want to say too much. He'd seen it all before. The desperate people who only wanted to cry for help, not realising that even if they did have their stomachs pumped out they could have damaged their liver irreparably. He'd seen the relatives sat around the bedside of a failed suicide who wished they hadn't done it. Changing their mind after seeing the sorrow on their relatives' faces was too late when they only had a week left to live.

'I'll go in with Eileen,' he said to Adele and Viv. 'I'll make her a cup of tea and make sure she's alright.'

'I'll inform Cameron,' Adele said. 'He's a good friend to Miles, he'll want to know.'

'And all we can do now is hope for the best for Miles,' Adele passed Eileen over to Rory and he touched her hand for assurance on the way past.

'Don't worry, I'll try to reassure her Adele. You get used to knowing what to say in my job.'

Adele left the group to make her call. She said her goodbyes to Eileen, Rory and Viv in the lane. Upstairs in her kitchen a pair of eyes watched her vigilantly. They scanned her body language and scrutinized gesticulations. The eyes couldn't be wrong. It was there in front of them painting a picture of deceit. They ignored Eileen and Viv standing in the background blanking them out completely, for they saw only what they wanted to see.

Chapter Twenty Four

Of all the neighbours in Orchard Court Rory was the least likely to have ended up in Eileen's kitchen, let alone to be looking after her and making her a cup of tea. Eileen's crying seemed to have taken a grip on her. She had her head on the table resting on her arms and she shook with the sobbing. Rory began to wonder about the extent of her grief. Surely there was nothing going on between her and Miles. Rory had seen Eileen trying to hang on to Miles in conversation and feed him up with her rock buns, but had they been engaging in any other activities inside their two houses? No, he told himself, not Miles and Eileen, but the crying wouldn't stop. He quickly made a pot of tea and then sat with her at the table.

'Eileen, it might not be as bad as you think. Providing they get Miles to hospital quickly he should have a chance. Then they'll keep him in while they do a few tests and sort him out for some counselling. He should have been having it all along really, but there was probably no one to push for it in his case You know what the health service is like for saving money. If patients say or even indicate that they don't want drugs or a certain service, the NHS won't push them to have it.'

Rory poured the tea into two mugs and pushed it towards her along with a box of tissues he'd found on the window sill. Eileen took a tissue and blew her nose. She picked up the mug of tea and stirred a spoonful of sugar into it. She wouldn't normally have used mugs to drink tea from, preferring a china cup and saucer. She didn't normally take sugar either, but she hadn't been herself of late. It had been building up ever since Claire left. She'd received a thank you note from Claire in the post about a week after her return, but nothing since. They hadn't talked in detail about what Claire had found in the box on her last evening and Eileen constantly worried about the consequences of Claire's new knowledge. She yearned for her to come back so that they could talk properly. The weeks had gone by. Eileen had made the weekly call to Robert and he talked as he usually did with her. At least it was likely that Claire had kept quiet on the information she'd uncovered. Surely Robert would be different with her if he knew. Well yes, she was sure that he would have wanted to talk to her about it, ask questions and delve deeper. The thing was she'd never intended for Robert or anybody to find out. The members of her family who did know about her secret were all dead now. They had taken the secret with them and she thought she was safe. She should have burnt the evidence, and then no one would ever have found out.

'Eileen, Eileen, can you hear me?'

Eileen realised she was staring right ahead, right through Rory and out of the window.

'We can ring the hospital tonight about Miles. I'll ring and find out for everyone, so don't worry. You don't need to get yourself distressed like this.'

Eileen paused for a second, and then she looked at Rory.

'It's not just Miles. There are other things.'

'What sort of things Eileen?'

'Don't misunderstand me Rory, I think a great deal about Mr Miles and I really hope that he'll pull through, but it's not just about him.'

Eileen paused again. She was thinking back to something her mother had told her years back. *If you want to keep a secret Eileen you don't tell a soul. People say that they won't tell anyone, but they always do and your story will become more and more warped on each time of its telling. It's like a game of Chinese whispers. Folk like to gossip and the more that they can spice up the tale the more they will be pleased with themselves. You keep your business to yourself my girl.*

She looked directly at Rory.

'Let's just say Rory that I have a few issues to sort out with my niece, Claire. I'd rather not say any more than that.'

'Fair enough Eileen. I understand teenagers well enough. How old did you say your niece was?'

'Eighteen.'

'Gone through the worst of it then. Although I don't know what girls are like in comparison to boys. I've got all boys myself and they've been bad enough lately.'

Rory continued with his sagas of Justin and his friend sleeping out and poor Drew getting beaten up at school. Eileen was pleased that he'd been side tracked and she listened intently to his problems. She was sorry that she'd run his children down before and chided herself for her narrow-mindedness. Rory finished with a touching sentence.

'Of course Viv always wanted a girl. That's why she was so upset when she lost the baby recently. And I had to go and make things worse by pre-empting events and having a vasectomy. I could have ruined everything and I'd be lost without my Viv. I'm still not sure that she's forgiven me.'

Eileen was amazed at Rory's openness with her, but on the other hand most of Rory and Viv's business was shouted out live in the lane at some point. They seemed to thrive on their open air arguments.

'I'm sure Viv will forgive you eventually Rory. What about your son, Drew? Is he alright now?'

'Yes. He's still recovering from the injuries, the bruises are gradually fading. They found the culprits and the community police are involved. They're going to interview the little sods, sorry Eileen, but when it's your own...'

'I understand Rory, I'd feel the same if it were my son.'

'Anyway, they hope to involve their parents and eventually organise some sort of punishment, like supervised community service. When Drew comes back he'll be in a different class and have a different timetable for his lessons, which means that he won't bump into the lads that bullied him very often, if at all.'

'Well Rory, it sounds as if they've done their best to correct the situation.'

'Yes, I can't really complain. They've even got an in house counsellor for the kids at school now. Mr Nichols, the principal came to see Drew at home and he said that he could go and chat to the new counsellor about how he felt and anything that worried him.'

Rory got up to leave, feeling satisfied that his conversation with Eileen had calmed her.

'I'll let you know about Miles's condition Eileen. I'll be ringing early this evening. I'll let everyone know as soon as possible.'

Eileen watched Rory through the kitchen window walking back to his cottage at the top end of the lane. She wondered what he would think of her if he was privy to her secret. Perhaps it had been a good thing that Claire had unearthed her past. It had reminded her that she wasn't flawless herself and prompted her to consider other people once more. Her judgemental attitude hadn't done her any good with her neighbours. They were ordinary folk, just like her doing their best to be honest and kind. If she couldn't

153

make allowances for them and quell her bigoted opinions it was a pretty poor show, a poor show indeed.

Adele let herself in and went upstairs to her own part of the house. Bradley stopped her on the stairs.

'What's going on down there? I heard the siren.'

Adele briefed him on Miles.

'I can't recall the man. I don't think he came into the shop very much.'

'No, he probably didn't. He didn't go out very much at all. He never really recovered from his wife's death. He was devoted to her.'

'Can't say I really understand folk who do that sort of thing though, suicide I mean.'

Adele stared at him in disbelief that he could make such a statement when the tragedy was so fresh.

'You've obviously never been that desperate Bradley,' she replied and she walked off and back to her own house.

She wondered whether Ben had heard the siren or whether he'd even woken up from the drunken stupor yet. As she walked into the kitchen he stood there in his dressing gown waiting for the kettle to boil. He had his arms folded and glared at her.

'So you decided to drag yourself away then did you?'

'Did you hear the siren Ben?' She asked as he was obviously unaware of Miles's collapse.

'What siren? Don't try and change the subject Adele. I've been watching you.'

Adele ignored his strange comments and retold Miles's story for his benefit.

'Well I'm very sorry that Miles felt that desperate.'

Ben made his obligatory statement of sadness for Miles and then latched back into attack mode.

'So I suppose your idol was the hero of the day was he?'

'What are you talking about?'

'Rodney, he was the hero. I bet he barged down the door and you swooned in admiration.'

'Ben, Miles could be lying in the morgue by now for all you know and you're making up stories about Rory. All Rory did was his duty as a sincere and caring citizen.'

'Well you would stick up for him wouldn't you? I saw you Adele, through this very window.' Ben pointed to where he'd been standing. 'You were talking to him for a while, so don't try and tell me that you're not interested in him.'

'Rory is a nice man, but I really am not interested in him.'

'That's it Adele, lie through your teeth. I know what I can see with my own eyes.'

'And you probably did see me talking to Rory in the lane a few minutes ago, along with Eileen and Viv.'

She paused to look at him, but he stood there defiant with his arms folded. He poured the water into the tea pot and folded his arms again.

'Anyway, I'm not sticking around today. I've had a call and I'm off to Birmingham for the rest of the day so you can go and chat to lover boy for as long as you like.'

Adele was generally a patient girl, but Ben's accusations infuriated her. Before she knew what she'd said it was out.

'It's not Rory you ought to be worried about it's Bradley.'

'And what do you mean by that? Bradley's my mate, he's one of the lads, he wouldn't let me down.'

'That's why he waited until you were well out of the picture before he really started on me.'

'What do you mean, started on me?'

Even though Adele knew she was implicating herself, she felt a strange satisfaction in crushing Ben's perfect image of his so called friend.

'Ringing me to offer to keep me company and then coming round with plenty of wine to seduce me.'

'So are you saying that you've been shagging Bradley?'

'Yes,' Adele replied. She took an odd kind of pleasure from two counts. One was that she could tell Ben that he was wrong in the judgement of Bradley and two was that she had flattened Bradley's iconic existence. And he had the cheek to tell her about putting someone on a pedestal. She held in a slight laugh, but this time Ben could no longer hide his anger. He slapped Adele hard across the face.

'I'm going before I do something I regret,' he said. He ran up the stairs to get changed. Then he picked up his car keys and didn't even bother to say goodbye to Adele. He simply grabbed his black gentleman's umbrella and left slamming the door.

Chapter Twenty Five

Bradley stood outside the entrance to Adele and Ben's flat. He heard every word of their agitated conversation and winced when his own name was mentioned. Shit, why the hell was she coming clean? He of all people knew that that was the last option unless you really wanted out. He heard Ben stomping around the place and at this point made his escape downstairs, promptly changing his mind when he reached the door to his flat, leaving the building instead. What if Ben came to seek him out? He couldn't stay now, he knew that much. He crept up the lane and hid behind the entrance to the garden steps. He could peer out from here and check that Ben's BMW had gone. Within minutes he heard the thud of Ben's footsteps vibrating the ground; they collided with the sound of his own shuddering heart pounding against his chest. His throat tightened and he prayed that Ben wouldn't come looking for him. Ben threw his briefcase into the back of the car, slammed the door and screeched off. Bradley stayed in his hiding place for a few more minutes before making a move to his flat. He had a lot to sort out and he had to move fast. Someone else walked past as he came out, but whoever it was didn't see him and walked straight past. He crept into the lane and saw that it was Rory. Bradley followed him as he walked with a purpose in the same direction as Rory, to Adele's. He listened as Adele came to the door.

'How is Miles?' she said, trying hard to quell the shakiness in her voice.

'There's no news. I rang the hospital, but they won't give out any information until they're sure of his condition.'

'You will let me know Rory, as soon as you hear.'

'Of course I will. It'll probably be tomorrow now. Are you alright Adele? You look pale.' Rory squeezed her hand.

'I'm fine Rory.'

'Sure?'

She nodded.

'Okay, so I'll see you tomorrow Adele.'

She smiled back at him.

'See you tomorrow Rory.'

Ben stopped at the traffic lights at the edge of town thrusting his fist into the palm of his other hand. Taking his anger out on the accelerator he pulled away in a cloud of exhaust fumes. Thoughts inside his head jumbled like a furious whirlpool and unable to extract them and place them in any order he started to repeat the slogan for the conference he'd attended recently in a frustrated rap on his steering wheel.

'Make the connection' – with our new summer selection from 'It Fits!'

He tapped out five steady beats on the wheel.

'Make the connection'

'Make the connection'

He rose to shouting and thumping the steering wheel.

'Make the connection'

'Make the fucking connection, shit the fucking connection. It was there all the time staring me in the face.'

A sudden sickness came over him and he had to look for somewhere to pull in. He swerved into a lay-by just in time to dive out of the car and vomit in the hedge. Urging three or four times until his stomach was empty he wiped his mouth with a white silk hanky from his trouser pocket. He poked the vomit with a stick from the hedge.

'That's just what you're worth, a pile of puke in the gutter.'

A lorry driver had parked in the lay-by to relieve himself. He'd seen Ben and started to walk over to him.

'Are you alright mate?'

'I'm okay, I'm okay.' Ben put his hand up in a waving gesture resembling a thank you and he quickly got back into the car.

'Heavy drinking session was it?'

Ben ignored him and pulled away. Let him think it was a hangover. It was better than anyone, even a stranger knowing he was married to a whore.

Bradley waited for Rory to leave before going upstairs to knock on Adele's door.

'I heard the argument earlier. Are you okay?' He leaned on the door frame waiting to be invited in.

'Did you actually hear what was said?' she answered, wary of his reaction to her earlier words.

'Are you going to let me in and I'll tell you,' he said.

'Come in then Bradley, come in.' She dragged him inside and checked the corridor in angst before closing the door and bolting it.

Adele walked through to the kitchen and Bradley followed. She made coffee and handed him a mug. He took it, but then put it down on the work surface so that he could take her in his arms. He kissed her on the lips and hugged her tightly.

'Don't you worry about him and his threats. He's got no right ...' She silenced him, kissing him back. She pulled his shirt out of his trousers and ran her hands underneath, relishing the warmth of his bare skin. He responded kissing her neck and undoing her blouse. Then he scooped her up in his arms and carried her to the bedroom. They spoke no words, concentrating their energies on their immediate passion for each other. Clothes flew into a scrambled pile on the floor and their tangled emotions twisted their naked bodies in crazed excitement. She screamed her pent up frustrations in shameless ecstasy and he indulged in pure carnal enjoyment. They lay panting in exhaustion under crumpled sheets, wet with perspiration. He leaned on his elbow stroking her hair.

'Where did you say your husband was going when he stormed out?'

'Birmingham.' She pulled him back down on the bed next to her and wrapped her arms around him. She'd tried to push the feelings away, but just now had proved she wasn't strong enough to resist.

'I don't like this Adele. He could come back. I'm not happy about being here with him in that raging mood.'

'He won't come back. He never has before.'

'But you told him didn't you?'

'About us,' she hung onto his arm stroking him gently. 'Yes, I did. I couldn't hold it in. I wanted him to find out and to know that you are more than just one of the lads as he makes out.'

'Well he knows that alright now doesn't he?'

Bradley got up and started untangling the pile of clothes. He threw Adele's at her.

'Come on. Let's get dressed and have that coffee.' He kissed her on the cheek and started dressing himself.

Adele made fresh coffee and handed it to Bradley.

'You've got a lovely rosy glow on those cheeks now.'

Adele blushed herself even redder and put her arms around Bradley's waist.

159

'So what about us now Bradley, where are we going from here?'
He didn't answer at first, looking down at his shoes.

'I know where I'm going,' he replied.

'What do you mean? Where?'

'To Manchester. I've been offered another job. I'd planned on turning it down. I wanted to be near you, but now it's out, about me and you I mean… it would make sense to take up the offer.'
Adele stared at Bradley with her mouth open.

'You've never mentioned a move to Manchester before.'

'I didn't think I'd have to. You can come as well Adele. Divorce him and come with me. You'd probably get quite a packet with your half share of this place. It would buy us a great place in Manchester, property's cheaper up there.'

'When are you going?'

'As soon as I can. I'll go up there and suss out the joint and when everything's more settled I'll send for you. You can sort out your marital arrangements here, get your half share from the stupid bastard and we're made.'
It all sounded a bit far fetched to Adele. She knew that she'd fallen in love with Bradley, but to rip up her roots again and run off with him was a different matter. She hadn't known him for long, not long enough to judge what he was really like. He finished his coffee and put his mug in the sink. He drew her towards him for a final hug.

'Look Adele, I'll be off as soon as I can, but I'll be in touch and I'll be back.'
He kissed her cheek and left.

Ben drove on and joined the duel carriageway filtering onto the motorway. He'd arranged to meet up with Ruby today, but thought better of it. He was too angry with Adele for the embarrassment she'd caused him. He'd carry on to Head Office and get involved with some work there. Ruby could wait; he'd call her and make his excuses later. Ben felt no guilt about his previous meetings with Ruby, after all he was a bloke and that's what blokes were like. They couldn't help it, it was in their make-up, but for a woman to behave in a promiscuous way – well that was different, different altogether. What if they did end up getting divorced? What would the company say? What about his immediate boss?
Two lanes expanded into three.

How would all this affect his position and would it jeopardise any future promotions? Globules of sweat formed on his forehead and the vortex of rage swirled around his brain and churned the acid in his stomach. The tongue that had hours ago uttered vicious and livid words lay dry and parched like paper scorched in the oven ready to crumble into the dust of his worthless future.

60...

All those years with her wasted, when he could have been with someone decent. His mother had been right. A dreamy girl could never be a virtuous one. Great, not much traffic on the road yet. Only another half an hour or so until his turn off.

70...

What would his mother say? And then there was the course on sales techniques he was due to go on next month. He would have got her out of the house by then. After all, why should he leave? He hadn't done anything wrong. Speed limit flashing 50. He wished they wouldn't do that. It never meant anything; they just wanted a valid excuse to give someone a speeding ticket.

80...

Watch out for police just in case.

All his work colleagues had honourable and respectable wives, some with children. His mother had always warned him to watch her and he'd always assumed it was something to do with the mother –favourite son bond.

Sod the bloody caravans. Get in the other lane.

Always knew that Bradley was one for the women, but not 'Del. No wonder he'd had been so keen to rent the downstairs flat. He should have seen it coming. Ben wondered whether Bradley would be around when he got back or whether he'd try and hide. Well he can't hide from me forever.

90...

When he got hold of him he'd beat the shit out of him. Compulsive shaggers like him never did an honest day's work. They were like cuckoos moving on to other people's nests depositing their seed. Better work out a reason for deciding to drop in at Head Office. He couldn't reveal the real reason just yet.

Slow down, lorry hogging outer lane.

SHIT IT'S STATIONARY!!!

0...

161

Bradley packed the rest of his belongings and sat on the suitcase to close it. He wrote a cheque out for the rent he owed and left it in an envelope on the table by the entrance to the flat. Then he picked up the carrier bags with the rest of his worldly possessions, popped the keys to the flat inside the envelope with the cheque and left.

Chapter Twenty Six

Claire drove cautiously at a steady speed of 60 M.P.H. in the slow lane of the M5. She'd past her driving test four weeks ago and it was only her second time on a motorway. The journey wouldn't be too long from Glastonbury to Devon. She had a note of her aunt's address and hoped that she could remember how to get there from when dad had driven there before. She'd told her mum and dad that she was visiting an old school friend for the weekend and she hadn't told her Auntie Eileen she was coming. It was seven weeks since she'd last seen her, but Claire hadn't stopped thinking about what she'd discovered in that box. She'd kept it to herself and mulled over it day and night. She'd been on the brink of telling dad on several occasions, but stopped herself. She needed to talk to her aunt first, now that all the information had sunk in. There was a certain rapport with Claire and her aunt, even though she hadn't spent an awful lot of time with her. Claire found her slightly old-fashioned and quaint but at the same time her aunt surprised her at times with an uncharacteristic remark, such as the time when Claire had been reading an article on the model, Jordan. Claire had remarked that Jordan always flaunted too much of her body and her aunt had replied with 'Well if I was her age dear and had bosoms like that I think I'd like to show them off.' Claire had been flabbergasted into silence. After that her aunt had placed tea on the table in her rosebud china teapot, along with milk in a jug and the sugar bowl with its little lace covering to keep insects off. The remark and the following actions didn't match up somehow and it made her think that there were definitely two sides to her aunt.

Claire pulled the chain on the green woodpecker and waited for the door to open. Eileen stood with the door handle poised in surprise.
  'Are you going to let me in Auntie Eileen?'
Eileen threw her arms around her niece and hugged her until she screamed for breath.
  'Sorry Claire, I wondered whether I'd see you again. How did you get here?'
Claire jangled the car keys and beamed proudly at Eileen.
  'I drove myself, in mum's car.'

'So soon after passing your test. Your dad told me a few weeks ago you'd past and first time you clever girl. Well done.'

She wiped a tear from her cheek and held Claire's hand leading her to the kitchen where she put her bag down and they both spoke together.

'Can I stay?'... 'Are you staying?'

Eileen put the kettle on and Claire sat at the table.

'So auntie has anything interesting been happening in Orchard Court?'

Eileen told her about the apple tree waiting to be examined by the arboriculturist and the latest on Miles.

'You must have been so frightened when you found him. Have you heard if he's okay?'

'No, it only happened yesterday and they wouldn't tell Rory anything last night. We should know something today. Poor Mr Miles, he really loved his wife. I'm praying he'll be alright.'

Eileen put the tea pot on the table and sat down.

'You're not really here to ask about the neighbours though are you Claire?'

Claire fiddled with the coaster on the table nervously.

'I'm not sure that I took in the whole story from my brief look in that box.'

'You got the main idea though didn't you?'

'I think so, perhaps we should talk about it to make sure I haven't come to any wrong conclusions.'

'Were you shocked when you discovered all my secrets Claire?'

'I don't know about shocked. I was intrigued. And...I think mum and dad should know. I think they have a right to know.'

'No, no please Claire. Let's talk about this first. I don't think that's a good idea.'

'And I don't want to fall out with you about it.'

Claire picked up her bag.

'It is alright if I stay with you isn't it auntie?'

'Of course dear, you're welcome anytime you like. Only I was afraid after what you'd discovered that you wouldn't want to come back.'

'Can we talk about it later auntie? I'm tired from the driving at the moment, could I take a shower? And by the way, I told mum and dad that I'm staying with a friend from sixth form who moved to Cornwall. As I said I've got mum's car and I bet she'll be checking how many miles I've done.'

'Won't she try and ring you at your friend's house?'

'I haven't given her the number and besides she'll ring me on my mobile. That's the beauty of mobiles auntie, you don't always have to be where you say you are.'

Eileen didn't have a mobile phone and didn't want one. Her phone had a cord so you had to sit on the draughty stairs while the phone sat on the hall table.

'I'll make the bed up while you're in the shower Claire.'

'Okay, thank you.' Claire kissed her aunt on the cheek and went upstairs. She lay for a few minutes on the bed. The pink floral bedspread was laid across the mattress, but there were no sheets underneath. Everything in the room was quaint and whimsical. It didn't always match in colour and design. The curtains were purple floral and the wallpaper a green leafy pattern. It was neat and tidy, but behind the times. There was a clock on the wall in the shape of a gold star and Claire reminded herself that she must take the battery out of it before she got into bed that night. It had kept her awake last time with its loud ticking. Eileen came into the room with some sheets.

'Oh, you're not in the shower yet.'

'No, I was just having a rest. I'm a bit tired after driving down from Glastonbury. It's my longest drive since I past my test.'

'Then I'll leave you to it dear.'

Eileen went downstairs to see what she had in the freezer for a meal later on. She remembered when she'd lived in Glastonbury for a while to be near to Robert and Carmel. She didn't miss it now. Personally she recalled it as rather a strange place with some odds vibes about it. She took out a vegetable lasagne and some bread rolls and made up a salad from bits and pieces in the fridge. In her larder Eileen found a bottle of gooseberry wine, a prize from the raffle at a WI function last year. She put it into the fridge with the salad and went back upstairs to make Claire's bed.

Eileen pulled the pink bedspread straight and went to pull the curtains. Outside in the lane she glimpsed a woman she'd never seen before being invited into Viv and Rory's house. Now who could she be? She leaned to one side of the window, but she still couldn't see. Viv ushered the woman in and then closed the front door. Eileen wondered if it was the tree specialist. Yes that would be it. She hung on behind the curtain in case they came outside again and she could have a better look, but they stayed where they were. The bathroom door clicked open. Claire must have finished her shower. Eileen pulled the curtains closed for Claire's privacy. They collided with each other as Eileen went to leave the bedroom causing Claire to drop her towel on the way into the room. Eileen picked it up for her, but as she got up she came face to face with Claire's array of embellishments to her tender young body. Claire pulled the towel from her auntie's grasp and wrapped it around her quickly. Eileen stood there in silence for a few seconds and then burst into an explanation of what she'd planned for supper.

'So are you sure that you like vegetable lasagne Claire?'

'Yes it's fine. I'll get dressed and be down in a moment to chat to you.'

Claire gently pushed her auntie out of the room and closed the door. How much had she seen? She'd better not tell her mother, or her father for that matter. She pulled on her jeans and a pink t-shirt, brushed her wet hair and went downstairs.

Auntie Eileen was at the door when Claire came downstairs. She was talking to the man who worked in the hospital. Claire noticed that she'd already poured two glasses of gooseberry wine and left them on the kitchen table. She sat at the table and waited. She couldn't quite hear what they were talking about, but guessed that it was probably about her auntie's neighbour, Miles. She took a sip from one of the glasses of wine while she waited. It was sickly sweet and quite flowery. She poured a bit of it down the sink and washed it away. She wouldn't want to offend her auntie. She looked at the label on the bottle – Gooseberry Wine. The date was only last year and there was a sticker on it saying First Prize. She wondered what the second and third had tasted like. Auntie Eileen had made such an effort even at such short notice. The kitchen table had a smart gingham cloth in mauve and white squares and she'd lit an old cream church candle in the centre. On one side was a salad with a bottle of French dressing and on the other some crispy baked rolls revived from the freezer. She'd even made butter curls in a glass dish to go with the rolls. Claire could smell fresh basil and melted cheese and she peeked inside the oven to see the lasagne gently bubbling. She hoped that Miles would be okay, auntie Eileen seemed to be quite fond of the old guy. She wondered whether she held a flame for him, but no, at their age it was probably just companionship she was looking for.

Claire sent a text message to her mother to tell her that she'd arrived safely. Hopefully that would keep her off her back and she wouldn't ring her up and start asking difficult questions. She heard the front door close. She waited.

'Well? Is he okay?'

Eileen didn't have to reply. It was painted all over her smiling face. She picked up the full glass of wine and took two large slurps.

'I'm drinking to his recovery, but he's out of danger. And the hospital said he was lucky that his neighbours acted swiftly.'

'That's great news. How long will he be in hospital?'

'Rory said that they weren't sure yet, but long enough to monitor him and take some more blood tests.'

'So you'll be able to go and visit him.'

'I hope so, but you don't know how glad I am that he's made it dear. Anyway, let's eat.'

Eileen pulled the lasagne out of the oven to cool and they sat down together.

'Claire?'

Claire looked at her aunt avoiding eye contact. Eileen picked up her glass and took a sip of wine.

'Yes?'

'This wine is rather sweet and sickly isn't it?'

Claire laughed.

'I'm glad you said it auntie. I was half afraid to tell you and I thought, I thought…'

'You thought I was about to tell you off about those piercings and the tattoo.'

'You mean you saw everything?'

'Everything and I'm amazed your mother has allowed you to do it.'

'She hasn't, that's the problem. Well, apart from the naval piercing. She knows about that, but she hit the roof when I showed her. That's why I decided not to tell her about the rest.'

'What about your father? Does he know?'

'He only knows the same as mum.'

'Well I must say that I did quite like the tattoo.'

'You did?' Claire was pleasantly surprised again by her aunt's liberal attitude.

'I'm not sure about the piercings though. Still, I suppose you can always remove them if they become unfashionable or you get bored with them.'

'So you won't tell them?'

'I don't see any point in telling them dear. It's only going to cause an argument and it's not as if you're causing yourself any harm. You're only decorating your body. You can't even see them when you have your clothes on.'

'I never thought that you'd be like this Auntie Eileen. You're so open-minded for...'

'For an old-fashioned spinster auntie you mean. Well dear, I suppose a lot of things have happened around here lately. A lot of things to make me think about what's really important to me and what I value most of all. You know that nice man, Rory who called just now on his way home from work to tell me about Mr Miles? Well I used to run him and his family down. Then one day I talked to him and I realised how narrow-minded I'd become. And I certainly don't want to lose you dear over being intolerant of teenage fashions and trends.'

'And you wouldn't lose me over what was in the box either auntie.'

'Are you sure about that Claire? Maybe it's time that we talked about what you saw and understood from what was in the box. I didn't put it back in the loft after you found it last time. It's here in the larder.'

Eileen got up and cleared the dishes to the draining board and then she went to the larder to find the box. She placed it in the middle of the gingham cloth and sat down opposite her niece.

Chapter Twenty Seven

Ruby paced up and down the main reception area of Strensham services. He was half an hour late already. Where the hell was he? She checked yesterday's text messages and he'd definitely said northbound and not southbound. Well she wasn't staying more than another fifteen minutes. She could pick up on that cancelled appointment again in Evesham and the afternoon wouldn't be wasted. She got herself another espresso and sat in the café area. She sent Ben a text *'where r u?'* and fumbled through her briefcase to locate the owners of the garden in Hinton-on-the-Green, near Evesham. On the next table were two policemen and one policewoman. The woman sat with her head in her hands while the men tried to feed her with coffee. One put his arm around her and eventually she took his handkerchief, blew her nose and took the coffee. The other man started reconstructing some sort of incident with the packets of sugar, salt and pepper. They all shrugged their shoulders and the woman dried her eyes, then they became silent and drank their coffee staring at each other.

Ruby found her phone so that she could rearrange her appointment. It flashed a message at her *'unable to send'*. It was the message to Ben. Maybe she'd ring him instead. The phone clicked into the automated message – *'this number is unavailable, please check and try again.'* If she was honest with herself she wasn't particularly bothered, he wasn't that good in bed anyway, but she didn't like being given the brush-off. Perhaps he'd had to change his phone number. Whatever, she wasn't going to hang around looking like a lost sheep any longer. She walked quickly to her car and took the A road to Pershore, avoiding the motorway. As she drove across the bridge she looked down onto the traffic crawling along the M5 underneath. There were road works, but it appeared worse than ever today. It was possible that he'd been held up, but 45 minutes was long enough for any woman to stand around jilted with no explanation. She put her foot down on the accelerator leaving the motorway behind and looked forward to the usual night with Dave tomorrow night in Gloucester. Dave was a long distance lorry driver who met up with Ruby every three weeks on his way back from deliveries in Scotland. Dave always appreciated the trouble she went to with her appearance. He brought flowers with him and told her she was stunning. He'd spend a night with Ruby before heading back to Merthyr Tydfil to be with his wife and kids. Dave looked after his body working out with weights in the gym. Now there was a bloke worth waiting for.

Adele wondered whether she should pack some of her clothes and go to stay at her mother's for a while. She didn't know what sort of a mood Ben would be in when he returned. Looking on the kitchen floor at the two plates he'd thrown at her she wished now that she hadn't told Ben about Bradley. It had all come out of her mouth on the spur of the moment and now her life was a tangled mess. She had been in a good position before she admitted her own adultery and it had been a big mistake to think that a man as bigoted as Ben would understand why she'd done it. Bradley hadn't turned out to be the knight in shining armour that she'd been hoping for. In fact he was as big a bastard if not worse as the one she already had. As soon as the heat was on and the affair was out in the open he was off like jack rabbit with a firework tied to his tail. She wondered whether he would keep in touch or indeed come back for her. She half hoped that he would and that possibly she could be wrong about him. Perhaps he did care about her and maybe he would stand by her. Anyhow, no matter what was going to happen, she plumped for the idea of going to her mother's for a few days. It would be quite a good idea in the light of everything, so she pulled a suitcase down and packed a few pieces of underwear before she heard the doorbell.

'Hell, who is that now?' she closed the suitcase and went to open the door. It was Rory with a woman she didn't know. The woman had blonde hair tied neatly back into a bun and wore a dark suit.

'Can we come in Adele?'

Adele stood back allowing them into the hallway. The woman looked official, like a police officer. Miles! It must be about Miles. Adele looked at Rory and then the policewoman.

'It's about Miles isn't it Rory. Please tell me it's not bad news. We were too late and he's gone hasn't he?'

Rory closed the door and guided Adele to a chair in the lounge.

'Rory tell me. Is he okay?'

Rory finally spoke.

'Miles is going to pull through Adele. He'll be okay, but I want you to brace yourself for some other news. It's Ben.'

Rory allowed the policewoman to deliver the rest of the news.

'Mrs Parker, I'm afraid your husband was involved in an accident on the M5 earlier today. Several cars ploughed into a lorry on the outside lane. Ben was taken straight to hospital and I'm so sorry to have to tell you this – despite the paramedics' efforts to revive him Ben died on the way.'

Adele sat very still in the armchair. Rory held her hand and she stared straight ahead. The policewoman knelt on the floor beside her. She waited for some sort of reaction, but none came. On other occasions she'd seen women burst into spontaneous floods of tears when she'd told a wife that her husband was dead. Adele kept her mouth closed and her breathing shallow. Her eyes didn't move. They focused on nothing in the air in front of her.

Rory let go of her hand.

'Look after her while I make some tea.'

The policewoman sat down very warily next to Adele. She didn't attempt to put her arm around her. She was stiff like a statue and it was as if the tenderness of a stranger was unwelcome. Rory beckoned to the policewoman. She followed him to the kitchen. He pointed to the handset of the phone, where Adele's mother was first on the list of known numbers.

'I'll phone her and let her know what's happened. She'll know what to do. Adele's very close to her.'

The policewoman stayed with Adele while he made the call and after she had left, Rory sat by Adele's side. He said nothing, he was just there. He only got up to answer the door to her mother about an hour later.

Adele watched her mother while she swept the terracotta tiles, emptied the remnants of the two smashed dinner plates into the bin and made a drink for the two of them. She sat in silence while she held her hand and drank hot tea. She knew that it would be a strain for mother to sit still for this long. At home she had never sat still for very long and preferred to be up and about, focussed on a task of some sort. Adele also knew that she would find the house in spotless order with few jobs that she could occupy herself with. She hadn't felt like speaking very much, but managed to get out the plea for her to stay with her for a while. Cynthia had gone straight to the car to collect her bag and promptly made the bed up in the spare room as well as changing the sheets on Adele and Ben's bed. She seen her mother changing the sheets and said nothing.

She was lucky that her mother had no pressing commitments at home and she'd heard her whispering the few cancellations to the Oxfam shop and to her friend for the church toddler group next week. Cynthia had lived by herself for ten years now, since Adele's father died of a heart attack on his allotment. She remembered the day that they had been alerted by father's friend, Harold. They'd all run up the hill together, getting there seconds before the ambulance did. They found him lying face down amongst all his cabbages. He still had his trowel gripped tightly in his hand. The ambulance staff knew that there was nothing that they could do to save him and when they transferred him to the stretcher he looked as if he had a smile on his face. Her mother told them to leave the trowel with him. At least he had died in a place where he loved to be. It was a place where he could be away from mother's bossiness.

Adele laid her head on her mother's lap, both of them keeping the silence. It was strangely comforting for Adele to recall her father's death at a time like this. Her mother had felt guilty about her bossiness after father died, but she had always ruled the roost. She'd dictated to him the exact time that meals would be served and shouted at him when he forgot to take off his muddy boots before he came into the kitchen. He'd suffered mother's domineering behaviour since the day he married her, but that was the sort of man that he was. He was quiet and submissive and Harold always said that father probably liked her mother organising him and telling him what to do. It meant that he didn't have to think of how to bring order to his own life. He was happy for her to do it for him.

Adele yawned and moved her head on her mother's lap. She wouldn't tell her about her troubles with Ben, not now, there was no point now, but all mothers and hers included had intuition when it came to their children. Her mother had picked up on her lack of appetite when she last visited for tea and she'd told her how pale her skin was and how she ought to get some more sleep to stop dark patches around her eyes. She always asked after Ben and noticed how he'd made himself scarce in the past year or so. Adele

172

made excuses for her husband saying that he was busy with his work, but things were certainly different since she had first brought Ben home to introduce him to her mother. It must have been at least seven years since Adele brought him home. He was charming then and mother had taken to him instantly. He had a good job and was very well dressed. He was polite and he thought the world of Adele. She was convinced that this man would look after her. That was then.

Adele allowed herself to be guided by her mother to the bedroom. She changed into the pyjamas she'd found for her and slid under the crisp clean sheets. Her mother sat with her and held her hand until she finally fell asleep. As she was drifting in and out of sleep she could hear her mother scurrying around the house washing the last few cups and pulling the washing out of the machine to hang out the next day. She heard her come back into the room to check she was asleep before retiring to bed herself. Finally she heard mother whispering to herself as she lay in bed. She'd done it since father died, like a sort of pep talk to herself. *'You're going to have to be strong for that girl of yours in the next few months Cynthia. She'll need you to help sort things out, but don't you go bossing her around mind. She's her father's daughter and don't you forget it.'*

It was cold on the landing at 4.30 a.m. as Adele subconsciously made her way to the spare room. She got into bed next to her mother and snuggled up against her. She wrapped her arms around her and her mother pulled her closer, settling her for a while until at around 5.00 a.m. the crying came.

Adele sat bolt upright and wailed for the world to hear. She held her hands over her eyes and the tears tumbled through her knuckles trickling over her wrists. She sobbed, rocking her body backwards and forwards. Her mother waited with her arm around her shoulders. The grief broke free from her body as she wept to oblivion, but the words wouldn't come. The crying enveloped her in a watery dirge, but still, still no words.

Chapter Twenty Eight

Crispin read the email three times before he could believe it. Poor Adele and she was traumatised according to her mother. It was only in the last few days that Adele had emailed him to tell him about Miles and to explain that with the upset in their lives they hadn't been able to concentrate on sorting out the tree problem. He made up his mind to call or email her mother with his condolences after the meeting. Perhaps it was just as well that Adele didn't have the BNG team trampling over the garden at the moment.

Ruby chaired today's meeting and she sat, crossed legged at the head of the table. She wore a cobalt blue wool suit and she tapped her matching blue patent stilettos against the table leg in agitated fashion. She hadn't had time to straighten her hair this morning and it surged over her collar in a fiery lava flow to her waist. She waited to open the meeting, strumming her bronze painted nails on the table. She made sure that the meeting didn't go on a minute longer than the scheduled thirty minutes. She was due for a nail infill and couldn't be late for the beautician. Ruby snapped her notepad shut and made for the door. Crispin stood by her chair ready to speak.

'Before you disappear Ruby I have something to say if you could wait just a few minutes.'

Ruby tutted and stood listening with her hand on her hip. The whole of the usual BNG crew were in the room now ready to listen.

'I'm sure that you all remember Orchard Court and their problem with the protected tree. I've been informed this morning that Adele Parker from Orchard Court has lost her husband. He died in a road accident yesterday. It's quite tragic and Adele only told me recently that another of the neighbours is seriously ill in hospital. So obviously we will have to shelve the ideas for their garden for a while. I only wish I could think of something I could do to help.'

Ruby shifted from foot to foot, checking her mobile in her bag.

'So that's why he didn't turn up yesterday,' she said quietly to herself. Crispin turned around. He must have misheard what she'd just said.

'That's it everyone, just to keep you up-to-date.'

Ruby stood behind him sending a text to her beautician.

'Right I must go,' she said and she flew from the meeting room without a care in the world.

Rory and Viv sat at their kitchen table eating a late breakfast. It was a good feeling to have all four boys safe at school and no trouble fizzing in the background. Justin had settled down to work in his last year at school. Spending more time with his girlfriend, Laura had helped. She was steadfast and sensible. She even helped him with his homework. Drew had settled into his new class and said he'd only seen Eric Bullen once since he'd been back. Harry and Jake hadn't been up to any major upheavals in the house and they hadn't even been hitting each other as much recently.

All in all Rory judged it as being a good a time as any to bring up the dreaded subject of his vasectomy again. He buttered another slice of toast and poured them both fresh mugs of tea.

'Viv,' he said slowly. 'How are you feeling lately? I mean how are you feeling inside your head?'

'Inside my head? I haven't had any headaches for ages Rory.'

Rory rephrased the question to suit her practical outlook.

'But you definitely feel physically better after the miscarriage?'

'Yes, I'm okay and I'm due for a check up at the end of next week.'

'Ahh, well…' Rory still seemed unable to get the conversation started. The telephone rang and Viv jumped up.

'I'll get that, you finish your toast.' She rushed to the lounge to answer it. Rory spread marmalade on top of the butter and waited. She didn't come back and after five minutes he started the washing up. Where the hell had she put the washing up liquid? There was always a bottle by the sink and a spare one in the cupboard under the sink. He turned the tap off and waited for her return, collecting the plates and bowls together in a heap to wash. Viv finally walked back into the kitchen holding the phone.

'What have you done with the washing up liquid Viv?'

'What have they done you mean.'

'Who?'

'Harry and Jake, that's who I mean.'

Viv paused for a moment before continuing.

'That was Harry and Jake's school. Apparently they rampaged in the playground before lessons this morning.'

'What do you mean, rampaged?'

'With washing up liquid bottles. They took the two bottles from here. They emptied the washing up liquid into the new water feature in the environmental garden and flooded the place with foam. Then they filled the bottles up with water and ran around the playground squirting other children.'

'Well at least they've joined the family team. We're all either a bunch of trouble makers or sad cases with problems.'

'I don't think it's anything to jest about Rory. And they didn't wash the liquid out of the bottles properly, which meant that the school had at least ten children in the medical room having their eyes rinsed. We could have been sued by the parents of those kids.'

'Oh, don't panic Viv.'

'Don't panic! They want the boys collected and taken home for the day.'

'I'll come with you Viv. It's better that there's two of us.'

'Thanks, I'll get my coat. We can go now and get it over with.'

Harry and Jake stood in the head-teacher's office looking extremely sheepish. They hung their heads in shame when their parents walked in.

'Good morning Mr and Mrs Cunningham, do take a seat.'

Rory and Viv took their places on the rather hard seats opposite the two boys. The head-teacher stood up and paced the room. The two boys faced their parents and as the head-teacher walked through the middle of them Rory couldn't decide who was on trial. Was it the boys for their mischievous deeds or them as examples of bad parents? They all stayed rigid and silent in their places until the lecture on bad behaviour, the importance of good examples and respect for people and property had been delivered. Rory was the first to speak. He tried to keep calm and smooth the waters over. If Viv thought that she was being accused of anything she'd be on the warpath, head-teacher or not.

'I'm sure that Harry and Jake are sorry that they've caused harm to other children and damage to the environmental garden, aren't you boys?'

They both nodded. The head-teacher waited for more, before he turned to Rory and Viv and replied.

'I hope that you're in agreement if I ask the boys to write a letter of apology to all the children who ended up with washing up liquid in their eyes. It would be a start on making amends.'

Viv joined in the discussion.

'Of course we'll see that they do that if you could give us a list of the names.'

Rory added, 'And we'll pay for the damage to the water feature.'

The head-teacher thanked Rory and Viv and showed them out. It was agreed that the boys would be suspended from school for the rest of the day.

The boys were quiet as they walked up the hill from the school back to their house. They had to pass the mini-market on the way and as they approached it Rory stopped Harry and Jake. They looked up at their father as he handed them £1 each. Viv stared in annoyance at her husband.

'They've just been hauled over the coals by the head-teacher and you're giving them money to spend?'

'It's not for treats Viv.'

He turned to his two sons and told them quite calmly.

'There'll be no pocket money for you two this week, except for the £1 each that I've given you. I want you to go into the shop and buy a bottle of washing up liquid each, since you wasted ours from home. Then you're going to your room for the rest of the day. Understood?'

The boys went meekly into the shop and came out a few minutes later clutching a bottle of washing up liquid each. They handed it to their father and said 'Sorry Dad,' in unison.

When they got inside Viv told them to do as dad had asked and they could come down for something to eat at lunchtime.

'Maybe it will give you time to think about what you did,' she said.

She slumped into a kitchen chair and breathed out in a huff of exhalation.

'I thought you handled that quite well, for you anyway,' Viv said with a hint of praise to Rory.

'What do you mean "for you anyway,"?'

'I thought you were going to let them get away with it and not give them any form of punishment. I know it was only devilment and they probably didn't think about the residue of washing up

178

liquid or that they'd ruin the water feature, but they need to realise that what they've just done was stupid and thoughtless.'

'Well perhaps I'm good for some things Viv. I must admit that I was slightly worried that the head teacher was going to give *us* some form of punishment.'

'So did I. He was quite intimidating wasn't he? I was glad to get out of there. What do you think he would have in mind for us?'

'Oh I don't know. Maybe something like detention and 100 lines of "I must be a more responsible parent" or perhaps he'd make us clean the swimming pool or sell raffle tickets for the summer fayre.'

'Do you remember what you did last year at the school summer fayre?'

'Yes, I had a brilliant job. I ran the bar.'

'Yes and right next door to the beef burger stall. How convenient.'

'I didn't even have any washing up to do. It was all plastic cups and disposable containers.'

'Well at least we can do our own washing up now we've all had our turn of sadness and trouble. Perhaps we can wash all our troubles away at the same time.' Viv put her rubber gloves on and she and Rory cleared away the breakfast dishes. At the end while Rory was still drying mugs Viv sat down and hung her gloves over the chair.

'You know Rory I've been thinking.'

Rory held on to the mug tighter.

'Yes, I've been thinking very seriously Rory. About losing the baby and how much I had wanted that child. And about how much I love small children anyway. Maybe it *was* fate trying to tell us something. Trying to tell us that we have enough to contend with already. Let's face it our four boys are quite a handful aren't they?'

'So what else do you think fate was trying to tell us?'

'That I should accept our loss and make the most of my, I mean our life.'

'And?' Rory said hopefully.

'And that I should forgive you for having the vasectomy. Even though that was your own daft idea and nothing to do with fate intervening.'

Rory sat down next to her.

'Do you really mean that Viv? That I'm forgiven. I couldn't believe my bad luck when you lost the baby. I mean I wouldn't have minded you having another baby if that's what you wanted and I would have loved it just like all the others.'

'I know you would Rory.' Viv put her hand in his and continued.

'There's something else Rory. It's something that I want to do. I could get recommendations for it, especially with my previous experience of nursing and bringing up four children of my own.'

Rory sat in trepidation waiting for her to unveil her plans. Surely she didn't mean surrogate motherhood or God forbid that she wanted him to have his vasectomy reversed.

'Go on Viv,' he urged.

'I've been thinking of registering as a child minder. That way I could look after babies and small children for other people who work. I'd be getting paid for it and I'd be able to hand them back at the end of the day. It would allow time for our boys when the children had been collected and we'd have some time together in the evenings.'

'That sounds a great idea Viv,' Rory relaxed his hand in hers. It was perfect. Viv could overdose as much as she liked on babies all day, cooing with them, reading them stories and singing songs with them.

'I'm glad you think so,' she said. 'I was also thinking of the garden. It would be so convenient to have the garden refurbished by the team that Adele organised. They could make it child friendly, a sand pit maybe and a nice soft lawn to sit on. They only put it on hold because of the tree being protected didn't they?'

'Yes, although I don't think she's going to feel like arranging anything after the accident.'

'No, the poor girl. You know I always thought that he appeared slightly rough towards her. He bossed her around a bit and bullied her. I watched him at that drinks party when the Breaking New Ground team came down to visit.'

'I think you're right Viv and maybe if things weren't right between them it'll make her feel guilty, although she shouldn't need to. She's a lovely girl.'

Viv let go of Rory's hand and a frown settled on her face, sifting away her excitement over the new venture. Rory put his arm around his wife.

'Not as lovely as my girl though,' he said. 'You're the loveliest girl in the world.'

Chapter Twenty Nine

Miles was still under a cloud when Rory and Viv visited the next day. Cameron had been to visit the day before and squeezed out the answers to the questions they all wanted to know. He'd be arriving home next week and only allowed to stay the extra time in hospital because he lived alone. Social Services had organised a grief counsellor to visit him at home and his GP would monitor his progress on the anti-depressants. It would be a long haul but the team of people looking after him would be meeting and checking up on him at regular intervals. If only they could persuade him to be patient then they'd be on a winning streak.

Miles didn't have very much to say in this early stage of his recovery and Rory and Viv found conversation slightly stilted, Rory less so than Viv as he was used to speaking to patients. They decided on the way into hospital not to tell him of Adele's tragic circumstances just yet. He wouldn't be ready to hear of a death by road accident when this was the very thing he was grieving over himself. However, Gina, his counsellor had said to Cameron that this could be something which could help him at a later stage. Perhaps he could offer support and sympathy for Adele when he was on the road to recovery himself. She said it would help him to rebuild his confidence by helping someone else in the same position. They managed to raise a smile to his face when they mentioned Eileen.

'Eileen would like to visit you Miles. Would you mind?' Rory asked knowing full well Miles's views on the sweet, but interfering lady.

'Tell her I'd like to see her if she makes me a promise.'

'What's that?'

'That she promises to stop calling me *Mr Miles*.' He laughed and Rory and Viv laughed with him. 'I suppose she's of the kind who believes that just because I'm a solicitor I'm a cut above the rest. Well I don't think like that. I'm a normal chap just like anyone else. Being a solicitor is just my job, so tell her nicely to stop calling me Mr Miles.'

'Don't worry, we'll tell her for you. Are you ready for the crate of rock buns she's probably already made to bring in?'

'He sounds like he's going to be alright don't you think?' Rory said as he reversed out of the parking space.

'He will be if everyone keeps their promise to visit him. Eventually he'll be able to return to work. Cameron will keep something open for him I'm sure.'

'Are you okay to see Adele? Her mother's still there. I wonder how long she'll be staying.'

'At least until after the funeral I should think.'

'Her mother said that should be at the end of next week. She's taken control of most of the arrangements and will let us know as soon as it's been finalised. It's going to be a quiet service with Adele's immediate family and the neighbours that knew him.'

Rory parked the car at the end of the lane and walked with Viv to Adele's house.

Adele had started to talk to her mother today. She'd thanked her for what she'd done so far and said that she was so glad that she would be staying to help with the arrangements. She sat at the kitchen table holding her mobile phone. She hadn't heard from Bradley since he'd left for Manchester on the same day as Ben had the accident. Unless he'd been back to the shop without her knowing there was no way he would have heard that Ben was dead. Up until now as she'd been suffering from shock it hadn't crossed her mind to contact him and their agreement had been that he would be the first one to contact her. Under the circumstances though she felt that she should tell Bradley and it wouldn't come as such a jolt when he came back home. She connected to his number and listened to the ring tone. There was no answer and it finally clicked onto the answer message. She hung up, composed a short message in her head and rang again leaving a brief note in her own voice. *'Brad, I know you said that you'd ring me, but I have some very serious news to report. Ben was killed in a road accident on the day that you left for Manchester. I've been suffering from shock, but don't worry I think I'll be okay and my mother is here to help me. Hope to speak to you soon, lots of love. A.x'*

Adele heard the telephone in the lounge and allowed her mother to answer it. This particular call seemed to have her mother perplexed and Adele eventually worked out that it must be the arboriculturist. Cynthia took down his number and said that someone would call him back. She walked into the kitchen.

'Adele, what on earth is an abreecuturist?'

For the first time in days Adele broke into a smile.

'It's an arboriculturist mum. He's a sort of tree expert. He was coming to inspect the apple tree in the middle of all the gardens. I can't remember when he was supposed to be coming. Did he say?'

'Next Wednesday, but do you feel like dealing with him at the moment?'

'If I'm honest, not really. I suppose he could be put off.'

'What about Rory and Viv. They telephoned this morning to see how you were. Couldn't we ask them to deal with the tree chappie? They wondered if they could visit you, so I invited them round this morning. I hope that was okay, but you were asleep when Rory telephoned this morning.'

'Of course it is mum and it's a good idea to ask them to see the arboriculturist.'

The doorbell rang and Cynthia went to answer it. Rory and Viv stood outside with a large bunch of pink chrysanthemums.

'Come in, come in,' Cynthia stepped aside to let them in. 'she's expecting you, she's in the kitchen.'

As they entered the kitchen Adele already had the kettle on. Viv gave her a hug and placed the flowers on the table. Adele made a pot of tea and Cynthia took over with the pouring and the talking. She talked in quite a matter of fact way about the funeral arrangements. It was an open and in some ways a cold conversation, but Rory and Viv were glad that they only had to listen and nod rather than ask delicate questions.

'You will come to the funeral won't you?' Adele turned to Rory and Viv. 'It would be a great support to me and there won't be a huge crowd of people there, only Ben's mother and sister, his work colleagues and a few neighbours. We hadn't had time to make many friends in the town.'

'Adele doesn't want any flowers,' Cynthia added, 'but if anyone would like to make a donation to the NSPCC we'd be grateful.'

'And after the service,' Adele continued there will be a light tea, sandwiches, sausage rolls and such things at The Hexbury Green Hotel.'

Cynthia joined in again. 'Yes, Adele and I thought that a hotel would be better than inviting everyone back here. I always think that's the worse part of a funeral, when you have to go back to the person's house. You see all the photographs and memories still lingering. It's upsetting for everyone.'

Viv moved closer to Rory and picked up her tea.

'You seem to have everything sorted out Adele and of course Rory and I will be there. We'll bring Eileen with us. Miles will still be in hospital; he's coming out the following day.'

'How is he?' Adele asked.

Rory and Viv explained the morning's account.

'We even persuaded him to allow Eileen to visit him.'

'Well I can see why he wanted to avoid Eileen, but she is a sweet lady and she has the best intentions.'

'She's about the same age as Miles isn't she?'

'I don't know. It's very difficult to tell with a slightly old-fashioned woman such as Eileen.'

'They could be really good friends if Miles would only give her a chance.'

Viv put her cup down on the table. She didn't want the conversation to go any deeper and risk upsetting Adele.

'We'll just have to wait and see won't we. Let's hope that they both give a little bit and only time will tell.'

Viv picked up her handbag and coat. She gave Adele a final hug and promised she'd be there for support next Friday. Cynthia showed Viv and Rory out, but before they walked away she stood outside the door with them.

'Would you two do something for Adele?'

They listened intently.

'Of course, what is it?'

Cynthia explained about the arboriculturist and that they merely needed to phone him and rearrange the appointment, then be on hand to speak to him and show him where the tree was when he arrived.

'She was so excited about the garden project before all this tragedy and if we could just keep it going until she feels better.' Cynthia lowered her voice to a whisper. 'Between you and me,' she said holding her hand up against her face, 'I don't think that things were going too well between Ben and Adele. I only hope that she won't bear any guilt for his death.'

Viv held Cynthia's arm.

'Don't worry, we'll keep it going for her after all when it's finished we'll all be able to benefit from our own little paradise.'

186

Chapter Thirty

Eileen still hadn't replaced the box in the attic. She wondered whether she should bother now. Maybe she should leave it in her wardrobe and look through it occasionally. She sat down at the kitchen table and tipped the contents out. There used to be a time when she couldn't even bear to think about the box and all its contents. She couldn't imagine how she'd found the courage to put it all together in the first place. At the time when it had all happened everything had been so raw and painful. She did vaguely recollect wrapping the Crown Derby egg cup in newspaper and placing it with the collection. She was only a girl at the time and the collection had been made so that one day the truth would be known. Now she was sure that it should remain a secret. It was a secret known only to her and Claire. She'd told Claire that if she died before her, which taking her age into account she probably would, Claire could do as she thought best. She was so lucky that Claire had understood and most of all had respected her wishes.

Eileen took everything out and placed it carefully on the table. She would have to leave in fifteen minutes to catch the bus to the hospital. There wasn't enough time to muse over something as great as this. She covered the box contents with a clean linen tea towel, made sure that Bertie the cat couldn't get into the room and made haste to go and visit Miles.

Sheryl locked up at the shop. The stand-in manager had gone home early tonight. Sheryl had been completely nonplussed at Bradley's swift resignation from the manager's job. She knew that when he was in trouble that he would always try to run away from it, but to go to Manchester was taking it a bit far. Surely things couldn't be that bad. He must have known about Adele's bereavement because he'd sent a card in the post for her. He'd sent it to the shop c/o Sheryl. She found that slightly strange. Why hadn't he sent it direct to Adele at her house? It wasn't as if he didn't know the address, he lived in the same building himself for God's sake. She put the card, along with her own in her bag ready to give it to Adele tonight. She picked up a bunch of mixed flowers from the shop and locked the main door.

The bus had gone the long way around all the villages and houses on the way to the hospital. It had taken much longer than Eileen had allowed for and to top it all she felt extremely sick from the bumpy twisting and turning ride. She got off the bus and took herself on wobbly legs past the main reception area in the hospital to the lift. Miles would be on the fifth floor, so Rory had pointed out, but looking at her face in the thin shard of mirrored tile on the inside of the lift she couldn't go and see him with the face of a ghost. She took the lift to the café on the seventh floor. She remembered from when her friend from the WI had been in hospital having her hysterectomy that the café was really only for staff and relatives looking after patients, but she didn't think they'd notice. She bought some still water and dry Jacob's crackers. She sat still and ate the crackers and sipped the water slowly. Gradually the colour crept back to her cheeks and she gathered her thoughts for visiting Miles. She swept the crumbs from the table and tipped them into her glass. 'Now I must remember not to call him Mr Miles,' she said to herself. Rory had explained nicely to her earlier. She hadn't got upset; it just hadn't occurred to her that her choice of name would annoy him. She got up and took her glass back to the counter. Looking at her watch she could see that it had taken her nearly two hours to get to the hospital and to recover from the harrowing ride. There would hardly be anything left of visiting time now. She made her way down to the fifth floor and asked the ward clerk where Miles Harper was. He was asleep, but Eileen said she'd sit by his side for a while and wait. The nurse who showed her the way seemed to think that Eileen was Miles's wife and before she could put her right she disappeared down the corridor to answer a buzzer.

Eileen waited. She read the newspaper left on top of the locker and then waited again. Miles still slept. Eileen didn't want to disturb him and she watched his relaxed body ebb and flow with his deep slumbering breaths. An afternoon trolley of drinks arrived and still Miles didn't stir. The auxiliary nurse asked if Eileen would like a hot drink.

'Is he still asleep? He's been asleep for most of the day. Still they say it's the best healer don't they?' She handed Eileen a strong cup of tea. The nurse who had shown her in arrived and looked at Miles's chart. She smiled at Eileen.

'At least you can be with him, even though he is asleep,' she whispered and she put the chart down to go on to the next patient. Eileen quickly followed her.

'I'm not his wife,' she whispered back frantically. 'My name's Miss Dolce, I'm a neighbour and friend.'

'Oh, I see. I'm sorry I haven't been properly briefed on Mr Harper yet.'

'He tried to take his own life. His wife died in a terrible road accident on the A30 a few years ago. He hasn't got over it, not only her death but the way that she died.'

'I think I remember reading about it in the newspapers. It was pretty horrendous wasn't it? Poor man, I'm glad you talked to me Miss Dolce. I hope he gets the right help.'

Eileen sat down again and began sorting out her handbag. Although she'd left the bulk of her collection on the kitchen table, she did grab a couple of photos and put them in the zipped compartment at the back of her bag. There was one of her when she was just fifteen. She wore a white cotton dress and her long dark hair was loose. There were flowers interwoven in her hair, like a crown. Davey's sister had made it and he'd given it to Eileen as a present for her birthday. He'd also given her a brooch. It was a black cat with sparkly green eyes. She could see it pinned on the lapel of her dress. She sat on a swing, well it wasn't really a proper swing. It was a piece of rope attached to a huge horse chestnut tree with an old chair top that his father had found at the tip. The other photo was of both of them. She'd written on the back 'Davey and Me'. He was sixteen at the time. He had his arm around her. His hair was slightly long and jet black, as black as the darkest cave and his eyes matched the darkness. She remembered falling headlong into the pools of pitch black like the midnight sky lit by occasional sparkles of stars. In the photograph she could just about make out the gold hoop of his earring. She'd wanted to have her ears pierced at the time. Davey's mother said she'd do it for free, but her mother wouldn't have any of it. She said it was bad enough that Eileen had got involved with the likes of them anyway. She was reminded of how handsome Davey was. The photograph captured his warm smile. He was smiling down on her and in his hand he had a small bunch of wild bluebells and campions to offer her. He had little else of monetary value to offer, but she didn't mind about that. It was Davey himself that she wanted, not his possessions.

Miles had stirred in his sleep, but Eileen hadn't noticed. He opened his eyes and saw her there, sat on the chair next to him, staring at a couple of old photographs.

'Eileen! How nice to see you. How long have you been waiting to see me?' He propped himself up and ruffled his hair out of the sleepy style.

She didn't answer immediately and then quickly put the photographs back in her bag.

She touched his arm. 'I expect you're feeling better after all that sleep. I've made you a date and walnut cake and don't worry if you don't feel like eating it just yet I'm sure that all the nurses in here would be only too happy to help you out.'

He grinned to himself inwardly. She meant well and she seemed to think that everything could be smoothed over with the help of a home-made cake. He knew now that it was going to take an awful lot more than a few home-made cakes to sort his life and his head out, but he also knew that he would have to let people such as Eileen in. He would from now on have to open the door to his heart again. It would be painful, but with the pain would come new friendships accompanied by peace and understanding.

'Thank you for coming,' he said. 'And thank you for the cake.'

She must have sat there for ages. It was way past visiting time now. She was so quiet and enraptured by the photograph she'd been looking at when he woke up to find her there. Perhaps there was a different side to this woman that he'd found so annoying over all these months. She chatted to him in an energetic fashion over the next half an hour until the trolleys came round with supper. He apologised for not being able to match her conversation at the moment, but said that he had been feeling more like talking every day.

'Perhaps you could come and have a cup of tea with me at my house when you're feeling more up to it,' she said, stopping herself just in time from calling him the old familiar name.

'That would be very pleasant Eileen and will you allow me to order and pay for a taxi for you rather than have to put up with the dreadful bus journey you had earlier.'

She prepared to resist, but Miles thrust the money into her hand, explaining that one of the nurses would make the call for her.

'Please,' he said 'after all the time you've spent getting here and sitting with me. It's the least I can do.'

She finally nodded and accepted. As she waved goodbye supper arrived and Miles raised his hand back to her with a hint of a smile. Eileen walked towards the hospital lift and for the first time she felt that the door to Miles's closed-in world had been left ajar. He'd let her in and sanctioned her sympathy and kindness. She'd never wanted to patronise or feel sorry for him and today she had allowed that feeling to trickle through in the conversation. Maybe she'd never be able to fully understand how he felt or comprehend the trauma he'd suffered, although she knew what it was like to have loved and lost and she knew that life had an uncanny knack of providing unexpected help of some kind around the next corner.

Chapter Thirty One

Viv held the telephone number for the arboriculturist in her hand. She'd welcomed the chance to help Adele, but something stopped her from making the call. It wasn't just the fact that she knew nothing about trees or gardening for that matter. Nor was it fear of actually using the telephone. It was a slight feeling of sickness in her stomach; a feeling that had come on since she'd lost the baby. She used to feel so sure of herself, but now there was an underlying sensation of doubt. On the piece of paper with the telephone number was another name and number. *Crispin at Breaking New Ground 02081469270.* He was the man who came to the drinks party wasn't he? She'd chatted to him for a while. She remembered thinking on that evening how relaxed and gentle he seemed, especially compared to his brash and garish looking assistant. Viv picked up the handset again and this time dialled Crispin's number. She had no idea of what she was going to say to him, but maybe she'd just chat in general and then she'd feel better about having to deal with the arboriculturist. Damn, the phone rang followed shortly by an answerphone message.

'Hello, this is the answerphone service for Breaking New Ground…**Hi can I help?**' A welcoming voice chirped in at the end.

'Is that Crispin Grainger?'

'It certainly is, how can I help you?'

'My name is Viv Cunningham from Orchard Court.'

There was no need for Viv to have any worries when talking to Crispin. He explained in detail what she would need to say to the arboriculturist. He asked after Adele and Miles and was pleased when she told him how Adele had been coping.

'So there's no need to worry about phoning the arboriculturist Viv.' Crispin waited for her response. He'd found the plans for Orchard Court on his file and he looked at the design brief on his screen. There were sketches of the proposed changes. He closed his eyes for a moment to picture the finished garden with its archway entrance and central pond complete with fountain. They'd planned an attractive walled-in sand pit in one corner surrounded by an interesting patio to include replica glazed fossils of fish and birds. The pond was the main feature with its lilies and a few silver koi carp and the seating built into the stone wall. The residents of Orchard Court deserved to have a garden like this to enjoy. He began to close his conversation and say goodbye to Viv, but then it came to him – he could help.

'Before you go Viv, would you prefer it if I rang the arboriculturist? I've dealt with this kind of problem many times before and I'd know how to follow it up.'

'Well, isn't it our responsibility? I mean, you must be busy enough already.'

'Strictly speaking yes, it should be the residents themselves that deal with a situation like this, but I'd like to help all of you. Especially as Adele has had such a dreadful time and Miles I understand has been suffering.'

'That's very kind of you Crispin. Are you absolutely sure?'

'Yes, I'm positive about it. I've been trying to think of a way I could help Adele after her awful news and besides you're all nice people in Orchard Court. You need something like this to give you a boost and lighten the load.'

Adele sat over her bowl of muesli, stirring, but not eating.

'Come on, eat up my girl. You need to sustain yourself. I know it's difficult, but if we can get through the next few days.'

She knew that her mother meant well, but she couldn't explain to her what she really felt. There was the guilt that Ben had died following the revelation of her brief fling with Bradley and even more guilt that her heart still yearned for Bradley when she should be grieving for her husband. There had been no telephone call from Bradley since she'd left her message informing him of Ben's death. She'd checked her mobile every few hours for texts and messages, but nothing. She gulped down a few more mouthfuls of muesli to please her mother and then took her coffee to the computer to check her emails. There were ten junk mail items, one from her auntie and one from Breaking New Ground gardening team - Nothing from Bradley. Perhaps something had happened to him, something that prevented him from contacting her. What could it be? She could think of very few reasons that would excuse him from sending condolences and concerned wishes. She read the other emails. Her auntie sent her sympathy and said she hadn't been able to telephone as the line was engaged. She would be there at the funeral on Friday. Breaking New Ground had already sent a card in the post but further condolences were sent from Crispin. He told Adele that matters were in hand for sorting out the protected tree and asked if she would mind if he attended the funeral on Friday to represent the wishes of the team. She replied.

'Dear Crispin, Thank you for your help and concern. Of course - come to the funeral on Friday. It's very sweet of you to pay respects on behalf of the team. You are also welcome to join our family and friends at the Hexbury Green Hotel afterwards. Adele.'
Adele couldn't help thinking that in life it was always the quiet, genuine people like Crispin that sunk into the background, while the phoney charlatans breezed in stealing all the limelight.

Cynthia came into the room having been downstairs to check on the ground floor flat.

'There was a bit of junk mail on the mat. I'll put it in the bin shall I? Oh, and this.' She handed a brown envelope to Adele and took the rest of the mail away. The envelope was addressed to Mr B Parker and felt bulky. She opened it. Inside were the keys to the flat along with a cheque and a letter.

The letter was very short and to the point.

Dear Ben

Please find enclosed a cheque for £225 to cover my rent until the end of the month. I was hoping that you would waive the notice normally required to quit the tenancy. My keys are also enclosed.

Yours Bradley Blake

It couldn't be – he said he'd be coming back. She read the letter again. It couldn't mean anything else. He'd tied up all the loose ends and it looked like he was gone for good.

Sheryl took the flowers out of the jug of water. She hadn't found the time to visit Adele last night, but today she told herself she must make the effort after all the kindness Adele had shown to her. She had the day off today and by mid-morning had finished all her washing and housework. She wrapped some kitchen towel around the wet flower stems and checked that the cards were still in her bag. The sun was shining on her back as she walked and the warmth of the day made it feel bright and cheerful, until she got to Orchard Court. She looked up at the garden from the bottom of the lane and the gnarled old apple growled down on her. She watched for a while as its branches swayed like arms in the breeze; arms that blighted the joy of the sunlight and shielded its frowning trunk from the pleasure of warmth. It was certainly an ugly specimen and she couldn't understand why such a hideous tree should be protected.

Adele and her mother had only just returned from a walk into the town when Sheryl got there. They stood outside with the key half way in the lock.

'Sheryl, how lovely to see you,' Adele put her bag down. Sheryl quickly off-loaded the flowers to Adele's mother and gave Adele a huge hug.

'How are you Adele and I'm sorry I haven't called around earlier?'

Cynthia ushered them inside.

'I'll put these in water and make you a drink. You go and talk to your friend. Is tea okay for both of you?'

'Thanks mum,' Adele led Sheryl through to the lounge.

'She's a gem your mum isn't she?'

'She certainly is.'

Everything was so tidy in the house. Nothing of Ben's had been touched as yet and Cynthia would have told her daughter that it lacked respect if she'd tried clearing out too early. That could wait until a few weeks after the funeral. Then it was a task that had to be done, so that one could start afresh. Adele could get on with her life then. Sheryl felt dubious about sitting on the sofa. The cushions were so perfectly puffed up and arranged so neatly. Adele sat in an armchair and her mother came in with a tray of tea.

'Sit down my dear. You don't need to wait to be asked.'

She left the room again and let the two girls catch up.

'I've got two cards for you in my bag Adele.' Sheryl produced them and handed them over. Adele opened Sheryl's card, a simple sympathy note with embossed lilies. She put it on the mantelpiece with the others.

'Thank you Sheryl. So who has sent the other one?'

'Oh, I think it might be…' Sheryl didn't finish her sentence as Adele had already ripped open the envelope. It was a small plain white card with a cross on the front and the words 'In Sympathy'. The words were few inside the card and Adele sat still in her chair staring at the card. Sheryl looked over her shoulder.

'To Adele, Sorry to hear about Ben, Bradley.'

'Is that all he could think of to say?' Sheryl chirped in without too much of a thought.

'Apparently so.' Adele still held the card tightly.

'Mind you I was quite surprised to hear about his resignation.'

'Resignation?'

'Yes, didn't you know? I suppose you haven't been into the shop to find out. He resigned from the job and as they owed him some holiday it meant that he could go straight away.'

'But I thought…he told me that they'd offered him a better job in Manchester. He said he was coming back for a while after it was all settled.'

'Oh he won't be back if I know him. It is true what he said about Manchester though. That's where he's gone. We have got quite a few stores located in the north and sometimes he would cover for other managers on holiday. It just happened that two of the stores were in Manchester. And it just happened that he met Sharon there. I thought that it was quite a casual relationship, but according to the manager in our store up there that's where he's gone.'

Adele put the card down on the table. She went to speak, but her voice came out as a croak.

'To be with Sharon you mean?'

'Yes, and Sharon's been quite lucky apparently. She had a lottery win recently. She won half a million. She paid off her small mortgage and she still has bucket loads of it left. She divorced her husband two years ago so she told our area manager that she's going to enjoy spending the rest of it now.'

Adele couldn't speak at all now. She stared into space. Sheryl carried on blithely, completely unaware of how much pain she was inflicting on her friend and workmate.

'So I suppose Bradley will hurry his divorce along now that Sharon's on the scene.'

'Was he married?' Adele squeezed from her throat.

'Oh yes, if you could ever call it that. You know what he was like; I mean it was obvious to all wasn't it? His wife thought he was having an affair with me at one time. We used to have a bit of fun together, me and Brad, but I never really took him seriously. She kicked him out in the end after he'd stayed at my house for the weekend. We'd been clubbing with a few of my mates and he was too drunk to go home. When he finally did get back his clothes were in the front garden and her hard case of a brother was standing watching Brad from the window.'

'He didn't have… have any children…' Adele stammered.

'Kids, yes just the one, little Tommy. He must be two and a half by now and so cute. His wife used to bring him into the shop when she was still speaking to me and to him for that matter.'

'I didn't know…'

'You didn't get to find out much about Bradley at all really did you?'

Adele didn't answer and she'd turned a putrid shade of pale green. Sheryl stopped talking.

'Are you okay Adele? You don't look well.'

Adele still didn't speak and stared straight ahead.

'I'll go and get your mother.'

Cynthia came in and held Adele's hand. Sheryl put her arm around her.

'We were talking about work and things, or rather I was talking. Then she clammed up and went this awful colour. Oh God, I hope it wasn't anything I said.'

'Don't worry my dear. Grief can have this affect on people sometimes. It's a very strange animal, grief. I think she needs a lie down.'

'I'll go now and leave you to it. I hope I didn't upset her.'

'Thank you for coming around dear and you will come to the funeral tomorrow won't you?'

Sheryl nodded and made a quick exit. Cynthia took her daughter to the bedroom to lie down. She lay with her for a while, smoothing her beautiful auburn hair. It would all start to get better after tomorrow she told herself. After the funeral it would all seep out of the festering wound of bereavement and when all the sadness, sorrow and regrets had been talked about and aired it would start to heal. Day by day mourning and wretchedness would fall away to be replaced by new friendships and fresh beginnings.

Adele slipped into a deep sleep and her mother left her, covering her gently with the duvet. She crept quietly into the lounge to retrieve the tray. She wiped the table and plumped up the cushions. A white card lay on the table and she read it. Bradley? That was Adele's boss at the shop wasn't it? Jolly decent of him to think of her and send a card. She placed it on the mantel piece with all the others and took the tray outside.

Chapter Thirty Two

Eileen opened her wardrobe and selected a few items to choose from for the funeral tomorrow. She remembered Adele's wishes for brighter colours and not for the usual sombre all black. Eileen didn't have a huge selection of fashionable clothes; she'd always considered them a frivolous waste. Besides she had no idea of what was in vogue at any particular time. It came down to a choice between a delicate pink blouse and a woollen skirt in a darker pink or a pale lemon dress with a thin strappy belt. She held them up at the window, having no wish to try them on in order to decide. Perhaps the dress was a tad cheap and cheerful. She put it back in the wardrobe and hung the skirt and blouse on the back of her bedroom door. Maybe she could add her old grey crimpolene jacket to it and black shoes and handbag. After all there was no need to throw sombreness completely out of the window. It was a funeral after all. She surveyed the outfit all together. It would do. She smiled to herself as she wondered what Claire would think of her mismatched apparel.

Eileen tipped out the contents of her one and only handbag on the bed. She added two packets of tissues so that she could assist any relatives who'd be upset at the ceremony and some smelling salts, just in case. She checked her purse for change for the collection and put in a plastic scarf for good measure along with her telescopic black umbrella. At least it would match the bag and shoes and one couldn't be holding up a garish bright red umbrella at a funeral, no matter what was all the rage nowadays. There, she was all ready for tomorrow. Rory and Viv would pick her up at 10.20 a.m. and they would drive into town and park near St Matthew's church. She was pleasantly surprised that Adele had chosen to have a church service after all although Rory had explained that Ben's mother requested a formal procedure at a Church of England church. She had also requested that Ben's ashes be interred at the church in his home town of Croydon. Rory said that he thought that was a bit much, after all Adele was his wife and she should decide on a matter as delicate as this. Eileen responded telling Rory that Adele was a kind, considerate girl and she had obviously thought about the dire grief of a mother losing her child at such a young age. She'd then changed the subject fairly swiftly, being attuned to Viv's recent loss. She wouldn't want Rory to think that she was criticising his views after they had left the stilted awkwardness of previous association behind them.

The two photographs that Eileen had taken to the hospital in her handbag lay forlornly on the bed. She picked them up and took them downstairs. The box and its contents were still on the kitchen table, covered loosely with a clean cloth. She still hadn't plucked up the courage to look through everything. Claire would tell her to bite the bullet and face up to it. She'd already told her that it wasn't so bad in the light of today's society, but Eileen had said that that's how it was back then and you couldn't change what folk thought in the past. She went to the kitchen window and pulled the curtains across slightly as she did whenever she left the house. Checking that the front door was locked she sat down resolutely at the table. Pulling the cloth off she folded it neatly and put it to one side.

Everything was taken slowly and purposely and one-by-one its memories were extracted. Each recollection was aired in her mind and replaced in the box. The delicate flower crown had almost disintegrated. It had been wrapped in tissue paper, but the colour had left the blooms years ago and she only had to touch the brittle buds for them to collapse into blue/grey dust. The black cat brooch was wrapped in the same tissue paper. It had survived the time well. The green eyes still sparkled giving the creature a look of mischief and devilment. Davey had had that wayward look. He was always game for an adventure of some sort. That's what had attracted her to him in the first place. She unwrapped an item in newspaper. It was the egg cup. It would probably be worth quite a bit now, being Crown Derby, but she wouldn't dream of getting rid of it. She ran her finger around the intricate pattern of red and black laced with real gold leaf. Davey had let her have it when they first started seeing each other. It was stolen of course, like most of the Crown Derby that adorned gypsy caravans. Eileen had been amazed when Davey had shown her his mother's collection. It filled a glass fronted cabinet. The cups and saucers had been passed down from Davey's grandmother and the some of the plates were a present from his uncle. Davey's father had stolen the remaining two plates from the local china shop on two separate occasions. Eileen and Davey were there when he arrived home full of glee with his loot hidden inside his overcoat. He'd laughed when he related the tale to Davey's mother about the dim shop assistants. The Crown Derby was so expensive that it was kept locked away in a glass cabinets in the china shop, but you'd need more than just a glass cabinet to stop gypsies from pinching it. Davey's father had taken his sister into the shop with him. He'd asked to inspect a piece of the Crown Derby before buying it for his wife's birthday. The girl had unlocked the cabinet and shown him the plate. While he examined its ornate patterns his sister asked the assistant to open up another cabinet further down the shop. While she was gone he slipped the plate inside his coat, moved another plate over and closed the cabinet. He thanked the girl, told her that it was a lot of money and he'd think about it and then he left. But as if this wasn't enough excitement for him he went back to the shop again. He hadn't missed that the assistant failed to lock the cabinet again when he moved the other plate. He told his sister to go back to the camp with the first plate. 'I'm going back for the second one,' he said. 'You can't you're bound to get caught this time,' his sister panicked, but he placed the expensive plate into her hands and said, 'Go.' The second one was easier than the first. The girl who'd served him previously had disappeared, probably on a tea break and the new assistant left him to browse while she served someone else. He waited for her to turn the corner towards the Royal Doulton display, then he slid open the unlocked cabinet door, quietly took the other plate, slid the door closed and left with the plate inside his coat for the second time in an hour. No wonder he'd been laughing when he got home.

Eileen threw the newspaper away and placed the egg cup back in the box without the protective wrapping. She picked up the selection of photos. They were all similar poses of her and Davey outside the caravan, sat on the grass with their arms wrapped around each other. In the last one Davey had her in his arms whizzing her around. Eileen recalled what had happened after the photograph had been taken. He'd fallen over, dizzy with the turning and she'd landed on top of him. She added the photos to the box. There were two more items. One was the large white handkerchief with the initial D. He'd given her this when the family were ready to move on. She'd known that they were getting restless. It was in a gypsy's nature and the family had become fidgety, like they'd overstayed their welcome. Not that they were welcome at all by anyone in the locality. They planned on moving to Northumberland for a while. Davey asked Eileen to come with them, but she knew she couldn't. Her parents would never in a million years give their consent and if she disappeared they'd have had the police on her tail before she crossed the border into England. She'd begged Davey to try and get a job locally and stay, but it was his way of life. She couldn't expect him to settle just like that after the nomadic way he'd been brought up. Eileen cried and cried. That's when Davey gave her the handkerchief and told her to dry her tears. They'd had one last night together, under the stars outside the caravan. Eileen lied to her mother and told her that she was staying at a friend's house. She could remember the warmth of his body next to hers even now after all these years.

It was a week later that she received the dreadful news from a friend who worked at the manor house. Davey and his family had stopped overnight nearby. He'd been in the woods with his father poaching for something to eat for supper. The game keeper should only have been firing warning shots, but he said that he slipped on a stone and fired lower than he should have done. Davey was killed by the shot that night. Eileen thought that her world had ended. Nothing could be worse, she would have found someway of killing herself, but for the redeeming event. She picked up the last item for the box and unfolded the certificate reading the details. *Robert David Dolce, born 19th May.* The birth certificate recorded Eileen's mother and father as the parents. They'd thought it best at the time. Eileen had stayed off school and feigned illness and her mother had managed to pull the whole thing off, even to the family doctor who wasn't informed until weeks after the birth. So to everyone else Eileen had a baby brother and only she and now Claire knew the real truth.

Chapter Thirty Three

The hearse arrived as arranged the next morning and Adele's mother drove them to the church. There was a small car park around the back and a place had been reserved for them by the vicar. Adele wore a pink dress with dark green accessories and her mother a wine coloured suit with a white blouse. Ben's mother was already there and ignoring her daughter-in-law's wishes she was dressed all in black, completing the picture with a black feathered hat. The hearse pulled up at the church's main entrance and the vicar waited for the family mourners to gather. Adele and her mother joined her auntie and Ben's mother stood with his sister and her husband. Adele kept hold of her mother's arm and Cynthia rested her hand reassuringly on top. Ben's mother and his sister wavered on the other side of the path glaring at her and Cynthia.

'Who is that woman with the garish blonde hair,' Adele's auntie whispered to her mother.

'Ben's sister,' she whispered behind her hand.

'You can certainly tell where she gets her sour face from,' she said nodding towards Ben's mother.

'Shh, Sheila be quiet,' Cynthia steered her sister behind them.

The funeral director stood by the hearse and watched the bearers slide the coffin out. They skilfully hoisted it onto their shoulders and prepared for the procession into church. The vicar stood in his place and the bearers followed. Adele and Cynthia prepared to follow the coffin, but Ben's mother forced herself to the front.

'I think you'll find it's senior members of the immediate family first,' she said.

'And I think you'll find that next of kin take priority,' Cynthia pushed in beside her, still holding her daughter. Adele sunk on her feet and held onto her mother more tightly. Ben's sister tapped her mother on the shoulder.

'Mother, not now. Don't make it any worse.'

His mother fell in behind them and got out her handkerchief.

'My son, my son,' she muttered, sobbing into her hands.

Adele followed the coffin with her mother. The agitation outside melted away when she saw the familiar faces in the congregation. Some of her friends had come down from Croydon and Ben's work colleagues were there. Sheryl stood in front of her friends.

She wore a bright red and orange patterned dress. Trust Sheryl to take the meaning of brightly coloured clothes to the extreme. She had tried her best to please Adele and although what she related yesterday had hurt her Sheryl would never mean to upset her intentionally. She wished that Sheryl had told her the truth about Bradley sooner. She might not be following her dead husband's coffin today. Crispin was beside Sheryl looking as sophisticated as ever in a dark navy suit and pink shirt and tie. He gave Adele a respectful glance. It was a very considerate act for him to come today, after all he'd only known the residents of Orchard Court for a short time and it wasn't as if he would normally keep in touch with all the people who participated in Breaking New Ground. Somehow though, it was as if she had known Crispin all her life. From the first day that they had met she'd felt at ease in his company. She didn't feel judged or intimidated and he coaxed out the true person inside of her. Thankfully Crispin hadn't brought his overbearing assistant with him. Adele couldn't bear the thought of her being here today, especially after what she'd been up to with Ben.

The bearers reached the front of the church and placed Ben's coffin down very gently and carefully on the stand. The vicar stood in front and the funeral director ushered everyone to the correct seats, before bowing before the coffin and seating himself. The service began and Adele sat next to her mother. The vicar's words passed through her head not sinking in, her ears recognising the sounds and not comprehending. Instead she went over the events of the last few months. Could she have changed anything? Was it her fault? Had she entered into the relationship with Bradley with eyes wide open or naively blinkered? Why had Ben changed from the vibrant man she'd married to the obsessive angry man who slept around with tarts like Ruby? She looked around the rest of the congregation as she mouthed the words to The Lord is my Shepherd. She watched Crispin as he adjusted his glasses to read the hymn book. Rory and Viv were on the opposite aisle along with Eileen. They all held their hymn books and sang the psalm. Candles flickered in the background, adding an air of tranquillity. She noticed Eileen genuflect with the sign of the cross and remembered her Italian religious background. There'd be little chance of her ever making a mess of her life like Adele had done. Adele would have laid a large bet that she'd been a 'goody two shoes' all her respectable life. She wondered whether Eileen was lonely, she knew that she felt lonely herself before the changes in her life had even started. She was scared by the thought of being constantly alone at her age, with no real friends around and no job. She felt that she couldn't go back to working in the shop with Sheryl and she couldn't picture her future at all. Her mother nudged her. The bearers were moving Ben's coffin around to leave. The vicar prepared again to lead the procession out of church. Ben's coffin followed, shadowed by the family mourners. Adele was looking as green as her jacket and she stood by with her mother as the coffin was loaded into the hearse for the journey to the crematorium. Ben's mother was ready to follow and had already instructed her son-in-law to fetch the car.

Adele sank on the stone wall outside the church and Cynthia saw that it was time to call a truce. She approached Ben's mother.

'I'm going to take her to the hotel to sit down for a while. She's not well, I think she's suffering from the shock.'

Ben's mother smiled and for the first time today a brief look of concern flashed across her face.

'That's alright. I'll attend with my daughter and her husband and if it's okay with you we'll make our way back to Croydon from there. I think we've had enough trauma for one day as well. Thank you for helping Adele with the funeral arrangements.' She turned to Adele and kissed her on the cheek.

'Goodbye my dear. I'll speak to you soon.'

She got into the car and her son-in-law drove off.

'I bet she'll speak to you soon,' Cynthia said relieved that Mrs Parker senior was out of the way. She took Adele's arm again and pointed her in the direction of the Hexbury Green Hotel. It was very close to the church and once inside the foyer Cynthia asked if there was a room they could go to in private for a few minutes before Adele had to face the guests. A charming young girl came along and showed them to a small lounge where they could sit for a few minutes behind a solid wooden door. She reappeared a few minutes later with a tray of tea. Cynthia poured and handed a cup to Adele.

'Now, that wasn't too bad was it? The funeral director was superb if you ask me. He organised everyone and everything was done with decorum. The vicar's service was pleasant.'

Adele spoke at last. 'And all the neighbours came and Sally and co from Croydon.'

'Yes and they'll be gathering in the function room now, eating sandwiches and waiting to speak to you.' Cynthia said with encouragement.

'I know mum. Thanks for being here for me, I don't know what …' she started to cry.

'Come on darling, hold out just a little longer and then it'll all be over.' Cynthia leaned over and wiped the tears away.

'Brave face sweetheart. Go and talk to your friends. They all feel for you, really they do and I hate to say it but we'll be all the better for getting rid of Ben's mother.'

'I never did get on with her mum, although I did notice her sorrow today. Sometimes people show their grief in the form of anger.' Adele put the cup down and stood up straightening out her dress. She took a deep breath and opened the door. It was the door to an unknown future, but she had to face it head on and she told herself that it would be alright.

Chapter Thirty Four

The air of tranquillity that resided in St Matthew's church yesterday had been blown by the wind to land on Orchard Court today. The wind dropped and the sun shone down on the garden and the lane. Even Harry and Jake sat quietly on the garden steps reading a picture book together. Adele could see them from her kitchen window and she smiled to herself as she watched them point out things to each other. Rory opened his front door and Crispin came out to sit on the steps with the boys. He'd been so kind to her yesterday at the funeral reception. She'd ended up confiding in him a little about Bradley. She'd by no means related all that had gone on, but enough to indicate to him how guilty she was feeling for her friendship with Bradley and how much to blame for the accident and Ben's death.

'If we hadn't had the argument that morning and I hadn't told him that Bradley had been interested in me he wouldn't have rushed off in such an angry mood. I'm sure that was why he was driving so fast,' she'd told Crispin.

'You can't blame yourself Adele. It probably would have happened anyway. And don't forget what he did with Ruby,' he said.

'He told me he was sorry about that and I can see how some men would be tempted by her.'

'I can't say I would be. She's a strange woman, so stark and clinical. She might be all chic and glamour to look at, but there's no warmth in her whatsoever. It's just as well she's leaving the team. She's going to work as a designer for a high class chain store in the London area, designing make-up display counters. That'll suit her just fine. She can look like one of those painted dolls, so silken and sheer that any hint of a facial expression would crack the war paint.'

He also told Adele that he was staying with Rory and Viv after the funeral for a few days. He'd grown to like this part of the country. He said it made him feel relaxed in comparison to London. On Monday morning he and Viv had arranged a meeting with the arboriculturist. He invited Adele to come along if she felt up to it.

Crispin took the boys inside and Adele heard a car at the bottom of the lane. It was Cameron bringing Miles back home. Miles got out of the car and Cameron carried his bag. He looked a different man already, even his skin had lost the pale wan appearance. He stood with his hands behind his back and surveyed the garden and the houses in Orchard Court before following Cameron back to his own home.

Miles had lost the washed-out feeling inside as well as outside. Nothing would ever be the same again without Janet, he had to accept that, but there were other people out there who cared about him. Cameron stayed for a while and they drew back all the curtains that had been closed while he was in hospital. Miles reached the landing and pulled the long red velvet swags to reveal the garden. It still looked a mess and there was that man from the television programme. He was prodding around the protected tree. It would make such a difference to Orchard Court to have a pleasant vista to look out on. Somehow the man from the TV show didn't manifest himself as such an interference or threat as he had a few weeks ago. He watched Eileen come out of her house and climb the steps to the garden to talk to the man. He'd make sure that he made the time to go and see her this afternoon. When Cameron had gone he'd go down to the mini-market and buy a small token to thank her for her kindness.

Miles and Eileen sat on two picnic chairs beside the bleached pathway. She held the posy of red and yellow daisy-like flowers to the sunlight.

'Gerberas are lovely flowers. They're so friendly, like dancing faces smiling in the breeze.'

He turned to Eileen.

'I'm glad you like them. I wanted you to know that I really appreciated the kindness that you showed while I was in hospital. By the way, Cameron told me this morning about Ben. I know why you wanted to keep the news from me. I only hope that Adele doesn't think that I don't care about what happened. How is she?'

'The funeral was only yesterday and I must admit that she wasn't looking well. Her mother's staying with her at the moment. Perhaps now that the funeral is over she'll be able to think things through more clearly.'

'I've bought a card for her. Now that I've spoken to you I'll put it through her door this afternoon. Poor girl, I hope she'll be okay.'

'Crispin, from the gardening team came to the funeral yesterday.'

'So that's the man I saw in the garden earlier. I never really got to meet him properly when the team came down last time.'

'He's staying for a few days. They're meeting with the arboriculturist on Monday. Let's hope that they get the permission to chop the rotten old apple tree down.'

'I hope so, it could be a breath of fresh air for all of us. Do let me know if you need any legal advice. I know Cameron has offered in the past, but I'm not as fraught as I was then. I could help now.'
Eileen spoke softly to him.

'I know and thank you. It's good to see you looking so well.'
He placed his hand gently on her elbow and nodded.

'It's good to be feeling so well Eileen.'

Eileen was feeling better herself, now that she'd put the lid tightly back on the box and placed it right at the back of her wardrobe. If she'd known that Claire was going to find the box and rifle through its contents, the mere thought would have rocked her world. Yet it was the discovery that had brought them closer together and built up a solid trust between the two of them. She was coming to stay with Eileen the following weekend and she'd asked her to cook something special for supper. She said she'd bring her cookery books with her and wanted some advice on how to make meringues. Eileen couldn't wait to help her and said they'd have a trial run with the meringues for dessert.

Viv had sent an application off to Ofsted to register as a childminder. She'd been told that it generally took 12 weeks to process, so in the meantime she and Rory could check the house to make it suitable to look after babies and small children. She already had two babies provisionally booked in with her to start the new school term in September. Their parents were part-time teachers and they lived nearby, so the caring hours wouldn't be too long. Rory had started to check around the house for safety measures. He'd bought cupboard locks and plug covers and he'd made a superb stair gate from some old furniture thrown out by Miles. An inspector from Ofsted would come and visit her at the house to finalise the application and after that she could enjoy the new job. They talked about it over dinner that night and Crispin offered some child-friendly suggestions to the garden plans.

'I've found some special stones to insert into the patio. They look like fossils of birds and fish. They'd be quite interesting for older children to look at and we could incorporate a small swing and a covered sandpit providing that the others agree.'

'Do you think that the arboriculturist will recommend the tree is felled?' Rory asked.

'I reckon so and then we can get on with it, and not before time.'

'Well I'm not celebrating until I hear his decision tomorrow,' Viv concluded.

Chapter Thirty Five

Crispin accompanied the arboriculturist, Mr Beazley to the garden the next morning. Viv visited Adele and they agreed that it was best that Crispin should talk to Mr Beazley by himself.

'I'm so pleased that Crispin suggested it. He knows what he's talking about and I'd only say the wrong thing,' Viv said as she looked down on the two men and the apple tree in the garden. Adele was grateful for the company this morning as her mother had gone home for the first time since the accident. She'd promised to come back regularly until Adele felt more settled, but today Viv's friendly chatter was most welcome and she gave a running commentary of the happenings below.

'He's taking photographs now Adele and now he's making notes,' she turned her head eagerly. 'Crispin's nodding his head.'
Adele smiled at her friend's enthusiasm.

'Come and sit down Viv, you can't tell what they're saying from up here.'

Mr Beazley took one of the limbs of the apple tree. It wobbled and creaked and he pointed to a weak point where it joined the main body of the tree.

'In my view Mr Grainger this tree is most definitely dangerous.'
He referred to his notes again. 'Now you said that you'd be planning to have small children playing in the garden from time to time didn't you?'

'That's right, one of the residents will be a registered child-minder and she intended to let them play here when the weather was fine.'

Mr Beazley took several photographs of the damaged limb, before examining the bark in greater detail. He found the area where Drew and Justin had carved their names.

'The bark is darker in this area around where someone has carved their name. You see Mr Grainger, this laceration would have created a favourable environment for wood rotting fungi. However, I'm surprised that there are no fruiting bodies of the fungi on the trunk.'

Crispin spotted a small white cloud-like attachment on the other side.

'Like this one you mean?'

'That's exactly what I mean.' Mr Beazley glanced to the floor. 'And here are the rest of them. They've obviously been scraped off by some well-meaning person in an effort to save the tree. I think it could be rather too late for that. This tree has been neglected for far too long. The location wouldn't help either. Your houses are very close to a densely wooded area over there.' Mr Beazley pointed to the copse behind Orchard Court.

'There was probably a whole orchard here at one time and orchards in the vicinity of woods may be at greater risk of infection from fungi than trees grown in a more open area. There is more than likely a huge range of wood rotting fungi residing in that woodland area over there.'

'So what's the conclusion Mr Beazley?' Crispin asked, unable to hold back any longer.

'The tree is dying and dangerous, which means that its condition overrides the Tree Protection Order and you can do what you like with it. You have to give five days notice to the local council enclosing my report and photographic evidence, so it should take about a week.'

'Well thank you very much for examining the tree Mr Beazley. Mrs Cunningham has provided the cheque on behalf of the residents. Will you send the report to her?'

'Yes, I think that's best don't you. Then it can all be sent by recorded delivery to the local council offices and you can start work as soon as you have their authorisation.'

Mr Beazley shook hands with Crispin, picked up his equipment and left.

Crispin held his thumbs up behind his back where he knew for sure that Viv would be watching from Adele's kitchen window.

Viv was so excited that she couldn't stay. She had to rush back and tell Rory when he returned from his shift. Crispin stayed in Adele's kitchen, telling her all the details of the tree examination.

'I'm glad that Viv decided to rush off today. It means that I can tell you about my proposal,' he said with excitement. He continued, 'Since you were the one that instigated this plan and I've been so impressed with your sketches and ideas...'

Adele frowned and looked slightly puzzled.

'Don't look bewildered Adele, my idea will give you something enjoyable to focus on. As you know I'm without an assistant at the

212

moment on the design team and I was wondering if, for the Orchard Court project that you could stand in and help me.'

He stopped to give her time to think. 'It's just having someone else to bounce ideas off Adele, one more opinion and another person to take some control of the organisation. I will be calling a meeting very soon to involve everyone and to make sure that everyone has a wish for the new garden. I also have to let everyone know about the proposed changes to the TV programme. So what do you say?'

Adele didn't hesitate in her reply.

'Well since I only have myself to answer for now the answer has to be yes, as long as you don't expect me to slot into the shoes of a long-standing experienced garden designer.'

'Now come on, compared to Ruby you'll be Hexbury's answer to Gertrude Jekyll.'

'Seriously Adele you have some great ideas and your sketches are better than a lot of fully trained garden designers.'

'Okay, I'll do it and you're probably right. It will give me something to focus on.'

Crispin drafted a letter to the council and Adele typed it in readiness for the report when it arrived from Mr Beazley. A meeting was arranged for later that evening for all the neighbours at Adele's house.

'I'll announce this for those of you that don't know. The apple tree has been declared dying and dangerous and as soon as authorisation is obtained from the council it can be removed from the garden.' Crispin sat on an upright chair with his design brief, while the rest gathered on Adele's sofas.

'Are you sure that the council won't create any more problems?' Eileen piped up.

'I'm quite sure Eileen. As soon as we get the report and photographic evidence back from Mr Beazley it's full steam ahead. However, before we proceed we need to iron out your wish list and I need to tell you about the changed format of the programme.' Crispin looked around the circle of neighbours. He handed out sketches of the proposed plans.

'Let's start with you Eileen. What would you like to see in the garden or what would you like to keep?'

'I know everyone is going to say that I'm old-fashioned, but I like my pink and white slabs in my patio.'

213

Viv and Rory looked at each other in dismay and then at Crispin.

'Okay, we had incorporated a patio area; you can see it on your plan on the right hand side as you enter the garden.' Crispin delved into his black bag and pulled out a catalogue. He thumbed through it quickly and knelt down beside Eileen. 'How do you like this type of stone Eileen?' He showed her a picture of a patio using pink and white stones with a more weathered look. She took the catalogue and frowned. She wouldn't be able to scrub those stones up to their original brightness. Miles looked over her shoulder and pointed to the models in the picture. It was an elderly couple on two wooden chairs with a small table in the middle sharing a cream tea.

'Ideal for afternoon cream teas Eileen,' he said.

She smiled and instantly conjured up a list of the baked goodies that she could serve to everyone. The stones did appear worn and battered, but it said in the catalogue, *'a more natural weathered stone in subtle colours for a cultured effect.'* Claire would approve of these, she'd tell her to get up-to-date.

'So is this the modern approach Crispin?'

'Oh very modern, these stones are up to the minute.'

'We'd better have them then don't you think everyone,' and she held the magazine up for everyone to see.

'And what about you Miles?'

'I'd like to keep something that we already have. It's the buddleia tree in the corner. It's in my share of the garden at the moment. Janet bought the tree. She liked watching the peacock butterflies landing on it; she always said it was so colourful.' Miles spoke of Janet with fondness now and without the despair that he'd initially been suffering. Crispin showed him on the plan where the buddleia tree was.

'How about a new wooden bench under the buddleia tree Miles?'

'That would be absolutely splendid, but no brass plate, I'll keep my memories to myself,' he added with a warm smile. Rory and Viv's glance between each other said it all. It was good to hear Miles bringing Janet into the conversation in an affectionate and positive way.

Crispin continued and turned to Rory and Viv.

'The bench will look over the area I mentioned to you last night Viv. We have a small storage shed for gardening tools and children's toys and by the shed a covered sand pit and the patio stones with a few inserts of bird and fish fossils. There's also a plan for a small swing which can be attached by a bracket to the wall and put away when not in use.'

'It sounds wonderful Crispin, but I'd like to ask if anyone else minds about these ideas. Everything can be put away if the garden needs to be used in a more adult way,' Viv said addressing the group.

'I don't mind for one Viv, especially as the toys can all be hidden from view when we want to change the usage of the garden,' Adele replied reinforcing the tidiness aspect. Everyone else nodded in agreement and Crispin finished his explanation of the plans.

'Beyond the swing bracket on the wall is another bench reflecting the one next to the buddleia bush. We have a stone wall here where something could be grown as well as the flower and shrub border on the opposite side of the swing. Finally, the garden is accessed by a central set of steps with handrails both sides and an archway of evergreen honeysuckle.'

Adele interrupted, 'have you included my request for the bleeding heart plant and some herbs?'

'The herbs could go in the small stone walled area and the bleeding heart in the flower border. What do you think?'

'It sounds perfect, but don't forget the piece de resistance. What will go in place of the old apple tree?'

'Thank you Adele. As we will have to treat the stump of the tree and the old roots will still be buried in the surrounding ground we had planned to put lawn in the remaining area and on top of the old stump, a raised pond with a central fountain and some fish and lilies. It will of course have a removable netted cover for when small children visit the garden,' he said turning to Viv.

'I'm sure that none of you can have any objection to that,' Adele added. 'Here's an illustration of what it will finally look like.' She held up two drawings of the pond.

'Can we sit near the pond Adele?' Eileen asked. Adele turned to Crispin for an answer.

'Yes, we've thought about that. We were planning to incorporate two small seating areas within the stone surrounding the pond.'

'So when can the work be started?' Miles asked enthusiastically.

'That's the next thing I have to explain to all of you,' Crispin replied. He paused for a while as if preparing them for a venture.

'Originally the Breaking New Ground team would take on the refurbishment of a garden following the discussion of plans with the owners. However, we have recently discussed a new format to the programme. It's an offshoot to the original and involves a different approach to the work for community gardens. The producer liked the idea of your shared garden in Orchard Court and wanted to film a series of shared gardens all over the UK. Yours would be the first in the series.'

'So what do you mean exactly when it comes down to the approach for the work?' Miles said with interest.

'Yes Crispin, who exactly will be doing the work?'

'The BNG team will be instructing and involving themselves in some of the skilled work such as building the stone walls.'

'But who will be doing the bulk of the work?'

Crispin paused again.

'You will,' he said looking hopefully at all the residents.

Chapter Thirty Six

Crispin and Adele finished typing up the work plan for the few weeks ahead. Authorisation should arrive from the council early next week and a tree surgeon had been booked to remove the apple tree. The reaction to the work force had not been as bad as Crispin first thought. Rory had stepped in and told the neighbours that it would be fun to be involved in the project and he'd roped in the help of his sons. Adele's mother had also offered to help and with a workforce of ten the job shouldn't be too arduous.

Adele welcomed the work from the project. It certainly took her mind off the sadness and regret surrounding Ben's death. Her mother had moved in for a few weeks until the garden project was over and she was looking forward to the excitement of the filming.

'Adele, what do you think of my new gardening gloves? And what about my navy shorts for the filming session?'

'Mum, it's not a fashion show. They're fine,' Adele said, 'but I'm sure that Crispin will tell us if anything looks out of place.'

Cynthia took the shorts and gloves to her bedroom, muttering about splashing them with mud to make them look more authentic.

The garden was stark as the tree had been removed earlier today. A bare patch stood in its place and the land around it was scarred. Work was due to start tomorrow and everyone had been informed of the schedules. The BNG team had booked into the Hexbury Green Hotel and Crispin had chosen to stay with Rory and Viv again. Adele stared out of the window at the half mutilated garden. Its fences had already been taken down and some of the larger weeds pulled and placed in a skip below in the lane. She had a clear picture in her mind of how the garden would look, but she couldn't see herself in this picture. She'd dreamt about the garden last night. She'd seen herself standing on a long never-ending pathway with a brick wall either side. The pathway was miles and miles of sameness winding its way until she became too old to walk it any more.

Cynthia came back into the kitchen. What do you think of this pale blue t-shirt Adele and should I wear my wellies or old trainers?'

'I don't know mum, perhaps we'll ask tomorrow morning,' Adele replied forgetting the walled path in the dream.

Colin and Barry had been invited back down with the team. They had archived some of the film from their last visit and could use it to start the programme, showing the viewer how the garden looked before the alterations. They filmed the removal of the apple tree and the bare stump in the garden afterwards. They were all set to film the group of neighbours and the refurbishment as it took place. The first job was to clear all the weeds, the old benches and any other rubbish on the surface. Then a team from BNG rotovated and levelled the surface. Harry and Jake carried some of the smaller stones for the raised pond. The surrounding stone wall was repaired in some places and the ground was marked out with sand for the patios. The patios were laid, the storage shed erected and the covered sand pit was put into place. A brick barbecue was built, the baby swing bracket fixed and the flower and shrub border filled to include a particularly large bleeding heart plant for Adele. The herb garden was finished and the new benches were put facing each other on opposite sides of the garden. The entrance archway was cemented into place by Justin and Drew and the pond filled with water, lilies planted and fish added. Eileen took delight in sweeping down all the patios and the final task was to lay the lawn. Everyone became involved in the last job and Colin and Barry filmed a chain of neighbours passing the turfs carefully along to Crispin and Adele who laid them neatly and firmly onto the finely raked topsoil. Miles planted the two honeysuckle plants on either side of the archway and they could finally stand back and survey their hard work.

It had taken four days to complete the project and now Colin and Barry filmed the final shots. Everything was in place and brought to order. The filming was finished. Barry switched off his camera and Crispin stood on the wall to make an announcement.

'Well done everyone. It's been a lot of hard work, but I'm sure that you'll agree the last four days of our extenuating efforts have been worth it when you look at our finished picture.'

Everyone cheered. Crispin had one more announcement.

'We have our party team arriving tomorrow. So you can all go home and have a relaxing soak in your baths, sooth those aching muscles, sleep away tired limbs and be ready to enjoy the reward of a champagne celebration tomorrow.'

Everyone cheered again and very quickly and quietly returned to their homes for the night. They were too tired to converse and too weary to stand up any longer.

Epilogue

The final scene was in place in Orchard Court. Champagne was flowing and everyone gathered on the fossils patio for the last few shots for the TV programme. A local reporter called to take a photograph of the group and they all posed smiles at the ready. The reporter jotted down a few notes about the TV programme and the problems that the residents had with the tree protection order on the apple tree. He made notes about them all pulling together and helping each other. The group started to disperse, trying not to stand on the newly established lawn. Adele sat on the cover for the sand pit. They *had* all pulled together over the past months and they'd certainly helped each other. Adele watched everyone leave the garden by the archway. The BNG team had set up trestle tables in the lane with a delicious buffet and more wine and champagne. It reminded her of Christmas when she was a little girl. When it finally came she didn't want it to pass because everything would be back to normal. The normality of everyday life would return with no more looked-forward-to anticipation. Adele's normality of everyday life had been turned upside down. There seemed nothing to look forward to. The neighbours were her friends of course, but she had no friends in Hexbury her own age, no job, no husband, no lover and no one to share her life with her. Her mother wouldn't always be on the scene. She remained seated on the sand pit while all of this dawned on her. This was reality and her future appeared as gloomy and miserable as the garden had before its makeover. She looked up and saw a hand, Crispin's.

'Come on. There's plenty of delectable food down there.' He pulled her hand gently and she got up. He put his arm around her to support her and guided her down to the lane and the scrumptious buffet.

Eileen examined the delicate cheese straws for evidence. Were they home-made or a packaged sort? She pointed out the quails eggs to Viv and they shrieked as Rory showed off and ate two in one go. Miles poured her another glass of champagne and she laughed when he accidentally poured it over her fingers. Miles had agreed to have the fountain for the garden attached to his power supply. He said that everyone in Orchard Court had been his lifeline and the garden project something for him to hang on to. He

221

insisted that he would pay for the power to run the fountain. Adele stood next to her mother and sipped her champagne slowly, the bubbles almost making her sneeze. Everyone looked so happy. Their problems had all been ironed out and hers were only just beginning. Crispin came over again with the champagne bottle in his hand.

'I wanted to thank you personally Adele for your help on this project. You've done a brilliant job with your sketches and with the organisation. In fact you've done so well I'd like to make another proposal to you. I'm offering you a permanent job as assistant garden designer on the Breaking New Ground team.' Crispin paused as usual and waited for her reaction. Adele stood still, poised over her champagne glass.

'You have enjoyed working with the team haven't you?' He added.

'Yes, but I didn't expect this,' Adele replied.

Cynthia soon added her comments making up for her daughter's silence.

'Of course she'll take the job, won't you darling. It's ideal for her and it's worthy of what she has to offer.'

Adele hung onto the champagne glass and glanced at her mother.

'Mum I can speak for myself.'

Then she turned towards Crispin.

'But Crispin...but what if...'

'There are no buts or what ifs,' Crispin replied determined not to accept no as her answer.

'Say yes Adele,' he said looking straight at her, gently.

And before she knew it she'd said it.

'Yes Crispin, I'd like to accept the job.'

He threw his arms around her and hugged her tightly. Then he picked up the champagne bottle, topped up their glasses and made a toast.

'Here's to a brand new year for Breaking New Ground!'

ACKNOWLEDGEMENTS

A huge thank you to ALL my friends and relatives that have given
me so much encouragement and friendly nagging to finish this
novel, especially to fellow writer, Myfanwy (Vanni) Cook
and my best friend, Rachel Willcock.
Love and thanks to my two sons, Adam and Paul
for their opinions on teenage dialogue.
Also to Natasha Buckley, Mike Gilmore, Chris Everitt,
Pete Hurford, Teresa Tyler-Smith, Chris Pithouse, Patricia Fawcett
and Becky Kodritsch for their interest and enthusiasm.
Thanks to Dr Rob Gardner for his help with the medical
information and to Tony Everitt for his ecclesiastical advice.
Lastly, but not least to Celia Duncan for her brilliant cover design.

Under the Bonsai Trees
By Anna West

Millie Bray is a happy-go-lucky bank clerk who is always ready to help anyone. Unfortunately, her friendly liaison with garden centre owner, Richard Greenway is not progressing as she calculated. Millie is hoping to change Richard's philandering nature, but there are many obstacles standing in her way; the most annoying being his intermittent young girlfriend, Yolanda. The story starts with an unexpected holiday in the Greek Islands, but what goes on later under the bonsai trees is **even more** out of the blue!

Due to be published in 2009.

GW01424379

Original title:

When Butterflies Become Thunderstorms

Author: Jude Lancaster

ISBN HARDBACK: 978-9916-90-834-1

ISBN PAPERBACK: 978-9916-90-835-8

A Flutter of Dreams Breeding Storms

In whispers soft, the night awakes,
With fleeting thoughts, the silence shakes.
A fluttering heart, a pulse unknown,
Breeding storms in the twilight zone.

Shadows dance upon the ground,
As dreams and fears begin to pound.
In tempest's grip, we find our way,
Through contours bleak, we choose to stay.

Merging Currents Beneath Delicate Wings

Here flows the river, wild and free,
A dance of currents, just you and me.
Beneath the wings, the world takes flight,
Merging whispers of day and night.

In every bend, a story swirls,
As dreams unfold and fate unfurls.
The soft caress of a gentle breeze,
Guides our hearts with tender ease.

Ruins of Peace Born from Vibrant Hues

Colors clash in a muted dawn,
Ruins of peace where hope is drawn.
Vibrant hues paint stories old,
In every shade, a truth unfolds.

Yet through the chaos, beauty thrives,
In shattered peace, the heart still strives.
From ashes rise a whispered song,
In ruins' grace, we all belong.

The Flutter of Daring Wings

With daring wings, we seek the sky,
A chance to dream, to soar, to fly.
In every flutter, courage calls,
To rise above where silence falls.

Through storms and trials, we chase the light,
With every heartbeat, we fight the night.
For in our veins, a flame resides,
The flutter of wings that never hides.

Whispers of Tempest Wings

In shadows cast by brewing clouds,
The echoes stir in silent shrouds.
A promise hangs in the tense air,
As nature breathes its whispered prayer.

The wings of twilight brush the ground,
In every rustle lies a sound.
An omen floats on winds that wail,
Their fervent song, a haunting tale.

Through branches twisting in the night,
The storm awakens with fierce might.
Yet in the chaos, life takes flight,
To dance beneath the waning light.

A symphony of wind and rain,
In solitude we bear the strain.
For when the tempest's song does cease,
We find our hearts in whispered peace.

Echoes of Colorful Storms

Beneath the skies of shifting hues,
A vibrant dance of rains ensues.
The thunder rumbles, colors clash,
And in that fury, dreams are splashed.

The lightning paints the world in streaks,
A tapestry that nature speaks.
With every pulse, the heavens roar,
As echoes bounce from shore to shore.

Yet in this tempest, beauty blooms,
As wildflowers break through the gloom.
Their heads held high, they greet the storm,
A testament to nature's form.

Each droplet tells a story shared,
Of longing hearts and souls laid bare.
In chaos, find the colors bright,
And let your spirit take to flight.

Fluttering Chaos in the Sky

A whirlwind spins, a dizzying flight,
Clouds swirling fast, no end in sight.
In the dance of chaos, dreams take wing,
As hope ignites, a fierce, soft spring.

Feathers drift on turbulent airs,
Whispers rise, dissolve in prayers.
Each gust unfolds a tale untold,
Of hearts that brave the gusts, the cold.

Glimmers of sun through stormy veil,
Chasing shadows in twilight's trail.
With every flutter of wild grace,
We find our truth in the storm's embrace.

Listen closely, the sky implores,
To seek the calm beyond the roars.
In chaos, life begins anew,
A vibrant spark, a chance to pursue.

The Dance of Delicate Resistance

With gentle steps, the flowers sway,
Against the winds that seek to play.
A dance of grace, fierce and refined,
In every movement, strength aligned.

The softest petals bear the strain,
Yet hold their ground through sun and rain.
In every breeze that bends their frame.
They whisper softly, fierce yet tame.

At twilight's call, they stand once more,
Rooted deep, they seek to soar.
In shadows cast by storms unseen,
They bloom anew, their spirits keen.

A testament to life's sweet fight,
Through trials faced, they find their light.
In delicate resistance, stand tall,
For even the softest can conquer all.

The Dance of Delicate Fury

In twilight's grip, fierce whispers rise,
A tempest brews beneath the skies.
With graceful steps, they twist and twine,
A fragile art, a starlit sign.

The shadows leap, a ballet bright,
Each movement charged with pure delight.
Yet in their grace, a warning hums,
For delicate hearts, the fury comes.

Fluttering Shadows in a Gloomy Sky

Amidst the clouds, they take their flight,
Soft silhouettes in muted light.
Whispers of dusk in swirling dance,
Echo the stories of lost chance.

They flirt with fate, a fleeting glance,
In heavy air, they weave romance.
Yet in their grace, a hint of sorrow,
Fluttering dreams of a brighter tomorrow.

Thunder's Embrace in Gentle Colors

Beneath the storm, a canvas swells,
With hues that blend where thunder dwells.
A soft embrace of sound and sight,
Where chaos births the peace of night.

In every clash, a promise grows,
Colors collide as nature flows.
Harmony sings in discord's face,
Thunder whispers of love's warm grace.

Wings Unleashed in the Tempest

A tempest roars, the skies aflame,
Yet in the storm, hearts stake their claim.
Wings unfurl, defying the gale,
In wild abandon, they shall prevail.

Through rain and wind, their spirits soar,
Embracing chaos, seeking more.
In every gust, a strength is found,
Wings unleashed, they dance around.

The Radiance of Chaos

In shadows deep where wildfires dance,
The glow ignites, a daring chance.
Whispers rise, a storm unfurled,
Chaos reigns, yet beauty swirled.

Fractured paths of light and dark,
In every flicker, a vibrant spark.
Through raging winds, a silent call,
In the chaos, we stand tall.

Petals and Turbulence in Nature's Theatre

Amidst the bloom, the tempest cries,
Petals drift under stormy skies.
Nature's stage, a dance so bold,
In chaos' grip, new tales unfold.

Colors clash in fleeting light,
Turbulent winds, a fierce delight.
A ballet sweet, then harshly tossed,
In beauty's wake, we find what's lost.

Tides of Change in Wooly Corners of Chaos

Wooly corners, tides collide,
Whispers of change, no need to hide.
The sea swells high, the land it sways,
In chaos' arms, we find our ways.

Each wave a laugh, each crash a sigh,
In the storm's embrace, hearts learn to fly.
Life's currents swirl, a playful jest,
From chaos born, we find our rest.

Shifting Harmonies in a Cacophony

Amidst the clamor, voices rise,
Shifting harmonies touch the skies.
In a cacophony, notes entwine,
Creating music, pure, divine.

Errors echo, laughter blends,
In noisy streets, the chaos mends.
Each dissonance, a tale to spin,
From every clash, new dreams begin.

A Kaleidoscope of Nature's Whimsy

Colors spill from petals bright,
Whispers lift the morning light.
In the breeze, soft sighs of trees,
Dancing leaves in joyful tease.

Mountains wear a blanket white,
Valleys bask in golden light.
Rivers laugh in silver streams,
Nature's magic, woven dreams.

Birds take flight on wings of grace,
Clouds drift by in gentle pace.
Every hue, a story told,
In each shadow, colors bold.

Underneath the vast expanse,
Life unfolds its wondrous dance.
A kaleidoscope we see,
Nature's song, wild and free.

The Electric Pulse of the Weary Sky

Thunder rumbles, shadows creep,
The weary sky, secrets keep.
Lightning strikes with vivid glare,
Painting stories in the air.

Fleeting moments, storm's embrace,
Time slows down, a gentle pace.
Raindrops tap on windows clear,
Nature's rhythm, loud and near.

Clouds collide in fierce display,
Heartbeats sync with skies of gray.
Each gust whispers tales of old,
Of dreams and fears yet untold.

As the dawn breaks, peace returns,
The weary sky slowly learns.
To breathe anew, to find its way,
In the light of a brand new day.

Transformation of Tranquil Dances

Moonlight spills on water's gleam,
Ripples weave a silken dream.
Stars align in whispered grace,
Nighttime casts a soft embrace.

Every shadow bends and sways,
In this quiet, woven gaze.
Dancing flames in distant fires,
Illuminating deep desires.

The world shifts in gentle flows,
In the stillness, magic grows.
Breath by breath, the night unfolds,
Transforming hearts with stories bold.

As dawn brings the light anew,
Tranquil dances find their due.
In every step, a tale takes flight,
Resonating day and night.

Convergence of Light and Fury

Fires clash in tempest's roar,
A storm brews, the heavens pour.
In this chaos, beauty found,
As elements whirl all around.

Vivid flashes in the dark,
Nature's voice ignites a spark.
Hope emerges through the strife,
From the clash, we draw our life.

Rain's embrace, the earth's loud cry,
Life and death, they intertwine.
In the tempest, strength bestowed,
From fury, light's own path is rode.

As calm follows the raging tide,
In the quiet, dreams abide.
Convergence brings both pain and bliss,
In every storm, there's light to kiss.

From Graceful Flight to Roiling Might

In skies of blue, the larks ascend,
With plumes so bright, on winds they blend.
Yet dark clouds gather, fierce and bold,
A tale of grace from light to cold.

The tempest brews, the thunders call,
From heights above, to earth they'll fall.
Wings once so free, now tightly drawn,
In swirling storms, a dance till dawn.

With shadows cast, the echoes cry,
Of soaring hopes that touch the sky.
But from their grace, a force ignites,
Roiling might beneath the flights.

So heed the winds, both soft and loud,
Embrace the change, be fierce, be proud.
For in the storm's unyielding flight,
We find our strength from grace to might.

Fluttering Shadows Across the Blackened East.

In twilight's grip, the shadows creep,
Across the land, where secrets sweep.
The whispers hum, a soft lament,
Of dreams once bright, now seldom spent.

With each flutter, the darkness looms,
A dance of fate, as silence blooms.
The eastern sky, in charcoal grays,
Hints at the night, where hope decays.

Yet in the dark, a spark remains,
A flicker bright amidst the pains.
These shadows weave a tale of old,
Of strength in dark, in light retold.

So let them flutter, let them sigh,
For in their passage, spirits fly.
Across the blackened, sorrowed east,
A promise lingers, joy released.

Whispers of Stormy Wings

Through the night, the echoes soar,
Whispers born from ocean's roar.
Stormy wings with secrets weave,
Tales of loss, and those who grieve.

In the moonlight, shadows play,
A haunting hymn of night and day.
With every flap, the winds respond,
To call of skies, to dreams beyond.

Nights of dread, yet hope ignites,
In the heart of stormy flights.
Whispers linger on the breeze,
Carried forth by drifting leaves.

So listen close, for they confess,
Stormy wings in their caress.
In every gust, a tale they bring,
Of life's embrace and love's sweet sting.

Tempest's Gentle Caress

Amidst the storm, a softness lies,
Where tempest meets the weeping skies.
A gentle touch, a calming breath,
In chaos born, there blooms a depth.

The raindrops sing, a lullaby,
While thunder rolls, yet bids good-bye
As nature sways to rhythmic beats,
A dance of storm in winding streets.

Yet in the gale, the heart finds peace,
A tranquil moment, fears released.
For through the wrath, a love shines bright,
Tempest's caress, a guiding light.

So hold it close, this tender space,
In wild embrace, there hides grace.
Through raging storms, we find our way,
To gentle shores, where calm will stay.

From Petals to Power: Nature's Shift

Soft petals fall in silence,
Colors fading from the day.
Nature breathes a deeper essence,
Whispers shift in bright array.

Roots entwined beneath the surface,
Strength lies hidden in the ground.
Life emerges with new purpose,
Transformations all around.

The trees sway in a bold embrace,
As every leaf claims its right.
The blossoms bloom, they find their place,
In the canvas of the night.

From the quiet, power rises,
Nature shifts with grace untold.
In the cycle, truth surprises,
Life's potential unfolds.

Fluttering Fear Before the Deluge

Whispers echo through the air,
Clouds gather in shades of gray.
The world pauses, senses aware,
As shadows dance and sway.

A fluttering heart, near the shore,
Waves crash with an urgent plea.
Tension builds, a primal roar,
Nature speaks, wild and free.

rays of light break into fragments,
Drenched hopes try to take flight.
Deceiving calm hides wide descent,
Fate awaits in stormy night.

With each pulse, the water rises,
A lesson etched in fear and grace.
From chaos stems the world's surprises,
In the churn, we find our place.

Shattered Calm and Fractured Light

Stillness cloaks a world asleep,
Yet dreams linger, vivid, bright.
In corners, secrets softly creep,
Distracting from the fractured light.

Silence cracks with sudden thunder,
Echoes swirl like autumn leaves.
Hearts awaken, torn asunder,
Searching for what truth believes.

The dance of shadows casts a spell,
Reflections twist and fade away.
A fragile peace, where echoes fell,
In fractured beams, we learn to sway.

Yet in the chaos, strength appears,
From shards, we grow and redefine.
Through shattered calm, we face our fears,
Becoming whole, one step, one line.

The Subtle Storm in Gentle Flight

A breeze whispers through the trees,
Softly weaving tales of night.
Wings in motion, like the leaves,
The subtle storm in gentle flight.

Colors swirl in twilight's glow,
Nature dances with delight.
Every flutter hints at flow,
In shadows cast by fading light.

Clouds drift lazily above,
While whispers tease the waiting ground.
In the calm, the heart will love,
As gentle storms resound.

With each breath, the world expands,
Unfolding secrets yet to see.
In delicate, embracing hands,
We find our place, we dare to be.

Harmonies Colliding in a Sky of Color

Colors dance across the sky,
Whispers of a gentle sigh.
Clouds collide in vibrant play,
Painting dreams in bright array.

Melodies of light and shade,
Nature's brush, a grand parade.
Harmony in chaos found,
Serenade the world around.

As the sun begins to fade,
Colors blaze, a bold charade.
Moments linger, time suspended,
In this realm, all fears are ended.

Each hue tells a tale untold,
In the twilight's arms, it's bold.
Fates entwined in light's embrace,
A symphony of endless grace.

Nature's Prologue to Thunderous Tales

Earth whispers secrets on the breeze,
Underneath the swaying trees.
The sky darkens, tension builds,
Awaiting storms, anticipation thrills.

Clouds emerge, thick and gray,
A prelude to the storm's wild play.
Nature's breath begins to roar,
Echoes of the ancient lore.

Raindrops fall like whispered prose,
Drumming softly, a rhythmic rose.
Each flash of light, a story spun,
In the chaos, hope is won.

The earth drinks deep, a thirsty soul,
Embracing thunder, bold and whole.
With every clap, a promise grows,
In the tempest, life bestows.

A Threnody for Gentle Beacons

Stars light paths in quiet nights,
Guiding dreamers, soft delights.
Whispered hopes on silver beams,
In the dark, they weave our dreams.

But time can take away their glow,
As shadows creep, the winds may blow.
A threnody for those we miss,
Their gentle warmth, a fleeting kiss.

Each beacon shines in hearts' embrace,
Fading slowly, leaving trace.
For memories hold what time belies,
In whispered winds, their spirit flies.

Though they dim, their love remains,
Time may cause such gentle pains.
In silence, we recall the light,
A threnody for stars so bright.

The Inception of Storms in Soft Shadows

In the hush before the storm,
Shadows stretch, a ghostly form.
Air grows thick, an electric thrill,
Nature's sigh, a waiting still.

As whispers turn to urgent calls,
Darkness deepens, softly falls.
Winds awaken, rise and sweep,
Stirring dreams from peaceful sleep.

Lightning dances, fierce and bold,
With every flash, a tale unfolds.
Thunder rumbles, a heartbeat loud,
In the storm, we're all allowed.

From soft shadows, power breaks,
In its wake, the earth awakes.
Life reborn with every drop,
In the storms, we learn to stop.

Wings of Change: A Thunderous Tale

In skies above, the eagles soar,
Their wings spread wide, forevermore.
With every gust, their spirits rise,
As thunder rolls across the skies.

The winds of fate begin to shift,
Carrying tales that storms can gift.
With every flap, they carve the air,
In search of dreams laid bare with care.

Beneath the clouds, the whispers cling,
The promise of what change may bring.
A dance of hope in stormy light,
Where shadows fade and dreams ignite.

Through tempests vast, they find their way,
With courage bright, they greet the day.
Each thunderous roar, a tale to tell,
Of wings that rise and hearts that swell.

The Majesty of Quiet into Tempest

In silence deep, where shadows dwell,
A stillness wrapped, a whispered spell.
The calm before the storm takes flight,
A transformation from day to night.

The clouds embrace the twilight hue,
As winds begin to stir anew.
With majesty, they twist and turn,
A lesson in the tides we learn.

From quietude to vibrant roar,
The heart awakens, craves for more.
As lightning cracks the sky in two,
The tempest's rage brings forth the true

Yet through the storm, the beauty glows,
In chaos, peace and power flows.
In every clash, we find our part,
The majesty that stirs the heart.

Colors Torn from the Cloudless Blue

From azure depths, the colors burst,
In vibrant strokes, the passion thirsts.
A canvas stretched across the sky,
Where dreams take flight and hopes still fly.

Each hue a whisper, soft and bright,
Pulling us in with sheer delight.
Yet clouds encroach, with thunder's might,
A dance of shadows, day to night.

The storm may rage, but colors blend,
In every drop, a story penned.
Torn from blue, the shades unite,
In tempests fierce, we find the light.

So let the skies ignite and sway,
In swirling hues, we'll find our way.
For every storm brings forth anew,
The colors torn from cloudless blue.

Fluttering Echoes of Tempestuous Hearts

Beneath the storm, our spirits quake,
With every rumble, fears awake.
Yet deep inside, a fire glows,
In fluttering hearts, the courage grows.

The echoes of the tempest call,
Through shadows cast, we stand tall.
As raindrops fall, we intertwine,
In storm's embrace, our souls align.

With each fierce clash, we learn to bend
Through trials faced, our hearts transcend.
In tempest's heart, we find our song,
A melody that rolls along.

Through every storm, we rise, we soar,
With fluttering echoes, forevermore.
In tempestuous dance, we'll stand apart,
As one, we beat, a tempestuous heart.

Transitions of Grace and Gall

In quiet whispers, shadows play,
A dance of light at end of day.
Where hope meets doubt, a fragile line,
The heart holds both, entwined divine.

A bittersweet embrace we find,
As sorrow sways, the joy unbind.
Through trials faced, our spirits soar,
In grace and gall, we learn to score.

Life's woven threads, both dark and bright,
In every tear, there shines the light.
The cadence shifts, a fleeting song,
In transitions, we find where we belong.

Serene Fragments in a Sudden Fury

A tranquil dawn, the world a breath,
Soft echoes linger, dance with death.
But storms arise with wild intent,
Disrupting peace, on chaos bent.

Fragile petals torn away,
In sudden fury, skies turn gray.
Yet in the clash, fragments shine,
In anger's wake, a spark divine.

From gentle winds to thunder's roar,
Nature's heart beats evermore.
In broken calm, we search for grace,
As serene fragments find their place.

Beauty and Beast in Broken Weather

Amidst the storm, a beauty sways,
In fractured light, the world decays.
A beast within, both fierce and soft,
In broken weather, souls take off.

Clouds gather round, a haunting sight,
Yet in the dark, emerges light.
The wild contrasts, a dance of fate,
From beauty's touch, the beast can wait.

In tempest's rage, we face our fears,
Through rain and tear, the heart endears.
In tangled paths of joy and pain,
We find the strength to rise again.

From Sighs to Sound: Nature's Lament

In sighs that echo through the night,
A sorrowed breeze, a muted flight.
The rustling leaves, a tune of woe,
In every breath, the heartbeats flow.

Yet nature speaks in subtle sound,
A melody of loss profound.
With every crest and every fall,
We hear the whispers, nature's call.

From silent pains to symphonies,
The world awakens, soft like trees.
In lament's hymn, we find our place,
In sighs, we learn of time and grace.

The Spectacle of Storm-Born Wings

In the sky, the tempest swirls,
Where thunder roars and nature twirls.
Wings emerge from clouds so gray,
A dance of power and wild display.

Colors flash in fierce delight,
Brilliant hues that chase the night.
In chaos, beauty finds its form,
A spectacle of storm-born wings, reborn.

Voices rise, a call to soar,
Through gusty winds, they explore.
Beneath the storm, life finds its song,
In harmony where hearts belong.

As shadows play, the dance evolves,
In quiet moments, problems resolve.
With every beat, the storm's embrace,
A flight of wonder, a daring grace.

Shadows and Colors Collide in Tornado Dance

Under dark skies, shadows creep,
Colors swirl in a wild sweep.
Nature's fury spins the storm,
A dance of chaos, a vibrant form.

Whispers merge with howling wind,
In this tempest, dreams rescind.
Every twist, a story told,
In the heart of a storm, daring and bold.

Lightning strikes with fervent passion,
In the chaos, a sweeping action.
Shapes blend as colors collide,
A tornado dance, wild and wide.

Among the storm's fierce embrace,
We find life's unpredictable race.
In shadows deep, the truth we trace,
As colors collide, we find our place.

The Quiet Before the Feathered Fury

In the hush just before the roar,
Whispers of wings begin to soar.
Nature holds its breath in fear,
An anxious thrill that draws us near.

Clouds gather, dark and deep,
While the world pauses, it seems to sleep.
In this stillness, power brews,
A calm before the storm ensues.

Hearts race with unspoken dread,
As silence blankets all that's said.
The feathered fury soon takes flight,
Ready to plunge in wild delight.

And when the storm finally breaks,
The world awakens, tremors shakes.
Transforming chaos into grace,
In the feathered fury, we find our place.

Swirling Dreams Caught in Thunder's Grasp

As thunder rolls across the plains,
Our dreams awaken, lose their chains
Caught in currents, wild and free,
Swirling visions call to me.

In the tempest, we find our way,
Where hopes ignite and shadows play.
Colors merge in a vibrant stream,
A moment's pause for a fleeting dream.

Lightning dances with a spark,
Illuminating all that's dark.
In the grasp of thunder's might,
Swirling dreams take daring flight.

When the storm relents its hold,
A tale of courage to be told.
In every rumble, every crash,
We find our strength within the flash

Hidden Worlds Between Benevolence and Rage

In shadows where soft whispers dwell,
A soft wind carries secrets to tell.
Benevolence blooms with a tender care,
Yet hidden beneath, there's a brewing flare.

From kindness' heart, storms gather, collide,
Humanity's dance, a delicate ride.
In the twilight, the calm meets the wild,
Both worlds entwined, innocent and defiled.

Hope's gentle hand can spark the flame,
While unquenched anger exudes its claim.
A fragile balance, the line that we tread,
Both love and fury, emotions widespread.

Caught in the silence, a thunderous sigh,
Echoes of turmoil are never too shy.
What lies in the heart where shadows now play?
Hidden worlds merge, in night and in day.

The Fragile Tapestry of Nature's Drama

Threads of color weave in the air,
Each moment a stitch, tender and rare.
Nature's art flows through the trees,
Whispering stories on the breeze.

Beneath soft clouds, the sun takes its bow,
While rivers below forget time, somehow.
In every bloom, a tale is spun,
Life's fragile dance has only begun.

Seasons hold hands in a graceful twirl,
An ever-changing, magnificent whirl.
With each gentle sigh and every loud roar,
Nature weaves drama, forevermore.

In the twilight glow, reflections take flight,
Mirrors of beauty, in dark and in light.
A tapestry woven with love and with strife,
In nature's embrace, we discover our life.

Flickering Stories in the Rain

Raindrops dance lightly on rooftops and leaves,
Whispers of tales that the vapor conceives.
Every splash holds a secret, a sigh,
Flickering stories that mingle and fly.

Puddles reflect dreams, a shimmering sheen,
In every droplet, a world to be seen.
Soft patterns emerge as the waters entwine,
Nature's own canvas, effortlessly divine.

As the rhythm of rain keeps the tempo alive,
Memories flicker, descanting to thrive.
Each journey unfolds with the softest embrace,
In the heart of the storm, we find our own place.

With each fleeting moment, the sky starts to fade,
Leaving behind all the magic it made.
In whispers of water, we wade through the night,
Flickering stories, a soft, guiding light.

Tornado of Feathers and Fury

A whirlwind of thoughts in chaos swirls.
With feathers of dreams, as each dread unfurls.
Fury ignites in the tempest's embrace,
A dance of wild power, no calm in this race.

Wings twisting upward, they scream to the sky,
The heart of the storm where the bravest will fly.
In shadows and light, the feathers confound,
A cyclone of passions, both lost and profound.

Through turbulent skies, the journey unwinds,
Where wishes collide with the harshness of minds.
In every fierce gust that breaks through the night,
Hope rises anew, a phoenix in flight.

Caught in the maelstrom, we learn to embrace,
The fury that forges our truest of grace.
For in the eye of the storm, we will learn,
A tornado of life, where the bright embers burn.

Vibrations of Fragile Flight

Wings whisper soft against the breeze,
Carried high with grace and ease.
Every flutter hums a song,
In the dance where they belong.

Beneath the sky, a gentle chase,
Threads of light in an endless space.
With every rise, a story told,
Of fragile dreams and hearts of gold.

Yet every gust might change the tide,
As they soar, their fears they hide.
But still they dare to greet the sun,
In the flight that has begun.

In summer's warmth, their spirits take,
Through unseen worlds, they weave and break.
In fleeting moments, they take flight,
Vibrations breathe in soft twilight.

The Metamorphosis of Nature's Wrath

Thunder cracks the silent night,
Nature's fury takes to flight.
Dark clouds gather, shadows loom,
Her power builds, a growing boom.

Rains cascade like liquid steel,
Each droplet's might, a primal feel.
Earth shakes under the fierce embrace,
Breath held tight in nature's face.

When the winds begin to howl,
Chaos reigns, majestic growl.
Yet within the storm, a change,
A quiet calm, a world re-arranged.

For in the aftermath of fright,
Life renews in borrowed light.
From devastation, blooms will sprout,
In nature's dance, we find the route.

Veils of Color in Churning Skies

Beneath the arches, hues collide,
As daylight fades, the colors bide.
Brushstrokes bold on canvas vast,
Moments fleeting, shadows cast.

Glimmers beckon from afar,
Promises whispered from each star.
With twilight's hand, a brush of grace,
Veils of color softly trace.

In the churning of the sky,
Every hue tells a lullaby.
Crimson whispers, sapphire sighs,
As day concedes to smoky skies.

From bright beginnings, shadows creep,
In twilight's arms, the world will sleep.
Yet dreams awaken with the dawn,
In colors' dance, forever drawn.

Symphony of Chaos in Winged Elegance

In the rush of unbridled flight,
Wings unfold, a pure delight.
Each motion sings of wild grace,
A symphony in time and space.

Color splashes on a whim,
Trills and cries, both bold and dim.
Amongst the chaos, beauty thrives,
In the dance where nature strives.

With every thrum and chase,
Harmony found in every place.
The world beneath, a breathtaking sight,
In winged elegance, ignites the night.

Through tangled branches, they glide with ease,
A fleeting moment, a gentle tease.
Symphony of chaos, their sacred plight
In every heartbeat, they own the light.

The Quiet Uprising of Nature's Heart

Beneath the soil, life stirs awake,
Roots intertwine, a gentle quake.
Whispers of green through cracks emerge,
Nature's pulse begins to surge.

Gentle hills breathe in the light,
Morning dew, a fresh delight.
The sun spills gold on tranquil streams,
As bluebirds sing of hidden dreams.

Petals flutter in the breeze,
A symphony among the trees.
Shadows dance in dappled rays,
Embracing warmth of verdant days.

In silence, power takes its stand,
Nature reborn, a healing hand.
Her heart beats softly, fierce and true,
Awakening wonders, ever new.

Subtle Universes in a Fiery Clash

Stars collide in cosmic fire,
Galaxies spin, their charge, desire.
Nebulae swirl, colors entwine,
In vastness, secrets intertwine.

A dance of planets, rhythms universal,
Gravity's pull, both soft and dispersal.
Black holes whisper their dark command,
While light years stretch through hidden land.

Comets blaze with trails of hope,
In celestial realms where dreamers cope.
Time unfurls in spirals tight,
Creating shadows that drink the light.

In each explosion, worlds are born,
From dust to dawn, creation's scorn.
The universe breathes, a fiery clash,
Where subtleties dwell in a luminous gash.

From Silk to Storm

Threads of silk hang in the air,
Soft as whispers, light as prayer.
But tempests gather beyond the veil,
As calmness yields to thunder's tale.

Rumbling skies weave tales of plight,
Lightning dances, a flash of fright.
The gentle wears a fierce disguise,
As rain falls hard from grief-stricken skies.

Nature's fury breaks the calm,
Tearing apart the fragile charm.
Yet in the chaos, life takes form,
From silk's embrace emerges the storm.

As winds howl, a fierce lament,
Sorrow mingles with a storm's intent.
But in the aftermath, new life will bloom,
From stormy shadows, the flowers loom.

Fractured Rainbows Over Darkened Fields

In twilight's grasp, colors collide,
Fractured rainbows, where dreams abide.
Over fields cloaked in shadows deep,
Whispers of hope through silence creep.

Faded hues of what once glowed,
A promise stirs where sorrow flowed.
Beneath the dark, a flicker thrives,
Resilient hearts, where courage strives.

Storm clouds linger, heavy with grief,
Yet in the pain, buds seek relief.
From murky depths, a light will break,
Transcending fears that shadows make.

So let the fractured colors reign,
Over fields that once bore pain.
In every drop, a prism's might,
Fractured rainbows spark the night.

The Quiet Before the Roar

Whispers linger in the dusk,
Shadows dance in fading light.
Hearts hold secrets, time will tell,
As silence wraps the world so tight.

A breath before the tempest hits,
The calm grows thick, like velvet night.
Eyes watch closely, senses keen,
Awaiting thunder's fierce delight.

Memories swirl in muted hues,
Of laughter held, of dreams once bold.
Yet still we wait, on hope's thin edge,
For stories yet to be retold.

Then comes the roar, a deafening sound,
Breaking the peace with primal force.
Yet in the chaos, beauty blooms,
A wild dance of nature's course.

Echoes of Change in the Breeze

Beneath the trees, the whispers flow,
Carried forth on a gentle breeze.
Stories weave through branches high,
Of changing times and bending leaves.

A fragile heart learns to let go,
In rhythm with the seasons' flow.
Each rustle sings of life anew,
With every gust, the past we sow.

The skies transform from gray to gold,
As winds declare their soft demands.
We shed our doubts, embrace the brave,
And join the dance life's path commands.

Echoes soft, yet loud they ring,
From valleys deep to mountains tall.
In every change, we find our voice,
Unraveling what we thought was all.

Where Calm Meets Cataclysm

Serenity weaves through the clouds,
A quiet face amidst the storm.
Nature balances on the brink,
Where chaos waits, yet peace is warm.

Silent prayers ride the fierce winds,
Voices hush as shadows grow.
In the eye, lies fleeting grace,
A fleeting glimpse in the undertow.

Thunder rumbles in the distance,
As darkness swells with endless might.
Yet still, a glimmer breaks the dusk,
The promise of a dawn's soft light.

In the clash of fierce and calm,
We find our strength, we face our fears.
For in the storm, we learn to breathe,
And rise anew from what endears.

Fluttering Dreams Amidst a Storm

Beneath the canopy of gray,
Dreams take flight on fragile wings.
In tempest tossed, they twirl and spin,
Echoing hope that fiercely clings.

Storm clouds gather, thick and loud,
As visions dance, then sway away.
Yet every gust ignites the fire,
That fuels our hearts in wild array.

Through raindrops' tears, we chase the light,
Each droplet holds a whispered plea.
For in the chaos, courage blooms,
And sets our souls forever free.

With every flap against the wind,
We learn to soar, we learn to rise.
In storms of life, our dreams take form,
Embracing chaos is the prize.

The Storm that Rides on Tender Wings

Whispers ride on the breeze,
A tempest cloaked in grace.
Eagles soar through the dark,
Lightning paints the sky's face.

With thunder's roar, they dance,
Clouds swirl in a wild embrace.
Gentle stillness before the rush,
Nature's heart starts to race.

Fields bask in muted light,
Rainfall soft like a sigh.
The storm arrives in wonder,
With tender wings, it flies.

And as it sweeps through the night,
Beauty sprawls across the land.
In chaos lies a secret,
A force understood, yet unplanned.

Delicate Beasts in the Eye of Wind

Fragile wings on the edge of flight,
Stirring dreams against the night.
Creatures of grace defy the storm,
In turmoil, they learn to transform.

Each gust a whisper, soft and low,
Guides the dance of shadows that flow.
Beneath the tempest's fierce embrace,
They find their strength, they find their place.

Feathers glisten, touched by rain,
Echoes call in wild refrain.
In the eye of the wind, they play,
Delicate beasts, not led astray.

With every twist and mighty turn,
There's a fire in their hearts that burn.
In this maelstrom, they take their stand,
And weave their magic across the land.

Gentle Whispers Turned Gripping Roars

Gentle whispers turn to flight,
As shadows weave through fading light.
The air thickens with untold tales,
Each breath walks where silence pales.

Echoes linger, soft and sweet,
Until the moment's heart will beat.
What once was still begins to roar,
The storm awakens at its core.

In the hush of twilight's charm,
Lies a power, wild and warm.
Whispers coalesce, merge and grow,
Turning tides that ebb and flow.

With every clash and raucous cry,
The world shakes, and spirits fly.
In the fury, life is born,
From gentle whispers to gripping roars.

Fractured Silence beneath a Wrathful Sky

Beneath the sky, so dark and deep,
Fractured silence begins to creep.
A rumble stirs the quiet long,
Breaking stillness with its song.

Clouds gather with a heavy breath,
Foretelling storms that dance with death.
Nature's warnings fill the air,
Beneath the wrath, a solemn prayer.

In every crack, in every flash,
Lives a world ready to clash.
Fragile earth, resilient still,
Draws upon a hidden will.

With every droplet's fierce descent,
Comes an echo of discontent.
Yet in chaos, beauty thrives,
Fractured silence brings forth lives.

A Flutter's Echo in the Heart of the Storm

A whisper dances in the night,
A heart beats softly in fright.
The storm rages, fierce and bold,
Yet warmth within, a tale unfolds.

Amidst the chaos, beauty thrives,
Silent echoes, where hope survives.
Fluttering wings in swirling air,
Strength is found in souls laid bare.

Each drop of rain, a note of grace,
In every shadow, we find a place.
The thunder rolls, a melody deep,
In the heart of storms, our dreams we keep.

Together we rise, hearts intertwined,
In the dance of danger, we are defined.
For even storms, in their wildest form,
Can nurture soft echoes, a love reborn.

Navigating Currents of Change

The river flows, a shifting tide,
In its embrace, we learn to ride.
With every twist, a chance to grow,
In the depths, we let our fears go.

A compass set to the heart's true call,
Navigating through the rise and fall.
Each current serves as a guiding light,
Illuminating paths in the night.

Though waves may crash and shadows loom,
Within our essence, we find room.
For change is but a dance set free,
A journey penned by destiny.

Together we forge a brand new course,
With courage gathered, a hidden force.
In every current, our spirits play,
Navigating life in a wondrous way.

Embracing the Thunder's Grace

In twilight's glow, the storms arise,
Through curtains grey, we hear the cries.
Yet within thunder, a heartbeat thrums,
In the echo of storms, our spirit hums.

Raindrops fall like silver threads,
Weaving tales of where hope spreads.
Embracing chaos with open arms,
Finding joy in nature's charms.

Lightning strikes with brilliant flash,
Moments of beauty in a fleeting clash.
Amidst the roar, peace finds its place,
In every storm, we find our grace.

Together we dance in the downpour's kiss,
With open hearts, we find our bliss.
For every thunder, fierce and grand,
Brings a melody we understand.

Sheltered in Wings Amidst the Tempest

When winds howl wild and shadows creep,
In the heart of the storm, we shall not weep.
For in the chaos, we find a home,
Sheltered in wings, no need to roam.

With feathers soft, we hold each other.
In the tempest's grip, a caring mother.
The world may rage, but here we stand,
Together, brave, hand in hand.

Clouds may darken, yet light still gleams,
In the shelter of faith, we weave our dreams.
Amidst the storm, love lights the way,
Guiding us through night into day.

So hold me close when thunder rolls,
In the dance of the storm, we're two interwoven souls.
With wings around, we bravely face,
All tempests bold, in our warm embrace.

Veils Torn asunder by Thunder

Raindrops collide, the sky grows dark,
Lightning flashes, a vivid spark.
Nature's voice roars, a powerful sound,
Veils of peace, now torn from the ground.

Winds howl loudly, trees bend and sway,
Storm clouds gather, holding at bay.
The world trembles in a fierce dance,
Thunder shatters the calm with a glance.

Hope stands firm, amidst the fear,
Knowing still, the end is near.
After the storm, colors will bloom,
Veils restored, dispelling the gloom.

In the wake, a tranquil scene,
Brightened earth, vibrant and green.
Veils no longer, they cheerfully sigh,
As peace returns beneath the sky.

Gentle Change on a Turbulent Canvas

Brush strokes blend, colors collide,
A canvas echoes the tempest inside.
Gentle whispers amidst the roar,
Transforming chaos into something more.

Crimson hues sweep through the night,
Soft blues dance in morning light.
Each layer speaks of battles fought,
Gentle change, the lesson taught.

Shadows linger, yet hope is near,
In each crevice, a voice to hear.
A gentle hand tames the wild,
Revealing beauty, serene and mild.

Art unfolds in the aftermath,
Turbulence giving a new path.
Change emerges, with every stroke,
A vibrant story in silence spoke.

Interlude of Calm in Nature's Rage

Beneath the storm, a quiet plea,
A moment of peace as wild winds flee.
The eye of chaos, where silence reigns,
Nature whispers through soft, gentle veins.

Leaves hold still, as time eludes,
In this interlude, nature broods.
Clouds part slightly, a beam breaks through,
As calm descends like morning dew.

Birdsong flutters, sweet and clear,
Amidst the echoes, whispers near.
Tension eases, the wild world waits,
In this heart of calm, serenity baits.

Then comes the thunder, a soft retreat,
The balance shifts, the rhythm's beat.
But fleeting joys, though they may shift,
In nature's rage, calm is a gift.

The Mighty Release of Colorful Souls

A burst of light from shadows deep,
Colors swirl, in joy they leap.
The canvas breathes, a life unveiled,
In vibrant hues, old fears curtailed.

From every stroke, a story spills,
Of laughter, whispers, and gentle thrills.
Each soul released, in colors bold,
Painted with love, and stories told.

They dance like flames, in the night sky,
Intertwined spirits, soaring high.
Each shade a memory, a thread drawn tight,
In the tapestry of radiant light.

The mighty release, a joyous roar,
Transforms the void, to something more.
In this symphony, they find their space,
Colorful souls, in a warm embrace.

Wings of Delusion

In shadows danced the fleeting light,
A whisper echoed through the night.
With fragile dreams that fade away,
I chase the dawn, but dusk holds sway.

The skies above are painted bold,
A story of the brave and old.
With wings of hope, I rise and fall,
Yet wander lost, within the thrall.

Mirages shimmer, blur the line,
Between the truth and dreams divine.
In silence, I find solace sweet,
While tangled thoughts beneath me fleet.

Oh, cruel illusions, vast and wide,
In you, I seek, in you, I hide.
With every brimming, half-lit chance,
I yearn to join the waltzing dance.

Dark Horizons

Beneath the cloak of endless night,
The stars have lost their shining fight.
I walk on paths where shadows creep,
And hold the secrets darkness keeps.

In silent whispers, fears arise,
As the horizon taunts my eyes.
The world ahead is painted grey,
Yet hope still lingers, finds the way.

In shadows deep, I find my grace,
A strength that time cannot erase.
With every step, the unknown calls,
To brave the night, to risk the falls.

But there within that dark embrace,
Lies beauty waiting to unlace.
A dawn that waits beyond the dread,
Where dreams and daylight can be wed.

The Art of Stormy Serenades

In winds that howl, a song emerges,
With thunder's pulse, the heart converges.
Each note a clash, a deep refrain,
Entwined with memories of pain.

The clouds compose a symphony,
With every drop, a harmony.
In rain's embrace, the world turns bright,
And chaos finds a spark of light.

The art of storms, both fierce and wild,
Resonates like echoes, mild.
Each tremor speaks of tales untold,
A beauty buried, fierce and bold.

Through violent shifts and sweet release,
I find a calm, a fleeting peace.
As waves crash down and spirits soar,
I seek the heart of the uproar.

Carnivals of Color in the Eye of the Storm

A circus spins in tempest's grip,
Where vibrant hues begin to slip.
In chaos blooms a wild parade,
Of colors rich where dreams are laid.

The winds may howl, the skies may blaze,
Yet in this whirl, I'm lost in daze.
The world a canvas, bold and bright,
A fleeting glimpse of pure delight.

As laughter mingles with the cries,
A dance of fate that never dies.
In every flash, a memory glows,
Within the storm, the beauty flows.

So here I stand, a part of all,
Embracing fate, I will not fall.
In colors bright, though tempests loom,
I find my heart, my vibrant bloom.

Tempestuous Hues and Calming Currents

In painted skies, the tempest brews,
As lightning strikes with vivid hues.
Yet in the maelstrom, calm resides,
A hidden strength the heart confides.

The ocean's roar, a primal song,
In chaos, I feel I belong.
With every wave, a story told,
Of dreams and fears, both brave and bold.

Through stormy nights, I swim the tide,
In swirling depths, I cannot hide.
Yet currents pull me to the shore,
Where peace awaits, forevermore.

In tempests fierce, I learn to trust,
That in the storm, I rise from dust.
With every change, I choose the way,
To find the calm in disarray.

Kaleidoscope Fury Unleashed

Colors clash in vibrant fight,
Swirling patterns burst to light.
Shadows dance, the chaos calls,
Through the storm, the silence falls.

Whispers rise, the tempest brews,
Echoes of forgotten views.
In the rage, a spark ignites,
Kaleidoscope of wild sights.

Crimson flames and azure skies,
Fury's heart beneath the lies.
Nature's canvas, torn and bold,
A story of the fierce, retold.

Beauty born from jagged strife,
In the fury, breathes new life.
Through the fragments, hope is found.
Kaleidoscope, where dreams abound.

Transformation from Breath to Roar

In the stillness, whispers grow,
Gentle breezes start to flow.
From the quiet, passions leap,
Waking dreams that lay asleep.

Softest murmurs turn to sound,
Power rises from the ground.
From the hush, a thunder's call,
Breath transforming, breaking all.

In the shadows, strength ignites,
Footsteps echo, daring flights.
From the silence born anew,
Roar of courage breaking through.

Bravest hearts, with fire and light,
Stand to rise from darkest night.
With each breath, the chains will sever,
Transformation, fierce forever.

Fragile Dreams in Thunder's Embrace

Delicate dreams on tempest's wings,
Twirling softly, wild heart sings.
Lightning flashes, shadows play,
In the storm, hopes drift away.

Clouds converge, a heavy sigh,
Fragile ties begin to pry.
Yet we dance in rain's caress,
Finding strength in nature's stress.

As the thunder cracks the air,
Breathless moments turn to prayer.
In the chaos, spirits rise,
Fragile dreams beneath the skies.

With each storm, new visions born,
Through the trials, beauty worn.
In the embrace of fierce plight,
Dreams take flight, hearts ignite.

The Unraveling of Serene Skies

Gentle breezes, calm and clear,
Whispers of the day draw near.
Clouds begin their slow retreat,
Sunshine spills on golden street.

Yet beneath the tranquil blue,
Tension brews, a hidden hue.
Threads of grace begin to fray,
Serene skies in disarray.

Moments quake, with colors warm,
Underneath, a brewing storm.
As the fabric starts to tear,
Beauty swirls in vibrant flair.

When the peaceful tapestry bends,
Life reveals its twists and bends.
In the unraveling, we find,
Serenity's not left behind.

Entangled in Turbulent Skies

Clouds collide in a stormy dance,
Winds whisper secrets of a chance.
Lightning flickers, a fleeting spark,
Thunder rumbles, echoing stark.

Darkness looms with a heavy breath,
Yet within chaos, whispers of faith.
Hearts race swift, as shadows creep,
In the tempest's hold, a promise deep.

Above the strife, where hope might soar,
Dreams entwined amidst the roar.
Holding on, as worlds collide,
In turbulent skies, we must confide.

Amidst the chaos, we find our grace,
Entangled hearts in this wild space.
Together we rise, through storm and rain,
In turbulent skies, love stays the same.

Halos of Color Amidst the Roar

In the midst of a restless roar,
Halos of color spill from the shore.
Waves crash with a furious might,
Yet beauty blooms within the fight.

Amber suns stretch across the blue,
Gilded rays weave through the dew.
Nature's palette, a vibrant song,
In chaos, hues where we belong.

Shimmering shades that dance and play,
As winds of change carry us away.
Our spirits soar on a canvas wide,
Halos of color, where dreams reside.

Amid the storm, we find our bliss,
A tapestry woven with every kiss.
In fleeting moments, joy ignites,
Halos of color, our sweetest sights.

Spirals of Flight and Fury

Across the vast and boundless sky,
Spirals twist, and eagles fly.
With grace and shadow, they intertwine,
In spirals of fury, an art divine.

Wings unfurl in the wildest dance,
Riding the winds, they take their chance.
Breathless moments in the air,
Where spirits rise without a care.

With each loop, a story told,
Of bravery cherished, and hearts bold.
Through storms' embrace and sunlight's beam,
In spirals of flight, we find our dream.

Fury may rage, but so does the peace,
As nature's song brings sweet release.
In endlessly soaring, wild and free,
Spirals of flight, just you and me.

The Heartbeat of a Flapping Tempest

Wings beat heavy against the night,
A tempest stirs, a fierce delight.
Echoes of thunder in boundless flight,
The heartbeat pulses in purest light.

Nature's fury, both wild and sweet,
In every flap, the universe meets.
With every gust, we rise and fall,
In this tempest's grip, we answer the call.

Feathers whisper secrets lost,
Of battles fought and dreams embossed.
The skies above, a stage so grand,
As tempests lead, we take our stand.

Boundless hearts, in wild embrace,
In a flapping storm, we find our place.
The heartbeat echoes, strong and bold,
In the tempest's heart, our story unfolds.

Flickers of Light in a Thunderous Heart

In shadows deep, a spark ignites,
A heartbeat echoes through the night.
With trembling hands, we grasp the fire,
Each flicker whispers of desire.

Beneath the storm, the silence stirs,
A soft resolve, the spirit purrs.
Against the winds, we stand our ground,
In every beat, our strength is found.

The pulse of hope, a glowing thread,
In thunder's roar, we're gently led.
With every flash, a promise made,
In this fierce dance, our fears do fade.

A tempest rages, yet we will soar,
Through flickers bright, our hearts will roar.
For in the clash of dark and light,
We find our way, our shining sight.

The Bifurcation of Delicacy and Might

In whispers soft, the strength reveals,
A tender touch, the armor heals.
Two paths diverge in silent grace,
A dance of power, a gentle embrace.

Where courage wades in waters clear,
With every step, we face our fear.
The delicate, it weaves the bold,
In stories told, our fates unfold.

With anchored roots, the branches sway,
In fragile blooms, the fighter's play.
The world unfolds in shades of rare,
Each clash of wills, a breath of air.

So let us walk this winding road,
In balance found, the truths bestowed.
For in this space, both firm and frail,
We write our tales, we shall prevail.

Beneath the Surface of Churning Tides

The ocean roars, a tempest calls,
Beneath the waves, a quiet stalls.
In rhythmic pulse, the depths abide,
Secrets held, like treasures wide.

The currents pull, both fierce and calm,
Each ripple sings a hidden psalm.
In shallow breaths, the mysteries sneak,
A symphony where silence speaks.

The surface breaks, the shadows play,
In the deep blue, dreams drift away.
With every splash, a story weaves,
Of lives intertwined in ocean heaves.

So dive into the ebb and flow,
Embrace the depths, let courage grow.
For in the tides, our truths reside,
Beneath the surface, hopes collide.

Celestial Wings and the Sound of Dissonance

In starlit skies, we spread our wings,
A fleeting dance, the cosmos sings.
With every beat, a story told,
Of dreams alight, of hearts so bold.

The echoes wane, a clash of sound,
In harmony where hope is found.
Yet dissonance, a symphony,
Draws forth the strength to just be free.

From shadows cast, the light will break,
In every note, our souls awake.
The celestial play, both dark and bright,
In every clash, we find our light.

So let us rise on wings of grace,
In the chaos, we find our place.
For in the dance of night and dawn,
Celestial hearts will carry on.

The Velvet Clutch of Stormy Graces

In shadows deep where whispers lie,
The velvet clutch of stormy sighs,
With lightning flickers in the night,
An echo blooms, soft yet bright.

A dance of clouds in muted gray,
Where secrets swirl and wild winds play,
The heart beats fierce with hopes untold,
In graces worn, both meek and bold.

With every gust, a story weaves,
Of past and future, lost on leaves,
Yet in this storm, a calm resides,
As velvet dreams the tempest hides.

So let the thunder crack and roar,
For in its depths, we'll seek for more,
A tapestry of life's embrace,
Within the velvet clutch of grace.

From Quiet Slumber to Resounding Chaos

From quiet slumber, dawn awakes,
A gentle stir, the stillness shakes,
The world, it shifts, from peace to sound,
In rising tides, the chaos found.

Waves crash hard against the shore,
As whispers turn to mighty roars,
Each ripple flows through heart and mind,
A symphony of ties that bind.

In every clash, a voice takes flight,
Emerging strong from muted night,
While shadows dance on trembling waves,
In urgency, the spirit braves.

Yet in this din, we find our place,
Each heartbeat thumps, a wild race,
From silent dreams to battles fought,
In resounding chaos, hope is sought.

Emblazoned Paths through the Storm's Heart

Through storm's heart, we forge our way,
On emblazoned paths where shadows play,
With every footstep, the thunder calls,
And into the tempest, courage sprawls.

Raindrops dance like stars above,
Each moment wrapped in fierce, bold love,
As echoes whisper through the gale,
We brave the winds, we'll never fail.

In flashes bright, our spirits soar,
Tracing lines on the ocean floor,
For through the fury, we shall find,
A spark of hope that ties mankind.

Emblazoned paths will guide our hearts,
Through storms that swirl, where adventure starts,
With every challenge, we will learn,
In storms and fires, our spirits burn.

The Pulse of Wings Against Thunder's Cry

The pulse of wings in thunder's reach,
A song of strength that storms can teach,
With beats that echo through the night,
In flight, they find their boundless light.

Amidst the clouds where tempests rage,
Each feathered soul turns a new page,
Resilience borne on turbulent air,
A testament to dreams laid bare.

Through roaring skies, they rise and bend,
As nature's chorus voices lend,
In perfect rhythm with the storm,
They dance and twirl, their spirits warm.

With every flap, a heart ignites,
As wings embrace the thunder's might,
An anthem strong against the night,
The pulse of wings, our hope in flight.

Milton Keynes UK
Ingram Content Group UK Ltd.
UKHW030750121124
451094UK00013B/810

9 789916 908358